LAW *for the*
EXPERT
WITNESS
Third Edition

LAW *for the* EXPERT WITNESS

Third Edition

Daniel A. Bronstein

CRC Press
Taylor & Francis Group
Boca Raton   London   New York

CRC Press is an imprint of the
Taylor & Francis Group, an informa business

CRC Press
Taylor & Francis Group
6000 Broken Sound Parkway NW, Suite 300
Boca Raton, FL 33487-2742

© 2007 by Taylor & Francis Group, LLC
CRC Press is an imprint of Taylor & Francis Group, an Informa business

No claim to original U.S. Government works
Printed in the United States of America on acid-free paper
10 9 8 7 6 5 4 3 2 1

International Standard Book Number-10: 1-4200-4673-X (Hardcover)
International Standard Book Number-13: 978-1-4200-4673-1 (Hardcover)

Library of Congress Cataloging-in-Publication Data

Bronstein, Daniel A.
　　Law for the expert witness / Daniel A. Bronstein. -- 3rd ed.
　　　　p. cm.
　　Includes bibliographical references and index.
　　ISBN 978-1-4200-4673-1 (alk. paper)
　　1. Evidence, Expert--United States. 2. Forensic scientists--United
States--Handbooks, manuals, etc. I. Title.

KF8961.B76 2007
347.73'67--dc22
　　　　　　　　　　　　　　　　　　　　　　　　　　　　　　　2006035161

Visit the Taylor & Francis Web site at
http://www.taylorandfrancis.com

and the CRC Press Web site at
http://www.crcpress.com

Dedication

Again, of course, to my wife, Lee, with all my love, and to the other important women in my life: my mother, Elaine Kinzler, my sister, Ruth Breindel, and the "kids," Dr. Linda Wennerberg and Dr. Judith Bronstein.

Contents

Part I
Before Trial

Chapter 1

Chapter 2

Chapter 3

Chapter 4

Chapter 5

Chapter 6

Part II
The Rules of Evidence

Part III
Suggestions and Hints for Expert Witnesses

Appendices and Case Listing

Preface to the Third Edition

There are several changes in this edition of the book, necessitated by changes in both society and the law since the last edition was issued in 1999. On the strictly legal side, the issues involving when expert testimony is accepted, which occupied approximately 12 pages of Chapter 8, now appear to have been settled. Thus that discussion has been reduced greatly in length.

At the same time, the courts are adjusting to the prevalence of computers in our society. For example, new rules have been issued regarding discovery of electronically stored data and a discussion of this now appears in Chapter 2. Similarly, courtrooms are becoming "wired" and a discussion of the implications of this has been added to Chapters 13 and 21. I would like to thank David Easterday, Circuit Court Administrator for Ingham County, Michigan, for showing me around the courtrooms and arranging for me to take the pictures that appear in Chapter 13.

In addition, the few typographical errors in the second edition have been corrected. Hopefully there will be no such errors in this edition.

Daniel A. Bronstein
East Lansing, Michigan

Acknowledgments

Since I appear to have reached that age at which one writes books that elucidate on the continuing themes of one's life, the time has also arrived for me to acknowledge those who have helped me reach this position.

For classroom training in trial law: Bernard Auerbach, John Brumbaugh, and James McElhaney; for practical training, Paul Berman, Sigmund Levin, and Bob Hochberg; and for restraint in advocacy, Hon. Edward Northrop — all in Baltimore. For encouraging my switch from legal practice to teaching: Garrett Power in Baltimore; Joe Sax, Paul Carrington, and Gordon Kane in Ann Arbor; and Raymond Vlasin and John Cantlon in East Lansing. For personal support and friendship when most needed: Angie and Dave Boyter, Gina Arents, Jim Durkay, Ileana Grams, Marguerite Williams, and Ted Rosenberg in Baltimore; Peter Waight, Frank Jackson, Gene Farber, John Freese, and Sharon and Gerry Lapkin in Ann Arbor; Gladys and Rupert Cutler, Don Erickson, and Karen and Eric Winston in East Lansing.

Introduction

When I entered teaching in 1972 I knew, based on my experience as a practicing trial lawyer, that there was a great need to familiarize professionals of all types with the process of giving expert testimony in legal proceedings. A course on that subject was one of the first that I developed, and I have taught it in alternate years ever since, attracting graduate and professional students from the entire Michigan State University campus. Starting in 1977 I also have given a two-day continuing education version of that course at various locations around the U.S. and under contract to many government agencies. This book is a revised version of the readings assigned to the students in that course, along with some of the professorial oral commentary. The book is divided into three major parts — procedural issues that an expert witness might need to understand; evidentiary issues that an expert witness might need to understand; and some hints for witnesses based on my experience as a trial lawyer.

Unlike my previous book, Demystifying the Law, which serves as an introduction to the legal system, Law for the Expert Witness is not discursive in nature. It deals with technical legal issues and is filled with quotes from various legal sources, particularly FRCP and FRE. Since rules are merely words on paper until we see how they may be applied to real life situations, edited versions of court decisions that show how the courts interpret the rules are provided where appropriate.

I used FRCP since that is the model on which most states have based their procedural processes. In different states the rules are numbered differently, but the substantive content is very similar to FRCP. I used FRE because it also served as a model for those states that have adopted rules of evidence. Even in states which do not have rules of evidence, however, the substance and interpretation of the rules are fundamentally the same; FRE is nothing more than a listing of the evidentiary principles that have evolved in U.S. courts over the past 200 years.

The extracts from FRCP, FRE, and from cases decided by courts have been edited. A standard ellipsis (…) indicates that less than a paragraph has been omitted. An asterisk ellipsis (* * *) indicates that a paragraph or more has been omitted. Footnotes that appear at the bottom of a page are those written by the court in its opinion. Notes I provided are set at the end of the chapter.

About the Author

Daniel A. Bronstein is a professor at Michigan State University where he teaches environmental law in the College of Agriculture and Natural Resources and medical jurisprudence in the medical schools. He received his bachelor of arts in biophysics from The Johns Hopkins University and his bachelor of law from the University of Maryland. After practicing trial law in his native Baltimore for five years, he decided to go into teaching. He received his master of law and doctor of jurisprudential science degrees from the University of Michigan. He has taught at Michigan State University since 1972.

Professor Bronstein was editor of Impact Assessment and Project Appraisal, the refereed journal of the International Association for Impact Assessment from 1993–2000 and is currently a member of its publications committee. He is the author of 5 books, 11 monographs and numerous journal articles, and is admitted to the practice of law in both Maryland and Michigan. He is an ex-officio member of the council of Section K of the American Association for the Advancement of Science and has served as chair of the Committee on Environmental Law and as a vice-chair of the Committee on Scientific Evidence of the American Bar Association.

PART I

Before Trial

Filing Suit, or Legal Paperwork

Before one can be an expert witness in court, somebody must file suit against somebody else. It is therefore useful to understand how a suit is filed and what happens in the early stages of litigation.

The rules of civil procedure govern trial preparation and conduct in the courts. The standard rules of civil procedure are those used in the Federal courts, the Federal Rules of Civil Procedure (FRCP). FRCP was adopted by the Supreme Court in 1938, and most states now follow the same general principles in civil procedure as do the Federal courts. The basic principle of FRCP is "notice pleading," which means that the papers filed in the courts do not require a great amount of detailed factual information but merely enough information to "put the opposing party on notice" of the issues to be contested at trial.

COMPLAINT

A trial commences with the filing of a complaint. The complaint is composed in numbered paragraphs, each of which details a different factual allegation. After jurisdictional allegations are made, each allegation again is made in yet another separately numbered paragraph. For example, assume we have a simple automobile collision that occurred at an intersection governed by a stop sign. The plaintiff, who was on the street that did not have the stop sign, was hit by the car of the defendant, who had the stop sign. The allegations might read as follows:

1. On December 5, 1988, at or about 9:00 a.m., the plaintiff was driving his vehicle westward on 1st Avenue, in the City of Absolute, in the State of Confusion.
2. At or about the same time the defendant was driving her car north on Elm Street.

3. That the defendant approached the intersection of Elm Street and 1st Avenue and failed to stop for the stop sign, which faced in her direction, as a result of which the cars came into collision in the middle of the intersection.
4. That the collision of vehicles was caused by the defendant's failure to stop for the stop sign, failure to keep a proper lookout for other vehicles on the road, and failure to fulfill the duty to operate a vehicle in a safe and proper manner.
5. As a result of the collision of vehicles, the plaintiff suffered a fractured right humerus, injury to his back and neck, and had and continues to have pain and loss of earnings due to the collision of vehicles and the resulting injuries.

The complaint concludes by detailing the relief requested — say, "wherefore the plaintiff prays that defendant be required to pay for plaintiff's vehicle, which was totally destroyed by the collision, pay for plaintiff's medical expenses, and pay for plaintiff's continuing pain and suffering and loss of earnings in the amount of $1 million." This last *ad damnum* clause always requests much more than one expects to receive since a court cannot award what is not requested.

Such a set of paragraphs does not really provide the other party with a great deal of information, but it does serve to give notice as to (a) the cause of the suit; (b) the injuries alleged; and (c) the relief sought.

ANSWER

When a party is served with a complaint the proper response is to make an answer. In the answer to the complaint the defendant typically goes through the allegations of the complaint paragraph by paragraph and either denies them, admits them, or states that the party has insufficient information to either admit or deny. The answer to the above complaint might read:

1. The allegations of Paragraph 1 are admitted.
2. The allegations of Paragraph 2 are admitted.
3. The allegations of Paragraph 3 are denied.
4. The allegations of Paragraph 4 are denied.
5. Defendant has insufficient information to either admit or deny the allegations of Paragraph 5.

In this way the defendant admits that the two cars were at the locations specified but denies that she was operating the vehicle in any improper way and states that she does not know what injuries the plaintiff sustained.

If the defendant wanted to assert what is called an "affirmative defense" the rules require her to present that in the answer. For example, if the defendant wanted to argue that the reason the vehicles came into collision was that she had to enter the intersection to make way for a fire engine behind her, a paragraph like the following would be part of the answer:

6. In addition, defendant alleges that the collision of vehicles occurred due to the failure of the plaintiff to observe an approaching emergency vehicle and yield to it.

The rules provide that inconsistent allegations may be contained in an answer. The classic story used to illustrate this concept for law students is something like the following: Mr. Smith filed suit against Mr. Jones alleging that Mr. Jones borrowed his black pot and returned it with a large crack in it, so Mr. Smith is therefore seeking money to repair the damaged pot. In his answer Mr. Jones made several allegations: that he never borrowed the pot; that he borrowed the pot but returned it in good condition; that the pot was broken when he borrowed it; that the pot was defective and broke in the course of normal use; and that the pot was broken by a burglar who entered Mr. Jones' house and ransacked the place. In any reasonable interpretation, these defenses are totally inconsistent with one another; nevertheless, it is perfectly permissible under the rules to file such an answer. Mr. Jones, of course, will have to choose one of these defenses for his main argument before the case goes to trial.

COUNTERCLAIMS, CROSS-CLAIMS, THIRD-PARTY CLAIMS, AND CLASS ACTIONS

A counterclaim is a claim that the defendant may assert against the plaintiff after the suit is filed or "counter" to the plaintiff's claim against the defendant. There are two types of counterclaims: compulsory and permissive. A compulsory counterclaim is one that arises out of the same incident, fact situation, or legal situation as the original claim by the plaintiff against the defendant. In our simple automobile collision case example, if the original defendant asserted a claim against the original plaintiff for the defendant's personal injuries and the damage to her vehicle, that would be a compulsory counterclaim. A permissive counterclaim, as the name implies, is a counterclaim permitted to be raised in the action, but it does not have to be raised. If, for example, the plaintiff in our automobile collision case owed the defendant money based on a loan made previously, that would be a permissive counterclaim for the defendant to assert against the plaintiff.

A cross-claim is a claim made by a party on one side of a case against another party on the same side of the case. As an example, let us assume that a small rented private plane crashes upon takeoff from an airport. The families of the pilot and passengers file suit against everybody they can think of who might possibly be liable: the plane's manufacturer, the company that sold the plane to the owner, the owner of the plane, the company that was responsible for doing the maintenance on the plane, etc. The families of the passengers could then file a cross-claim against the estate of the pilot, alleging that he negligently flew the plane. Similarly, the owner of the plane could file a cross-claim against the company that did the maintenance on the plane, saying that if the owner is liable for leasing a plane that was in poor condition it is because the maintenance company is liable for negligently performing maintenance and upkeep on the plane. This constitutes a series of cross-claims among parties who are already in the case.

A third-party claim is a claim by one of the parties in the case against someone not currently a party to the case. A third-party claim is handled exactly the same way that an original suit is handled; i.e., the third-party plaintiff must file a complaint against the third-party defendant and have the third-party defendant served with process, etc. Returning to our light plane crash example, the manufacturer of the plane, one of the defendants, might decide to file a third-party claim against the manufacturers of the engine and the propeller, alleging that the engine and the propeller were unsuitable for the use to which they were put, namely, to fly a plane (this is an example of a "products liability" claim). The manufacturer of the plane would file a complaint against the manufacturers of the engine and the propeller alleging, in separately numbered paragraphs, the various defects it believes were present. The third-party defendants, the two manufacturers, would then file answers to the complaint.

The only major difference between this third-party claim and the filing of a new suit by the manufacturer of the plane against the manufacturers of the engine and propeller is that the case is part of the original suit by the pilot and passengers, not a new and separate case. Once the manufacturers of the engine and propeller become parties to the case, other parties may file claims against them as though they were original parties. For example, the estates of the pilot and passengers could make a claim against the manufacturers of the engine and the propeller on the same basis as the claim by the manufacturer of the plane, and the other defendants could also file cross-claims against them. All this paper filing and the whole purpose of counter-claims, cross-claims, and third-party interpleading is to ensure, to the greatest extent possible, that all potentially involved parties have a chance to present their sides of the case before the case is resolved.

A class action is an action in which many individuals who have suffered a certain injury or who have an identical complaint against one or more defendants join together to file the suit as one. Rule 23(a) states there must be so many people involved that individual suits by each would be impracticable. There must also be a common question of law or fact in all the claims, enabling a class action to be maintained if there is a risk of inconsistent or varying adjudications among different parties who are identically situated. Many claims against medical device manufac-turers and pharmaceutical companies are class actions.

As a matter of actual fact, of course, the members of the class do not generally get together and decide to file suit; instead, an individual decides to file suit on behalf of the entire class. This is one of the hallmarks of a class action: the title reads something along the lines of "John Doe, on his own behalf, and on behalf of all other persons similarly situated, vs. the XYZ Corporation." "On his own behalf and on behalf of all others" clearly indicates the case is filed as a class action. Rule 23 also states that the plaintiff who files the action must be "representative" of the class; i.e., the injuries of that plaintiff must be similar to those suffered by all other members of the class.

Once a class action is filed and the court agrees that it is properly filed, various requirements must be met to notify the members of the class that a class action suit has been filed. Each potential member of the class must be informed of the class action in some way, either actually and directly or by publication in a newspaper or similar vehicle. Each potential member of the class has the option to continue to participate in the class action or to refuse to participate. Members of the class who refuse to participate are said to have "opted out." If a person who is a member of the class does not opt out of the suit, any judgment eventually entered in the case is binding against that person ever filing a similar suit for the same reasons. Like counterclaims, cross-claims, and third-party practice, the purpose of class actions is to consolidate in one place as many of the potential claims arising out of a given problem as possible and to resolve all claims at one time.

At this point in a suit, lawyers say that "issue is joined," which means all parties are before the court. Now the pretrial maneuvering begins, as the parties try to learn the details of their opponents' cases through discovery. It is at this point that expert witnesses frequently become involved.

CHAPTER 2

Discovery in General

Due to the lack of detail specified in the original filing of any lawsuit, which we noted in Chapter 1, some provision is necessary for the parties to find out what the lawsuit involves. This is the role of discovery. In the course of discovery, each side finds out the facts and opinions on which the other side is basing its case. The whole purpose of the discovery process is to ensure that each side knows exactly what the other side is planning to do and thus can develop the best possible counter presentations. It is virtually impossible to spring surprise witnesses or novel legal theories on an opponent who has taken the discovery process seriously.

From the perspective of the expert witness, discovery is the process by which the other side finds out what you think, why you think it, and what the weak points are in your opinion. For this reason, it is very important that you be familiar with discovery devices and processes and that you take them seriously and do your best to ensure that nothing happens that could return to haunt you. If you work for a bureaucratic organization — a government agency or a large industrial corporation — you may find yourself doing some of the discovery for your side in the course of the litigation. What frequently happens to experts who are employed by government agencies, for example, is that the discovery request filed by the other side eventually ends up on the expert's desk for appropriate response. If you find yourself in this position, the first thing you should do is contact your attorney to find out what he or she feels you should and should not answer.

Rule 26 of FRCP provides the general description of the discovery methods available and the legal technicalities common to these methods. For these reasons, and because it is the lowest numbered of the discovery rules, we shall start our examination with Rule 26. Note that I will interrupt the text of the rule with explanatory comments as we go along so you will not have to "digest" large doses of unadulterated legal language.

FRCP Rule 26. General Provisions Governing Discovery; Duty of Disclosure

(a) Required Disclosures; Methods to Discover Additional Matter.
(1) Initial Disclosures.
Except to the extent otherwise stipulated or directed by order or local rule, a party shall, without awaiting a discovery request, provide to other parties:
(A) the name and, if known, the address and telephone number of each individual likely to have discoverable information relevant to disputed facts alleged with particularity in the pleadings, identifying the subjects of the information;
(B) a copy of, or a description by category and location of, all documents, electronically stored information, and tangible things in the possession, custody, or control of the party that are relevant to disputed facts alleged with particularity in the pleadings;
(C) a computation of any category of damages claimed by the disclosing party, making available for inspection and copying as under Rule 34 the documents or other evidentiary material, not privileged or protected from disclosure, on which such computation is based, including materials bearing on the nature and extent of injuries suffered...

A key point here is that the word "privileged" used in (C) is a "term of art" for lawyers and includes attorney-client privilege, doctor-patient privilege, privilege against self-incrimination, etc. "Privileged" does not mean you do not wish to disclose information; it means there is a basis in law that allows you to avoid disclosing information.

FRCP Rule 26 (Cont'd.)

Unless otherwise stipulated or directed by the court, these disclosures shall be made at or within 10 days after the meeting of the parties under subdivision (f). A party shall make its initial disclosures based on the information then reasonably available to it and is not excused from making its disclosures because it has not fully completed its investigation of the case or because it challenges the sufficiency of another party's disclosures or because another party has not made its disclosures.

This section is fairly easy to understand. Each side has to make the disclosures. It is no excuse for one side not to disclose because the other side has failed to make its required disclosures.

Now comes the portion regarding you, the expert:

FRCP Rule 26 (Cont'd.)

(a)(2) Disclosure of Expert Testimony.

(A) In addition to the disclosures required by paragraph (1), a party shall disclose to other parties the identity of any person who may be used at trial to present evidence under Rules 702, 703, or 705 of the Federal Rules of Evidence.

(B) Except as otherwise stipulated or directed by the court, this disclosure shall, with respect to a witness who is retained or specially employed to provide expert testimony in the case or whose duties as an employee of the party regularly involve giving expert testimony, be accompanied by a written report prepared and signed by the witness. The report shall contain a complete statement of all opinions to be expressed and the basis and reasons therefor; the data or other information considered by the witness in forming the opinions; any exhibits to be used as a summary of or support for the opinions; the qualifications of the witness, including a list of all publications authored by the witness within the preceding ten years; the compensation to be paid for the study and testimony; and a listing of any other cases in which the witness has testified as an expert at trial or by deposition within the preceding four years.

(C) These disclosures shall be made at the times and in the sequence directed by the court. In the absence of other directions from the court or stipulation by the parties, the disclosures shall be made at least 90 days before the trial date or the date the case is to be ready for trial or, if the evidence is intended solely to contradict or rebut evidence on the same subject matter identified by another party under paragraph (2)(B), within 30 days after the disclosure made by the other party. The parties shall supplement these disclosures when required under subdivision (e)(1).

This merely means that you must finish your report and provide it to the lawyer you are working with so that the lawyer can send it to the other side. You must also provide all your qualifications as outlined in (B) within 90 days of the filing of suit (see Chapter 8 for an example of how to do this). I suggest that, when a lawyer approaches you to be an expert, you negotiate the question of the date when you must have the report ready.

FRCP Rule 26 (Cont'd.)

(a)(3) Pretrial Disclosures.

In addition to the disclosures required in the preceding paragraphs, a party shall provide to other parties the following information regarding the evidence that it may present at trial other than solely for impeachment purposes:

(A) the name and, if not previously provided, the address and telephone number of each witness, separately identifying those whom the party expects to present and those whom the party may call if the need arises;

(B) the designation of those witnesses whose testimony is expected to be presented by means of a deposition and, if not taken stenographically, a transcript of the pertinent portions of the deposition testimony; and

(C) an appropriate identification of each document or other exhibit, including summaries of other evidence, separately identifying those which the party expects to offer and those which the party may offer if the need arises.

Unless otherwise directed by the court, these disclosures shall be made at least 30 days before trial. Within 14 days thereafter, unless a different time is specified by the court, a party may serve and file a list disclosing (i) any objections to the use under Rule 32(a) of a deposition designated by another party under subparagraph (B) and (ii) any objection, together with the grounds therefor, that may be made to the admissibility of materials identified under subparagraph (C). Objections not so disclosed, other than objections under Rules 402 and 403 of the Federal Rules of Evidence, shall be deemed waived unless excused by the court for good cause shown.

(a)(4) Form of Disclosures; Filing.

Unless otherwise directed by order or local rule, all disclosures under paragraphs (1) through (3) shall be made in writing, signed, served, and promptly filed with the court.

Note that the above deals with pretrial disclosures, not immediate disclosures. It is probably safe to assume that by 30 days before the case goes to trial you will have all this information available and will be prepared to tell the other side about it.

FRCP Rule 26 (Cont'd.)

(a)(5) Methods to Discover Additional Matter.

Parties may obtain discovery by one or more of the following methods: depositions upon oral examination or written questions; written interrogatories; production of documents or things or permission to enter upon land or other property under Rule 34 or 45(a)(1)(C), for inspection and other purposes; physical and mental examinations; and requests for admission.

(b) Discovery Scope and Limits.

Unless otherwise limited by order of the court in accordance with these rules, the scope of discovery is as follows:

(1) In General.

Parties may obtain discovery regarding any matter, not privileged, which is relevant to the subject matter involved in the pending action, whether it relates to the claim or defense of the party seeking discovery or to the claim or defense of any other party, including the existence, description, nature, custody, condition, and location of any books, documents, or other tangible things and the identity and location of persons having knowledge of any discoverable matter. The information sought need not be admissible at the trial if the information sought appears reasonably calculated to lead to the discovery of admissible evidence.

In subsequent chapters, we will consider in greater detail each of the other discovery techniques set forth in Rule 26(a)(5). Note in (b)(1) that we again encounter the term "privilege," which has the same technical legal meaning here as we discussed earlier. Also important to note is the provision in the last sentence of (b)(1), that discovery is not limited to admissible evidence; discovery merely has to have a reasonable possibility of leading to admissible evidence.

FRCP Rule 26 (Cont'd.)

(b)(2) Limitations
(B) A party need not provide discovery of electronically stored information from sources that the party identifies as not reasonably accessible because of undue burden or cost. On motion to compel discovery or for a protective order, the party from whom discovery is sought must show that the information is not reasonably accessible because of undue burden or cost. If that showing is made, the court may nonetheless order discovery from such sources if the requesting party shows good cause, considering the limitations of Rule 26(b)(2)(C). The court may specify conditions for the discovery.

As can be imagined, there is currently a great deal of difficulty dealing with discovery of electronically stored information. The next case illustrates the issues that can arise and how at least one court has resolved them.

IN RE CV THERAPEUTICS, INC., SECURITIES LITIGATION, U.S. DIST. LEXIS 38909 (N.D. CAL. 2006)

BACKGROUND

1. Factual background

[Plaintiffs claim that] "Throughout the Class Period, defendants misled analysts, the investing public and even the FDA into believing that their novel anti-anginal drug, Raxena, was safe and effective for public use in an unrestricted population, and that the Company had conducted sufficient clinical studies to prove it." The complaint alleges that defendants' false and misleading statements artificially inflated the Company's stock [price].

* * *

2. Discovery: Backup Tape Stipulation

On September 20, 2004, plaintiffs propounded requests for production of documents on CVT. By agreement between the parties, plaintiffs' document requests cover the period from June 24, 2002 to June 5, 2004, which is broader than the class period. During the course of depositions in early 2005, plaintiffs learned that defendants had not produced documents contained on CVT's backup tapes. The parties' dispute concerning production of documents from the backup tapes culminated in the parties reaching a stipulation that the Court signed on May 18, 2005 (the "Backup Tape Stipulation").

Pursuant to the Backup Tape Stipulation, defendants agreed to make available to plaintiffs the catalogs (indexes) of tapes created in four time periods (June–August 2002; October–December 2002; June–August 2003; and September–December 2003). Plaintiffs were allowed to choose tapes from these catalogs for defendants to restore, and defendants were required to produce emails from these tapes. Defendants began producing emails from the tapes in a rolling production from late October 2005 until February 2006. According to defendants, plaintiffs received approximately 300,000 employee emails from this production.

In February 2006, plaintiffs confronted defendants about the existence of additional backup tapes that plaintiffs learned of from an undisclosed source. Defendants found these backup tapes, some of which cover the class period and one of which was created two months after this lawsuit was filed.

DISCUSSION

1. Plaintiffs' Motion to Compel and for an Order to Show Cause/Defendants' Motion for a Protective Order to Conclude Document Discovery

The parties' motions address many of the same issues. Plaintiffs generally contend that defendants have destroyed electronic documents and intentionally hid backup tapes that were only recently discovered after plaintiffs confronted defendants about their existence. Plaintiffs seek an order to show cause why defendants should not be sanctioned for spoliation. Plaintiffs also seek an order (1) ordering defendants to restore and produce all of the mailboxes of 20 witnesses identified by plaintiffs (not just the selected tapes that plaintiffs chose pursuant to the Backup Tape Stipulation), as well as all 26(a) witnesses of plaintiffs and defendants, without review or redaction, or "de-duplication"; (2) ordering defendants to immediately produce, without review or redaction, the newly discovered backup tapes, for restoration, and to pay for the costs of restoration; (3) ordering defendants to provide plaintiffs with immediate access to all documents from the "S" and "H" drives, "eRoom," and "Documentum"; and (4) plaintiffs' attorneys' fees and investigative fees incurred in "documenting CVT's contumacious actions" and preparing the motion to compel.

Defendants deny that they have failed to preserve, destroyed, or hid any documents. Defendants assert that CVT employees were instructed to preserve relevant emails and documents, that all documents were preserved either on the active server or on backup tapes, and that any apparent gaps in production are explained by standard technical processes employed by CVT and defendants' vendor such as the "de-duplication" process (described *infra),* technical procedures to prevent production of nonrelevant confidential information, and the manner in which certain mailboxes were stored on multiple servers. Defendants also contend that they have been engaging in good faith in the document production process, which has resulted in the production of nearly 1.4 million pages at a cost to defendants of over $4.3 million. Defendants seek an order concluding document discovery, arguing that the additional discovery that plaintiffs seek is too burdensome and costly...

B. Plaintiffs' Claims of Spoliation

*   *   *

The Court concludes that defendants have adequately explained, as a general matter, why there might be discrepancies between the number of emails contained on a catalog and the number of emails actually produced. Plaintiffs have not shown that CVT or defense counsel have intentionally deleted emails or otherwise destroyed evidence. For these reasons, the Court DENIES plaintiffs' request for sanctions.

However, because the Court is not satisfied that defendants have sufficiently explained the following specific examples of discrepancies in production, the Court will order additional briefing as set forth below:

(1) Colin Hislop

Plaintiffs assert that the December 8, 2003 catalog of Hislop's email box shows he had 47 emails in the "Ranexa Core Team" subfolder of his "inbox," but that defendants' production from the restoration of the December 28, 2003 backup tape includes only one email from the same folder. That sole email dates back to May 28, 2003.

Defendants respond that a new contract attorney did a poor job reviewing Hislop's December 28, 2003 mailbox on his first day at work. Defendants have identified over 150 emails improperly withheld, and these emails are now slated to be bates-stamped and produced to plaintiffs. Defendants have reviewed all the subsequent mailboxes reviewed by this contract attorney and confirmed that the quality of his review markedly improved after Hislop's mailbox.

It is unclear whether the 150 emails identified by defendants include the 46 emails referenced by plaintiffs. By April 10, 2006, defendants shall file a declaration with the Court clarifying whether the 46 emails referenced by plaintiffs are included in the 150 emails. If the 46 emails are not included in the 150 emails, defendants shall explain, with particularity, why those 46 emails were not produced, or alternatively defendants shall produce those 46 emails to plaintiffs.

(2) David McCaleb

According to plaintiffs, the catalog of the December 3, 2003 backup tape shows that McCaleb maintained a large "deleted items" folder with several hundred, if not several thousand, emails. McCaleb also maintained a "Ran Teams-Comm" subfolder housing what appear to be solely Ranexa-related communications, and at least 27 emails in this subfolder were entitled "Ranexa TM Core Team Minutes," which plaintiffs assert are clearly related to this litigation. Defendants produced one email for McCaleb from the

December 28, 2003 backup tapes dated October 13, 2003 and titled "Ranexa TM Core Team Minutes."

Defendants respond that they reviewed and produced two McCaleb mailboxes from two different servers from the December 28, 2003 backup tapes. Both were produced on January 12, 2006. Defendants state that a number of emails were removed through the de-duplication process, that there was no "significant inadvertent" failure to produce, and that they produced "several" emails titled "Ranexa TM Core Team Minutes." Although this explanation may fully account for the discrepancy, the Court is unable to reach this conclusion without more specific information. By April 10, 2006, defendants shall file a declaration explaining, with particularity, why the emails at issue ("deleted items" emails, the emails in the "Ran Teams-Comm" subfolder, and the balance of the 27 emails titled "Ranexa TM Core Team Minutes") were not produced. In lieu of such an explanation, defendants may produce these emails.

(3) Dan Spiegelman

Plaintiffs state that no emails were produced for Spiegelman's "inbox" or "outbox" from the December 28, 2003 backup tapes, and only 10 emails were produced from Spiegelman's "sent items," all but three of which were dated months earlier. Plaintiffs assert that Spiegelman deleted emails because the hard copy production of documents from Chris Chai shows receipt of an email with an attachment created and sent by Spiegelman on November 24, 2003, but no such email was produced from Spiegelman's box.

Defendants state that upon rereview of Spiegelman's mailbox, they discovered the email that plaintiffs asserted was in Chris Chai's hard copy production but missing from Spiegelman's mailbox. Defendants state that this email and its attachment were inadvertently withheld as privileged during Defendants' initial review, and that they will produce the email version. In light of defendants' agreement to produce the email version, and because the hard copy version has already been produced, the Court finds no further explanation by defendants is necessary. However, other than generally referring to the de-duplication process, defendants do not specifically address plaintiffs' charge that Spiegelman appeared to be deleting emails. By April 10, 2006, defendants shall file a declaration specifically addressing plaintiffs' charge that Spiegelman was deleting emails and explaining why no emails were produced from his "inbox" or "outbox."

(4) Lou Lange

As with Spiegelman, plaintiffs note that no emails were produced from Lange's "inbox," "outbox," or "sent items" for the August 3, 2003 backup tapes. Defendants respond that approximately 93% of the emails in Lange's mailbox were removed as duplicative. Defendants do not explain why the remaining 7% of emails were not produced. Defendants do not state that these emails were not responsive, or that they are privileged. By April 10, 2006, defendants shall file a declaration explaining why the remaining 7% of emails were not produced, or alternatively, defendants shall produce these documents to plaintiffs.

*   *   *

C. Documents contained on newly discovered backup tapes

Defendants sent the newly discovered tapes to its vendor for analysis. The Exabyte tapes appear to contain backups of desktop and laptop computers. According to defendants, the vendor determined that 170 of the newly discovered Exabyte tapes from the time period covered by the Backup Tape Stipulation (which comprise six sets ... [of] backups) are potentially restorable, and 16 of the newly discovered DLT tapes from August 2002 are potentially restorable (it is unclear if the September 2002 DLT tapes are potentially restorable).

. . .

Defendants assert that the majority of the Exabyte tapes only contain backups of "ordinary CVT employees' hard drives, not those of senior executives." However, plaintiffs correctly note that defendants have only located a catalog for one of the six sets of potentially recoverable tapes for the ... relevant time period, and thus nobody knows what is actually contained on these tapes. Moreover, plaintiffs assert that the catalog that has been produced lists the hard drives of each individual defendant, key CVT witnesses, and high-level executives identified in the case.

The Court concludes that plaintiffs have not demonstrated that defendants intentionally hid the existence of the backup tapes. However, it is undisputed that the newly discovered backup tapes should have been sent to the offsite storage location, and that if they had been, they would have been subject to the terms of the Backup Tape Stipulation. In light of the peculiar circumstances surrounding the discovery of the backup tapes, the Court orders as follows: no later than April 24, 2006, defendants shall review and prepare full catalogs for all Exabyte and DLT tapes from the time period covered in the Backup Tape Stipulation. Plaintiffs shall review these catalogs, and inform defendants by April 28, 2006, which documents plaintiffs wish to have produced. Defendants shall produce all requested documents, except those protected by a privilege, by May 19, 2006. Defendants shall prepare and produce a privilege log for any documents withheld on account of privilege by May 26, 2006. The parties may modify any of these dates through the meet-and-confer process. Defendants shall bear the full cost associated with all of this discovery.

D. Documents from "S" and "H" drives, "Documentum" and "eRoom"

Discovery from these sources is the subject of both plaintiffs' motion to compel and defendants' motion for a protective order. The "H" drive is a drive where CVT employees could store personal documents and emails, and it may contain FDA submissions and correspondence. The "S" drive is the drive on which employees can share documents, and it contains FDA submissions and correspondence. The "eRoom" was a form of communication at CVT used like email, and it was a place where people could work together electronically, and post, share, comment upon, and edit documents. "Documentum" is CVT's database management system which, among other things, stores FDA communications. All four sources contain primarily non-email document types, such as Word, PowerPoint, Excel, and Adobe Acrobat.

Although defendants previously represented to plaintiffs that these sources would be searched, defendants have not searched these sources for responsive documents. Defendants first told plaintiffs that they would not be producing any documents from these sources on January 19, 2006. Defendants contend that the burden and cost of searching these sources far outweigh any benefits to plaintiffs. Defendants estimate that it would take about 7,000 person hours to review the "S" and "H" drives, or put differently, a team of seven people, working 40 hours a week, over six months. Defendants estimate the cost of this review to be well over $1 million. Defendants estimate that it would take over 20,000 person hours to complete the review of documents on "Documentum" and "eRoom," taking a team of 13 people, working 40 hours a week, approximately 10 months. Defendants estimate the cost to be over $2.2 million. Alternatively, defendants request that plaintiffs be required to narrow their search and to pay for the costs associated with this discovery.

The Court is mindful of defendants' concerns regarding the costs and burden associated with this discovery. At the same time, the Court concludes that plaintiffs are entitled to some limited discovery from these sources because they have demonstrated that these sources are likely to contain relevant documents. In order to balance the competing concerns of the parties, the Court orders as follows: by April 24, 2006, defendants shall prepare and produce to plaintiffs an index of the documents contained on the "S" and "H" drives, eRoom and Documentum for the active server only. By April 28, 2006, plaintiffs shall inform defendants which documents that they wish to have produced. Plaintiffs are limited to choosing documents created between June 1, 2002 and December 31, 2003. Defendants shall produce all requested documents, except those protected by a privilege, by May 19, 2006. Defendants shall prepare and produce a privilege log for any documents withheld on account of privilege by May 26, 2006. The parties may modify any of these dates through the meet-and-confer process. Plaintiffs shall bear 100% of the costs of defendants' vendor incurred after the creation of the indexes. Defendants shall bear 100% of the costs of the vendor incurred in the creation of the indexes, as well as the costs of defense counsel associated with this discovery.

*   *   *

CONCLUSION

Accordingly, the Court DENIES defendants' motion for a protective order, GRANTS in part and DENIES in part plaintiff's motion to compel production and for an order to show cause and GRANTS plaintiff's motion to compel documents designated as privileged, and REFERS the in camera review of the documents claimed as privileged to a magistrate judge. Both sides have requested fees and costs associated with the instant motions. These requests are DENIED.

In addition to the question of what electronically stored information is discoverable, the issue of the form and format of the produced information has recently come to the attention of lawyers and courts. The issue of converting the data to be accessible by current programs and who would pay for that, as discussed in the previous case, is a hot topic. And, generating the most interest at the moment is whether the metadata in the files, showing, among other things, when and by whom changes were made, is also discoverable. So far, most courts appear to have ruled that the files should be produced in native format, thus including any metadata the program might generate.

FRCP Rule 26 (Cont'd.)

(b)(3) Trial Preparation: Materials.

Subject to the provisions of subdivision (b)(4) of this rule, a party may obtain discovery of documents and tangible things otherwise discoverable under subdivision (b)(1) of this rule and prepared in anticipation of litigation or for trial by or for another party or by or for that other party's representative (including the other party's attorney, consultant, surety, indemnitor, insurer, or agent) only upon a showing that the party seeking discovery has substantial need of the materials in the preparation of the party's case and that the party is unable without undue hardship to obtain the substantial equivalent of the materials by other means. In ordering discovery of such materials when the required showing has been made, the court shall protect against disclosure of the mental impressions, conclusions, opinions, or legal theories of an attorney or other representative of a party concerning the litigation.

The general rule is that materials prepared especially for court are not discoverable. Although you are entitled to know what evidence your opponent intends to use, you are not entitled to know how the opposing lawyer intends to use that evidence. This is part of what lawyers call the "work-product" rule; the work product of an attorney is not discoverable.

FRCP Rule 26 (Cont'd.)

(b)(4) Trial Preparation: Experts.

(A) A party may depose any person who has been identified as an expert whose opinions may be presented at trial. If a report from the expert is required under subdivision (a)(2)(B), the deposition shall not be conducted until after the report is provided.

(B) A party may, through interrogatories or by deposition, discover facts known or opinions held by an expert who has been retained or specially employed by another party in anticipation of litigation or preparation for trial and who is not expected to be called as a witness at trial, only as provided in Rule 35(b) or upon a showing of exceptional circumstances under which it is impracticable for the party seeking discovery to obtain facts or opinions on the same subject by other means.

(C) Unless manifest injustice would result, (i) the court shall require that the party seeking discovery pay the expert a reasonable fee for time spent in responding to discovery under this subdivision; and (ii) with respect to discovery obtained under subdivision (b)(4)(B) of this rule the court shall require the party seeking discovery to pay the other party a fair portion of the fees and expenses reasonably incurred by the latter party in obtaining facts and opinions from the expert.

Note that (A) and (B) relate to different types of experts: those the party intends to use at trial and those the party does not intend to use. If an attorney consults you for an opinion and you give one adverse to that attorney's side of the case, the other side cannot find out what your opinion was. Furthermore, you will probably not be allowed to testify for the other side even if the other side approaches you totally independently.

FRCP Rule 26 (Cont'd.)

(b)(5) Claims of Privilege or Protection of Trial Preparation Materials.

When a party withholds information otherwise discoverable under these rules by claiming that it is privileged or subject to protection as trial preparation material, the party shall make the claim expressly and shall describe the nature of the documents, communications, or things not produced or disclosed in a manner that, without revealing information itself privileged or protected, will enable other parties to assess the applicability of the privilege or protection.

(c) Protective Orders.

Upon motion by a party or by the person from whom discovery is sought, accompanied by a certification that the movant has in good faith conferred or attempted to confer with other affected parties in an effort to resolve the dispute without court action, and for good cause shown, the court in which the action is pending or alternatively, on matters relating to a deposition, the court in the district where the deposition is to be taken may make any order which justice requires to protect a party or person from annoyance, embarrassment, oppression, or undue burden or expense, including one or more of the following:

(1) that the disclosure or discovery not be had;

(2) that the disclosure or discovery may be had only on specified terms and conditions, including a designation of the time or place;

(3) that the discovery may be had only by a method of discovery other than that selected by the party seeking discovery;

(4) that certain matters not be inquired into, or that the scope of the disclosure or discovery be limited to certain matters;

(5) that discovery be conducted with no one present except persons designated by the court;

(6) that a deposition, after being sealed, be opened only by order of the court;

(7) that a trade secret or other confidential research, development, or commercial information not be revealed or be revealed only in a designated way; and

(8) that the parties simultaneously file specified documents or information enclosed in sealed envelopes to be opened as directed by the court.

A protective order is the way in which one protects oneself from the burden, oppression, or expense discussed above, as the following case illustrates. On the specific issue of "noninvolved" experts, this represents the view of the majority of courts, especially Federal courts, on the matter, but a growing state court minority appears to take a different view.[1]

BUCHANAN V. AMERICAN MOTORS CORP. IN THE MATTER OF RICHARD G. SNYDER. 697 F.2D 151 (6 CIR. 1983)

Appellant, a defendant in a federal, diversity, products liability, wrongful death action in North Carolina for injury arising from a claimed design defect in a Jeep manufactured by appellant, seeks to subpoena appellee, an expert residing in Michigan who has published a lengthy adverse research study about the safety of appellant's product. The subpoena reads in pertinent part as follows:

To Richard G. Snyder, Highway Safety Research Institute of the University of Michigan, Ann Arbor, Michigan.

You are commanded to appear at 290 City Center Building at the offices of Huron Reporting Service in the city of Ann Arbor on the 23rd day of July, 1981, at 10:00 A.M. to testify ... at the taking of a deposition in the above-entitled action pending in the United States District Court for the Western District of North Carolina and bring with you any and all research data, memoranda, correspondence, lab notes, reports, calculations, moving pictures, photographs, slides, statements and the like pertaining to the on-road crash experience of utility vehicles study by the Highway Safety Research Institute of the University of Michigan for the Insurance Institute for Highway Safety in which you participated.

Appellee is a stranger to the North Carolina litigation and is not an expert witness or adviser to any party to that litigation under Rule 26(b)(4) of the Federal Rules of Civil Procedure or to the Court under Rule 706(a) of the Federal Rules of Evidence. Appellant states that its reason for seeking discovery from the expert is that it expects its adversary in the North Carolina litigation to use the research study as one basis for expressing an adverse expert opinion about the safety of appellant's product.

Assuming without deciding that the expert here, whose testimony and data have been subpoenaed, has neither an absolute nor qualified privilege to refuse discovery and is subject to the same general evidentiary rules requiring discovery as any other witness, it is nevertheless clear that the question of the scope of discovery addresses itself to the sound discretion of the District

Court in the first instance. Our review of the record indicates that the District Court did not abuse its discretion in quashing the subpoena *duces tecum* in the instant case on grounds that it is unreasonably burdensome. Compliance with the subpoena would require the expert who has no direct connection with the litigation to spend many days testifying and disclosing all of the raw data, including thousands of documents, accumulated over the course of a long and detailed research study. Like the District Court, we note that the expert is not being called because of observations or knowledge concerning the facts of the accident and injury in litigation or because no other expert witnesses are available. Appellant wants to attempt to prove that the expert's written opinions stated in the research study are not well founded.

The District Court did not err in finding improper the practice of calling an eminent expert witness (who is a stranger to the litigation) under a burdensome subpoena *duces tecum* that would require him to spend a large amount of time itemizing and explaining the raw data that led him to a research opinion adverse to the interest of a party which is the author of the subpoena.

Accordingly, the judgment of the District Court quashing the subpoena in question is affirmed.

FRCP Rule 26 (Cont'd.)

(e) Supplementation of Disclosures and Responses.

A party who has made a disclosure under subdivision (a) or responded to a request for discovery with a disclosure or response is under a duty to supplement or correct the disclosure or response to include information thereafter acquired if ordered by the court or in the following circumstances:

(1) A party is under a duty to supplement at appropriate intervals its disclosures under subdivision (a) if the party learns that in some material respect the information disclosed is incomplete or incorrect and if the additional or corrective information has not otherwise been made known to the other parties during the discovery process or in writing. With respect to testimony of an expert from whom a report is required under subdivision (a)(2)(B) the duty extends both to information contained in the report and to information provided through a deposition of the expert, and any additions or other changes to this information shall be disclosed by the time the party's disclosures under Rule 26(a)(3) are due.

(2) A party is under a duty seasonably to amend a prior response to an interrogatory, request for production, or request for admission if the party learns that the response is in some material respect incomplete or incorrect

and if the additional or corrective information has not otherwise been made known to the other parties during the discovery process or in writing.

The courts take very seriously this duty to amend answers. Failure to do so may cause severe repercussions, as in the following case, in which the party that won the case had the decision reversed because it "played games" during discovery and failed to inform the other side when it discovered different information.

ROZIER V. FORD MOTOR CO., 573 F.2D 1332 (5 CIR. 1978)

The controlling issue raised by this appeal concerns the posttrial relief available to a party who has lost a civil suit after an adverse party failed to disclose relevant information called for by interrogatories and court order. For reasons not stated in its order, the district court denied plaintiff's motion for a new trial pursuant to Rule 60(b), Fed.R.Civ.P., timely filed when plaintiff's counsel, after adverse jury verdict and final judgment, learned of the existence of the undisclosed material. Aware of our limited role in reviewing this discretionary function, we nonetheless hold that the unique facts of this case require reversal and remand for a new trial.

The Facts

On March 13, 1973, the 1969 Ford Galaxie 500 in which William Rozier was riding as a passenger on a Georgia public highway was struck from behind by a faster moving vehicle driven by Benjamin J. Wilson, Jr. The impact caused the Ford's fuel tank to rupture, resulting in a fire which engulfed the car and severely burned Mr. Rozier. Within 24 hours, he died as a result of the burns he sustained. On August 26, 1974, his widow, Martha Ann Brundage Rozier, filed suit below against Ford Motor Company (Ford), based on diversity jurisdiction, alleging that Ford's negligent design of the 1969 Galaxie's fuel tank caused the death of her husband. After a one week trial, the jury returned a verdict for Ford. Judgment was entered on March 6, 1976, and Mrs. Rozier timely filed her notice of appeal to this Court. During the pendency of that appeal, counsel for Mrs. Rozier learned of the existence of a document prepared by a Ford cost engineer, A. Mancini, in 1971 and arguably covered by plaintiff's interrogatories in this case, as limited by an order of the trial judge entered on January 6, 1976. Because Ford had failed to produce this document in response to the court's order, Mrs. Rozier, on February 9, 1977, filed a motion for a new trial pursuant to Rule 60(b)(2), Fed.R.Civ.P., newly discovered evidence, and 60(b)(3), fraud, misrepresentation, and other misconduct. After hearing oral arguments and considering briefs and affidavits filed by the parties, the district court denied the motion on all grounds. Mrs. Rozier's appeal from this later order has been consolidated with her appeal from the original judgment.

* * *

The facts relevant to Mrs. Rozier's 60(b)(3) motion are as follows.

On August 25, 1975, counsel for Mrs. Rozier served her fourth set of interrogatories upon counsel for defendant Ford. Interrogatories 8, 10, 12, and 16 asked whether Ford had conducted "any cost/benefit analyses" with respect to four possible design modifications of fuel tanks for passenger cars, including full-sized sedans and hard-tops. Interrogatory 19 requested similar information not limited to "cost/benefit analyses":

19. In conducting "its own in-house research and development work on …
alternate fuel tank locations" over the last ten years has Ford Motor Company
prepared any written reports or analyses of the comparative advantages or
disadvantages of alternate locations (e.g., on top of the rear axle or in front
of the rear axle) for fuel tanks in full-sized sedans and hard-tops, including
the 1969 Galaxie 500?

The interrogatories also asked whether, in the event such documents exist, Ford would make them available for inspection and copying without the necessity of a request for production.

In response, Ford objected to these and other interrogatories on the ground that "the information sought therein does not relate to vehicles of the same size, chassis and fuel system as the 1969 Ford Galaxie 500." On December 11, 1975, counsel for Mrs. Rozier moved in writing to compel Ford to answer the fourth set of interrogatories. On January 6, 1976, the district court entered an order directing in part, as follows:

Defendant shall file with the Court and serve upon Plaintiff's counsel, no
later than January 21, 1976, answers to questions numbered 4, 5, 6, 7, 8, 9,
10, 11, 12, 13, 14, 15, 16, 17, 19, and 20 of Plaintiff's Fourth Interrogatories;
provided, however, that the aforesaid questions are limited to such written
requirements, cost/benefit analyses, and written reports or analyses which
are applicable to the 1969 Ford Galaxie 500. The fact that a written requirement, cost/benefit analysis or written report may also be applicable to vehicles
other than the 1969 Ford Galaxie 500 does not render it beyond the scope
of the aforesaid interrogatory and must be disclosed in response to the
aforesaid interrogatories.

Finally, on January 22, 1976, in purported compliance with this order, Ford filed amended responses to the fourth set of interrogatories. In answering interrogatories 8, 10, 12, and 16 concerning cost/benefit analyses of alternate fuel tank designs, Ford stated: "There would be no formal cost-benefit analysis with regard to this information." In response to interrogatory 19, concerning "written reports of analyses of the comparative advantages and disadvantages of alternate locations … for fuel tanks," Ford stated: "Defendant cannot find such written analysis covering the inquiry." Approximately one year after Ford filed these amended responses and ten months after the jury returned a verdict favorable to Ford, plaintiff's counsel learned of the document from Ford's files at issue in this appeal. Dated "2/9/71," this "Confidential Cost Engineering Report" states as its subject:

> Trend Cost Estimate Fuel Tank Proposals (30 mph Safety Std.) Prop[osal] I Tank Over Rear Axle Surrounded by Body Sheet Metal Barrier & Prop[osal] II Tank in Tank Filled With Polyurethene vs. 1971 Ford Design 1975 Ford/Mercury.

So far as we can determine from the face of the document and on the basis of remarks by counsel for Ford during oral argument, this "Trend Cost Estimate" was prepared in anticipation of a revised National Highway Traffic Safety Administration safety standard of 30 mph for rear-end collisions. It compares the costs of parts and labor associated with two proposed alternate fuel tank designs based on the design of a 1971 full-sized Ford. Without dispute the 1969 Galaxie 500 model was a full-sized Ford car. Apparently, Ford planned to begin using a new fuel tank design sufficient to satisfy the 30 mph standard in its 1975 full-sized models.

[T]he 1969 Ford Galaxie 500 is so similar in size, design, and fuel tank location to the 1971 Ford that the subject "Confidential Cost Engineering Report" is as applicable and valid for the 1969 Ford Galaxie 500 as it is for the 1971 Ford.

In response to Mrs. Rozier's motion to vacate, Ford produced an affidavit by Thomas G. Grubba, an attorney on the house legal staff of Ford Motor Company, who "was involved in" the case. Mr. Grubba swore that he was unaware of the Trend Cost Estimate when the answers to plaintiff's interrogatories were prepared, but that he became aware of the document on February 25, 1976. We note that although Ford's answers were filed on January 22, 1976, the trial did not begin until March 1, 1976, a week after Mr. Grubba discovered the document.

By any fair reading, the district court's January 6, 1976, discovery order called for production of this Trend Cost Estimate. Ford, in response to the motion to vacate and in this appeal, has urged that, as a term of art, a "trend cost estimate" is not a "cost/benefit analysis." Whether the document in question technically is or is not a cost/benefit analysis to our nonexpert eyes, the terms are synonymous, as alike as "Tweedledum and Tweedledee" is largely irrelevant in this case because plaintiff's interrogatories were not limited to "cost/benefit analyses." Interrogatory 19 asked whether Ford had "prepared any written reports or analyses of the comparative advantages or disadvantages of alternate locations ... for fuel tanks"; the court's January 6 order compelled production of all such "written reports or analyses which are applicable to the 1969 Ford Galaxie 500," specifically noting that written reports also applicable to vehicles other than the 1969 Ford Galaxie 500 were not beyond the scope of the discovery order "and must be disclosed in response to the aforesaid interrogatories." Undeniably, the Trend Cost Estimate is a report "of the comparative advantages or disadvantages" of alternate fuel tank locations, since the alternative which could satisfy the safety standard for the least cost would, in terms of Ford's interests, be the most advantageous.* Also, in light of the unchallenged assertions made in the Arndt and Bloch affidavits, this estimate based on the design of a 1971 full-sized Ford is applicable to a 1969 full-sized Ford.

---

* In his deposition, Ford engineer Stenning noted that one alternate location was disfavored because it would not allow different bodies to be installed on the same base, thus cutting down on "interchangeability."

We conclude that Mrs. Rozier has proved by clear and convincing evidence that Ford engaged in misrepresentation and other misconduct.* Plaintiff's interrogatory 19, as limited by the district court's order, called for production of the Trend Cost Estimate. In its written response, Ford stated that it could find no such report. A month later, an in-house attorney for Ford involved in this case discovered the Trend Cost Estimate but failed to disclose it or to amend the inaccurate response to interrogatory 19.** If Ford in good faith believed that the district court's order was not intended to compel production of this document, the appropriate remedy was to seek a ruling by the district court at that point and not a year after the trial and then only when, by chance, the plaintiff learned of it.

The more vexing question is whether nondisclosure of the Trend Cost Estimate prevented Mrs. Rozier from fully and fairly presenting her case. At trial, Mrs. Rozier contended that Ford was negligent in designing a fuel tank that could not withstand an impact such as that involved in the accident which took her husband's life. Prior to trial, she expressed an intention to rely on 14 theories to explain how Ford deviated from the appropriate standard of care. Inevitably, information developed in the discovery stages of the case influenced the decision as to which theories would be emphasized at trial. We are left with the firm conviction that disclosure of the Trend Cost Estimate would "have made a difference in the way plaintiff's counsel approached the case or prepared for trial," and that Mrs. Rozier was prejudiced by Ford's nondisclosure....Ford [also] argues in a related context, that the Trend Cost Estimate, if admissible at trial, would merely have been cumulative because plaintiff's experts testified at length as to the feasibility of alternative fuel tank

---

* In this respect we are not substituting our judgment for that of the district court. Unfortunately, the district court made no findings of fact, and its order denying the motion for a new trial stated simply: "the Court is of the opinion that said motion should be and is hereby denied upon each and every ground therein stated." Our conclusion that Ford engaged in misconduct is not inconsistent with the district court's holding because, conceivably, the court could have found that Ford engaged in misrepresentation or other misconduct but that a new trial was nevertheless unwarranted. ... [When] Ford attempted to argue that plaintiff's interrogatories were intended to discover only that which went into the design of the 1969 Ford Galaxie 500, the trial judge interrupted:

THE COURT: Wait a minute. But then if anything was learned by Ford between that time and the time of the death of Rozier that would have application to the safety of the '69 Ford, that would be relevant. That's why we limited it to the time of his death, didn't we?

Shortly thereafter the following exchange ensued:

MR. WEINBERG (for Ford): In any event, the Court's order, we contend, is clear and that there has been no violation of this Court's order by Ford.

THE COURT: Let me say this, you know. In a nontechnical sense, I would say it does, just by looking at it. I mean, they're talking about variable costs on the proposed design...

MR. WEINBERG: It doesn't have anything to do with the cost of tooling, the cost of production...

THE COURT: Whatever. It does have reference to variable costs.... It would seem to me to be a factor that would go into it.

** Ford's duty to amend its inaccurate response is based on Rule 26(e)(2).... Although we are unaware of the precise nature of Mr. Grubba's involvement in this case, he did not participate in the trial itself or in the appeal. The attorneys retained by Ford to represent the company at trial and in the appeal have assured this Court that they were personally unaware of the Cost Trend Estimate until Mrs. Rozier filed her motion to vacate almost a year after the trial. We accept their statements.

designs. Additionally, Ford contends that the document would have been inadmissible by virtue of Rule 407, Fed.R.Evid. We think that these arguments misconstrue the significance of the withheld document. The admissibility of evidence is irrelevant in the discovery process so long as "the information sought appears reasonably calculated to lead to the discovery of admissible evidence." Fed.R.Civ.P. 26(b)(1). The Trend Cost Estimate clearly satisfies this test. It was not an isolated document, but rather one in a series.

* * *

It is apparent, then, that the Trend Cost Estimate, far from being a cumulative tidbit of evidence already subsumed in the case presented to the jury, might have been the catalyst for an entirely different approach to the case on a theory that the plaintiff, lacking the document, let die before it reached the jury. Under these circumstances, we hold that Ford's wrongful withholding of information prevented Mrs. Rozier from fully and fairly presenting her case.

* * *

Policy Considerations

Our system of civil litigation cannot function if parties, in violation of court orders, suppress information called for upon discovery. "Mutual knowledge of all the relevant facts gathered by both parties is essential to proper litigation. To that end, either party may compel the other to disgorge whatever facts he has in his possession." *Hickman v. Taylor,* 329 U.S. 495, 507, 67 S.Ct. 385, 392, 91 L.Ed. 451 (1947). The Federal Rules of Civil Procedure substitute the discovery process for the earlier and inadequate reliance on pleadings for notice-giving, issue-formulation, and fact revelation. As the Supreme Court stated in *Hickman v. Taylor, supra,* "civil trials in the federal courts no longer need to be carried on in the dark. The way is now clear, consistent with recognized privileges, for the parties to obtain the fullest possible knowledge of the issues and facts before trial." 329 U.S. at 501, 67 S.Ct. at 389. The aim of these liberal discovery rules is to "make a trial less a game of blind man's bluff and more a fair contest with the basic issues and facts disclosed to the fullest practicable extent." *United States v. Proctor & Gamble Co.,* 356 U.S. 677, 683, 78 S.Ct. 983, 986, 2 L.Ed.2d 1077 (1958). It is axiomatic that "[d]iscovery by interrogatory requires candor in responding." *Dollar v. Long Mfg., N.C., Inc.,* 561 F.2d 613, 616 (5th Cir. 1977). Through its misconduct in this case, Ford completely sabotaged the federal trial machinery, precluding the "fair contest" which the Federal Rules of Civil Procedure are intended to assure. Instead of serving as a vehicle for ascertainment of the truth, the trial in this case accomplished little more than the adjudication of a hypothetical fact situation imposed by Ford's selective disclosure of information. The policy protecting the finality of judgments is not so broad as to require protection of judgments obtained in this manner.

Within a year of their entry, judgments obtained through fraud, misrepresentation, or other misconduct may be set aside under Rule 60(b)(3). Although the granting of such relief is within the discretion of the trial court, the rule "is remedial and should be liberally construed." Atchison, Topeka & Santa Fe Ry. Co. v. Barrett, supra, 246 F.2d at 849. In reviewing the instant denial of plaintiff's Rule 60(b)(3) motion for abuse of discretion, it is not without significance that the trial judge stated no reasons for the denial. We have searched for reasons justifying denial of the motion and can find none sufficient to sustain this exercise of discretion. Under the unique facts of this case, the policy of deterring discovery abuses which assault the fairness and integrity of litigation must be accorded precedence over the policy of putting an end to litigation.

We do not reach the question of whether the district court abused its discretion in denying plaintiff's motion for a new trial based on newly discovered evidence, pursuant to Rule 60(b)(2). Under that Rule, the moving party must show, inter alia, that the newly discovered evidence is "such that a new trial would probably produce a new result." To hold the plaintiff in this case to such a showing would be manifestly unfair:

> [I]t cannot be stated with certainty that all of this would have changed the result of the case. But, as said by the Supreme Court, a litigant who has engaged in misconduct is not entitled to "the benefit of calculation, which can be little better than speculation, as to the extent of the wrong inflicted upon his opponent." Minneapolis, St. Paul & S.S. Marie Ry. Co. v. Moquin, 1931, 283 U.S. 520, 521-22, 51 S.Ct. 501, 502, 75 L.Ed. 1243.

We hold that the district court abused its discretion in denying plaintiff's Rule 60(b)(3) motion and that a new trial is required.

Having examined the general principles that apply to all varieties of discovery, we shall now look at the specific discovery methods in more detail.

REFERENCE

1. Barinaga, C., Who controls a researcher's files, *Science,* 256, 1620, 1992.

CHAPTER 3

Depositions

The most common way in which an expert becomes involved in discovery is by having his or her deposition taken. Rule 30 sets forth the way depositions are to be taken.

FRCP Rule 30. Deposition Upon Oral Examination

(a) When Depositions May Be Taken; When Leave Required.

(1) A party may take the testimony of any person, including a party, by deposition upon oral examination without leave of court except as provided in paragraph (2). The attendance of witnesses may be compelled by subpoena...

(b) Notice of Examination: General Requirements; Method of Recording; Production of Documents and Things; Deposition of Organization; Deposition by Telephone.

(1) A party desiring to take the deposition of any person upon oral examination shall give reasonable notice in writing to every other party to the action. The notice shall state the time and place for taking the deposition and the name and address of each person to be examined, if known, and, if the name is not known, a general description sufficient to identify the person or the particular class or group to which the person belongs. If a *subpoena duces tecum* is to be served on the person to be examined, the designation of the materials to be produced as set forth in the subpoena shall be attached to, or included in, the notice.

A *subpoena duces tecum* is a subpoena that requires the production of documents as well as a person. If you receive such a subpoena you should review the documents to be produced and familiarize yourself with their contents so that you are not surprised at your deposition as was the witness in the following extract from a deposition in a "Superfund" case to recover the costs of clean-up from the defendants.

EXCERPTS FROM A DEPOSITION IN THE CASE OF *KELLEY ex rel MICHIGAN v. E.I. DuPONT, et al.*, E.D. MICH. (1991):

Q. Mr. Hoffmaster, I want to go back for just a minute to a few of the costs on the site. Before I do that I want to establish a little bit of groundwork. Were you the project manager responsible for the conduct of the RI/FS at this site?

A. Yes, I was the project manager for the conduct of the RI/FS at Stevens.

Q. That puts you as the person in charge for Michigan DNR of the specific activity?

A. Yes.

Q. Did you have some familiarity with the national contingency plan at that time?

A. Yes, some overall familiarity, yes.

Q. Can you explain what the national contingency plan is?

A. Basically it's a document that outlines the responsibilities and the roles of the Superfund law, CERCLA.

Q. Are you familiar with the phrase consistent with the NCP or not–inconsistent with the NCP?

A. Yes.

Q. Did you contemplate the possibility of cost recovery for the Stevens Landfill expenses at the time RI/FS was going on?

A. Yes.

Q. Was there an attempt on your part to determine that Michigan DNR would, in fact, incur expenses consistent with the NCP —

A. Yes, I believe so.

Q. — to facilitate cost recovery?

A. Yes, I believe so.

Q. Going back to Exhibit 12, the category of expenses, I just want to go down to a couple specific expenses. You've told us that Exhibit 12 lists, at least up to the time of its preparation, those expenses for which the State of Michigan is now suing DuPont and BFI of Ohio and Michigan, is that right?

A. Yes, that's correct.

Q. One of the categories of the expenses that our clients are being sued for is this miscellaneous expenses category; is that right?

A. Yes, I believe so.

Q. And within that miscellaneous expenses category, Exhibit 16, those are what the expenses are, that is right?

A. Yes, that's correct.

Q. So if it's on Exhibit 16 it translates onto Exhibit 12 and it's part of what we're being sued for?

A. Yes, I believe so.

Q. I want to identify a couple of specific things that are on Exhibit 16, if I could. I'll just mark these. I'm going to do them together.

Q. Mr. Hoffmaster, can you tell me what Exhibits 24, 25, 26, and 27 now are?

A. They appear to be phone bills, phone bill costs incurred from the Stevens Landfill project, and as the account number appears it appears that these are costs associated with the RI/FS work done at Stevens.

Q. So Exhibits 24, 25, 26, and 27 are copies of the actual phone bills for the trailer at the landfill together with the vouchers for their payment?

A. That's correct.

Q. Okay. And these appear to be genuine copies?

A. Yes, they do.

Q. Okay. And the expenses that are set out in these phone bills and paid through these vouchers are part of the expenses for which the State of Michigan is suing DuPont and Browning-Ferris Industries of Ohio and Michigan?

A. Yes, I believe so.

Q. And they're part of the cost recovery demand that was made in April of 1990?

A. Yes, I believe so.

Q. Just to try to determine what some of these expenses are for, do you see on Exhibit 24 on the fourth page there's some long distance communications?

A. Yes.

Q. Are you able to identify what any of those numbers are for?

A. I know what the first two numbers — well, the first number is an office call back to — 8166 is my secretary's phone number in Lansing.

Q. Okay. What about these numbers to this 900 exchange, are you able to identify those?

A. I'm not aware of what the 900 numbers would be to.

Q. These phone calls were made in October of 1986, is that correct?

A. That appears to be such, yes.

Q. Let me mark as an exhibit and hand you a magazine which is now marked as Exhibit 28.

Q. Does that appear to be a copy of the October 1986 issue of *Penthouse* magazine?

A. It says October 1986, yes.

Q. Can you turn in the inside back cover a couple of pages and see if there are some phone numbers listed? Right here.

A. Yes, there are several phone numbers listed.

Q. And do you find that any of the phone numbers that are listed on the inside of the October 1986 issue of *Penthouse* are some of the same phone numbers that appear on this bill for the expenses that you're suing — that the state is suing BFI of Ohio and Michigan to recover?

A. That appears to be some of the same numbers, yes.

Q. One of the numbers is 1-900-410-9999, is that right?

A. Yes.

Q. Can you tell me what *Penthouse* says you get when you call 1-900-410-9999?

A. I can't tell you, no.

Q. Does it say, Intimate sexual pleasure of Emmanuelle X?

A. Yes.

MR. FIRESTONE: Can we go off the record?

MR. BECK: In a few minutes. I want to go ahead and get these on the record.

MR. FIRESTONE: I just meant — I think the state would be willing to stipulate that these costs would not be consistent with the NCP, if that will speed things up and prevent us from having to leaf through *Penthouse* after *Penthouse*.

MR. BECK: There's only one *Penthouse*.

Q. Let's just go ahead and describe what some of these numbers are for. There is a call on this bill that our clients are being sued for to 1-900-410-7777?

A. Yes, that's correct.

Q. And what does *Penthouse* say that's for?

A. The caption reads, Hypatia Lee — sizzling, sultry sex star of the silver screen.

Q. And 1-900-410-7000, what's that?

A. It says, caption reads, Secret sex techniques — Advice on how to fulfill your ultimate sexuality.

Q. And then there's one for 1-900-410-3000. Can you tell us what that call is for according to *Penthouse*?

A. According to this it says, Forbidden fantasies of Alexis C — a seductive nymph.

Q. I trust, sir, that you will agree that the Forbidden fantasies of Alexis C — a seductive nymph, were probably not consistent with the NCP?

A. I would not think they would be, no.

MR. BECK: Your witness.

FRCP Rule 30 (Cont'd.)

(b)(2) The party taking the deposition shall state in the notice the method by which the testimony shall be recorded. Unless the court orders otherwise, it may be recorded by sound, sound-and-visual, or stenographic means, and the party taking the deposition shall bear the cost of the recording. Any party may arrange for a transcription to be made from the recording of a deposition taken by nonstenographic means.

(3) With prior notice to the deponent and other parties, any party may designate another method to record the deponent's testimony in addition to the method specified by the person taking the deposition. The additional record or transcript shall be made at that party's expense unless the court otherwise orders.

* * *

(6) A party may in the party's notice and in a subpoena name as the deponent a public or private corporation or a partnership or association or governmental agency and describe with reasonable particularity the matters on which examination is requested. In that event, the organization so named shall designate one or more officers, directors, or managing agents, or other persons who consent to testify on its behalf, and may set forth, for each person designated, the matters on which the person will testify. A subpoena shall advise a non-party organization of its duty to make such a designation. The persons so designated shall testify as to matters known or reasonably available to the organization. This subdivision (b)(6) does not preclude taking a deposition by any other procedure authorized in these rules.

(7) The parties may stipulate in writing or the court may upon motion order that a deposition be taken by telephone or other remote electronic means. For the purposes of this rule and Rules 28(a), 37(a)(1), and 37(b)(1), a deposition taken by such means is taken in the district and at the place where the deponent is to answer questions.

(c) Examination and Cross-Examination; Record of Examination; Oath; Objections.

Examination and cross-examination of witnesses may proceed as permitted at the trial under the provisions of the Federal Rules of Evidence.... The officer before whom the deposition is to be taken shall put the witness on oath or affirmation and shall personally, or by someone acting under the officer's direction and in the officer's presence, record the testimony of the witness. The testimony shall be taken stenographically or recorded by any other method authorized by subdivision (b)(2) of this rule. All objections made at the time of the examination to the qualifications of the officer taking the deposition, to the manner of taking it, to the evidence presented, to the conduct of any party, or to any other aspect of the proceedings shall be noted by the officer upon the record of the deposition; but the examination shall proceed, with the testimony being taken subject to the objections. In lieu of participating in the oral examination, parties may serve written questions in a sealed envelope on the party taking the deposition and the party taking the deposition shall transmit them to the officer, who shall propound them to the witness and record the answers verbatim.

As Rule 30(c) states, testimony will be taken subject to objections made to the evidence presented. The means the attorney objecting says "I object" and the objection is entered into the record. The reason for this is that, as already discussed, the testimony need not be admissible if it may lead to admissible evidence. The attorney notes the objection in the record because the deposition may be used later at trial. The witness should not allow an objection to interfere with his or her testimony; if the attorney wants to be certain that the witness does not answer the question (because of a claim of privilege, for example) the attorney will not make a "simple" objection but will instead direct or instruct the witness not to answer.

FRCP Rule 30 (Cont'd.)

(d) Schedule and Duration; Motion to Terminate or Limit Examination.

(1) Any objection to evidence during a deposition shall be stated concisely and in a non-argumentative and non-suggestive manner. A party may instruct a deponent not to answer only when necessary to preserve a privilege, to enforce a limitation on evidence directed by the court, or to present a motion under paragraph (3).

(2) By order or local rule, the court may limit the time permitted for the conduct of a deposition, but shall allow additional time consistently with Rule 26(b)(2) if needed for a fair examination of the deponent or if the deponent or another party impedes or delays the examination. If the court finds such as impediment, delay, or other conduct that has frustrated the fair examination of the deponent, it may impose upon the persons responsible an appropriate sanction, including the reasonable costs and attorney's fees incurred by any parties as a result thereof.

(3) At any time during a deposition, on motion of a party or of the deponent and upon a showing that the examination is being conducted in bad faith or in such manner as unreasonably to annoy, embarrass, or oppress the deponent or party, the court in which the action is pending or the court in the district where the deposition is being taken may order the officer conducting the examination to cease forthwith from taking the deposition, or may limit the scope and manner of the taking of the deposition as provided in Rule 26(c). If the order made terminates the examination, it shall be resumed thereafter only upon the order of the court in which the action is pending. Upon demand of the objecting party or deponent, the taking of the deposition shall be suspended for the time necessary to make a motion for an order. The provisions of Rule 37(a)(4) apply to the award of expenses incurred in relation to the motion.

(e) Review by Witness; Changes; Signing.

If requested by the dependent or a party before completion of the deposition, the deponent shall have 30 days after being notified by the officer that the transcript or recording is available in which to review the transcript or recording and, if there are changes in form or substance, to sign a statement reciting such changes and the reasons given by the deponent for making them.

Section (d), which provides for how the attorney can "call things off" in the middle of the process, is of little use to the witness. Section (e), on the other hand, is one of the most important points a witness must know about depositions. You, as the witness, have the right to read and sign your deposition *before* the lawyers see it. You should make it your practice, after giving your name at a deposition, to state "I insist on my right to read and sign this deposition." The following case illustrates the importance of this point.

INCARNATI v. SAVAGE, 329 N.W. 2d 790 (Ct. App. Mich., 1982)

Defendant appeals and plaintiff cross-appeals from a jury verdict in Wayne County Circuit Court which awarded damages to plaintiff for personal injuries suffered in a car-motorcycle accident.

Between midnight and 12:30 a.m. on June 8, 1974, plaintiff and a friend rode motorcycles on a two-lane road. As plaintiff reached a crest in the road, he noticed his friend was no longer by his side. As he proceeded down the other side of the slight hill, plaintiff heard a shout causing him to look over his shoulder behind him. At that point, plaintiff testified, he saw a car, driven by the defendant, coming down the incline towards him. The two vehicles collided. Plaintiff testified that he believed the car struck the rear of his motorcycle. Defendant testified that his car struck the front of plaintiff's motorcycle because it faced him broadside, straddling the road's center as if to make a U-turn. Attempting to avoid the accident, defendant testified, he swerved his car into the left lane.

Plaintiff suffered a fractured right arm. A rod was surgically placed in plaintiff's forearm and a cast put over the arm by Dr. James Ryan, an orthopedic specialist. The cast was removed in September or October of 1974. The rod was removed sometime between November, 1974, and January, 1975, the record being unclear. After the rod was removed and up to the time of trial, plaintiff complained of stiffness in his arm in damp, cold weather.

At trial, after the parties had rested and prior to closing arguments, the trial judge granted plaintiff's request to change a word in Dr. Ryan's deposition transcript, which had already been read to the jury. Defendant contends this was reversible error.

On the first day of trial, the following from Dr. Ryan's deposition was read to the jury:

Q. If he (plaintiff) were to indicate, Doctor, that his arm still becomes stiff and swells if any unusual activity is required, would that be inconsistent with your experience and understanding of the medical situation?

A. I would think so at this date.

The actual question put to the doctor was whether the symptoms were consistent. Through a stenographic error, the word "inconsistent" was inserted into Dr. Ryan's deposition transcript.

On the second day of trial, plaintiff's counsel apparently alluded to the transcript error when he told the court:

(Plaintiff's attorney): There is only one other matter. I believe there is a mistake in a transcript. I think it can be remedied by Wednesday. I don't want to point out yet what it is, but I am having the court reporter check it. And with the Court's permission, if there is — certainly I ought to be able to make that correction I believe at any stage prior to closing argument. I will have that by Wednesday. I am just having the court reporter check the shorthand notes. And I will bring it to the Court's attention prior to Wednesday.

(Defense attorney): I am not even entitled to know what he is talking about until Wednesday?

The trial court allowed the correction on the third day of trial after the parties had rested. The jury was informed that the correct word was "consistent." The trial judge read again to the jury the erroneous transcription and then the corrected version.

GCR 1963, 308.4 reads:

> As to Completion and Return of Deposition. Errors and irregularities in the manner in which the testimony is transcribed or the deposition is prepared, signed, certified, sealed, indorsed, transmitted, filed or otherwise dealt with by the person before whom taken under Rules 306 or 307 are waived unless a motion to suppress the deposition or some part thereof is made with reasonable promptness after such defect is, or with due diligence might have been, ascertained.

Under the court rule, the transcript mistake should have been deemed waived. Its last minute correction was reversible error requiring a new trial. Under GCR 1963, 308.4, errors in deposition transcripts are waived if not corrected within a reasonable time after the error was discovered or should have been discovered. Here, the error should have been discovered sooner. Plaintiff took the deposition nearly two years prior to trial. The transcript was 24 pages long. A party exercising due diligence would have discovered the error between the time of transcription and the time it was read at trial. The treating physician's deposition testimony in a personal injury lawsuit is important. GCR 1963, 308.4 does not contemplate only an express waiver, as plaintiff seems to believe.

Moreover, correction of the transcript after the parties had rested was prejudicial to the defendant. In his opening statement, defense counsel relied on the very part of Dr. Ryan's transcript which was later changed. Defense counsel informed the jury that plaintiff's claims of swelling were considered inconsistent by Dr. Ryan with the type of injuries sustained in the motorcycle accident. The defense sought to show that plaintiff's injuries were not serious and that defendant was not responsible for injuries to plaintiff which occurred after plaintiff fell while on a fishing trip. The plaintiff's counsel referred to the corrected part of the transcript in his closing and rebuttal arguments, reciting as damages plaintiff's residual problems with his elbow having stiffness. Thus, the late correction of the transcript destroyed the defense strategy. It is also impaired defendant's credibility with the jury.

*   *   *

Reversed and remanded.

The type of error illustrated by this case is generally referred to as a "transcription" error, in which the typing does not accurately represent what was stated in the testimony. If the witness reviews a transcript and finds such an error and the stenographer agrees that the transcription is wrong, the transcript is corrected before the lawyers see it. If the witness maintains there is a transcription error but the stenographer disagrees, or if the witness realizes that the testimony given is wrong, both the original testimony and the testimony the witness wishes to substitute are included on the copy sent to the lawyers. Nevertheless, it is still better to correct the matter at this stage rather than find yourself on the witness stand saying something and then be cross-examined about why you said something else at your deposition. One thing you can do to help the stenographer is arrive at the deposition with a list of correctly spelled technical terms you may use during the course of your testimony. When reviewing the transcript, however, do not attempt to correct grammar or syntax.

FRCP Rule 30 (Cont'd.)

(f) Certification and Filing by Officer; Exhibits; Copies; Notices of Filing.

(1) The officer shall certify that the witness was duly sworn by the officer and that the deposition is a true record of the testimony given by the witness. This certificate shall be in writing and accompany the record of the deposition. Unless otherwise ordered by the court, the officer shall securely seal the deposition in an envelope or package endorsed with the title of the action and marked 'Deposition of [here insert name of witness]' and shall promptly file it with the court in which the action is pending or send it to the attorney who arranged for the transcript or recording, who shall store it under conditions that will protect it against loss, destruction, tampering, or deterioration. Documents and things produced for inspection during the examination of the witness, shall, upon the request of a party, be marked for identification and annexed to the deposition and may be inspected and copied by any party, except that if the person producing the materials desires to retain them the person may (A) offer copies to be marked for identification and annexed to the deposition and to serve thereafter as originals if the person affords to all parties fair opportunity to verify the copies by comparison with the originals, or (B) offer the originals to be marked for identification, after giving to each party an opportunity to inspect and copy them, in which event the materials may then be used in the same manner as if annexed to the deposition. Any party may move for an order that the original be annexed to and returned with the deposition to the court, pending final disposition of the case.

(2) Unless otherwise ordered by the court or agreed by the parties, the officer shall retain stenographic notes of any deposition taken stenographically or a copy of the recording of any deposition taken by another method. Upon payment of reasonable charges therefor, the officer shall furnish a copy of the transcript or other recording of the deposition to any party or to the deponent.

Rule 30(f) indicates that, unless you make your desires known immediately, any materials you bring with you to the deposition can be lost to you for a considerable period of time. For this reason it is best to bring *copies* of such materials to the deposition (as well as the originals so the two can be compared) and ask to have the copies substituted for the originals.

CHAPTER 4

Other Discovery Techniques

As already noted in Rule 26, another major discovery technique is interrogatories. The relevant portions of the rules specific to interrogatories begin as follows:

FRCP Rule 33. Interrogatories to Parties

(a) Availability.

Without leave of court or written stipulation, any party may serve upon any other party written interrogatories, not exceeding 25 in number including all discrete subparts, to be answered by the party served or, if the party served is a public or private corporation or a partnership or association or governmental agency, by any officer or agent, who shall furnish such information as is available to the party. Leave to serve additional interrogatories shall be granted to the extent consistent with the principles of Rule 26(b)(2). Without leave of court or written stipulation, interrogatories may not be served before the time specified in Rule 26(d).

(b) Answers and Objections.

(1) Each interrogatory shall be answered separately and fully in writing under oath, unless it is objected to, in which event the objecting party shall state the reasons for objection and shall answer to the extent the interrogatory is not objectionable.

(2) The answers are to be signed by the person making them, and the objections signed by the attorney making them.

(3) The party upon whom the interrogatories have been served shall serve a copy of the answers, and objections if any, within 30 days after the service of the interrogatories. A shorter or longer time may be directed by

the court or, in the absence of such an order, agreed to in writing by the parties subject to Rule 29.

(4) All grounds for an objection to an interrogatory shall be stated with specificity. Any ground not stated in a timely objection is waived unless the party's failure to object is excused by the court for good cause shown.

(5) The party submitting the interrogatories may move for an order under Rule 37(a) with respect to any objection to or other failure to answer an interrogatory.

The requirement that answers be filed within 30 days is one "more honored in the breach than the observance." I doubt that any lawyer expects to receive answers to interrogatories within 30 days. If, for some reason (primarily bureaucratic), you must answer a set of interrogatories, the first thing you should do is call the lawyer who sent them and request an extension of time for answering; the request almost always will be honored. Once the lawyer grants an extension, send the lawyer a letter via regular mail, confirming the date when the answers actually will be filed.

FRCP Rule 33 (Cont'd.)

(c) Scope; Use at Trial.

Interrogatories may relate to any matters which can be inquired into under Rule 26(b), and the answers may be used to the extent permitted by the rules of evidence.

An interrogatory otherwise proper is not necessarily objectionable merely because an answer to the interrogatory involves an opinion or contention that relates to fact or the application of law to fact, but the court may order that such an interrogatory need not be answered until after designated discovery has been completed or until a pretrial conference or other later time.

(d) Option to Produce Business Records.

Where the answer to an interrogatory may be derived or ascertained from the business records, including electronically stored information, of the party upon whom the interrogatory has been served or from an examination, audit or inspection of such business records, including a compilation, abstract or summary thereof, and the burden of deriving or ascertaining the answer is substantially the same for the party serving the interrogatory as for the party served, it is a sufficient answer to such interrogatory to specify the records from which the answer may be derived or ascertained and to afford to the party serving the interrogatory reasonable opportunity to examine, audit or inspect such records and to make copies, compilations, abstracts, or summaries.

Rule 33(d) is very useful when you are faced with a request for "historical" or "archival" data. It means that you do not have to go out and do the other side's research for it; you merely have to provide the other side with the source material under reasonable circumstances and the time to do its own research. This can be a great time-saver for you and may even convince the other side that the information it requested is not really so important after all.

If, to reach a conclusion about the issues presented in a case, you need to inspect or copy documents, test objects, or enter upon land, the rules provide the means for you to achieve this.

FRCP Rule 34. Production of Documents, Electronically Stored Information, and Things and Entry Upon Land for Inspection and Other Purposes

(a) Scope.

Any party may serve on any other party a request (1) to produce and permit the party making the request, or someone acting on the requestor's behalf, to inspect, copy, test, or sample any designated documents or electronically stored information--including writings, drawings, graphs, charts, photographs, sound recordings, images, and other data or data compilations stored in any medium from which information can be obtained--translated, if necessary, by the respondent into reasonably usable form, or to inspect, copy, test, or sample any designated tangible things which constitute or contain matters within the scope of Rule 26(b) and which are in the possession, custody or control of the party upon whom the request is served; or (2) to permit entry upon designated land or other property in the possession or control of the party upon whom the request is served for the purpose of inspection and measuring, surveying, photographing, testing, or sampling the property or any designated object or operation thereon, within the scope of Rule 26(b).

If physical or mental examination of a person is required, Rule 35 provides for that to be secured during the discovery process:

FRCP Rule 35. Physical and Mental Examination of Persons

(a) Order for Examination.

When the mental or physical condition (including the blood group) of a party or of a person in the custody or under the legal control of a party, is in controversy, the court in which the action is pending may order the party to submit to a physical or mental examination by a suitably licensed or certified examiner or to produce for examination the person in the party's custody or legal control. The order may be made only on motion for good cause shown and upon notice to the person to be examined and to all parties and shall specify the time, place, manner, conditions, and scope of the examination and the person or persons by whom it is to be made.

(b) Report of Examiner.

(1) If requested by the party against whom an order is made under Rule 35(a) or the person examined, the party causing the examination to be made shall deliver to the requesting party a copy of the detailed written report of the examiner setting out the examiner's findings, including results of all tests made, diagnoses and conclusions, together with like reports of all earlier examinations of the same condition. After delivery the party causing the examination shall be entitled upon request to receive from the party against whom the order is made a like report of any examination....

*   *   *

If you, as an expert, are requested to perform a mental or physical examination for a pending lawsuit, the odds are very good that such a request is pursuant to this rule. There is considerable variation among courts concerning whether the person to be examined is entitled to have a lawyer present at the examination. In some jurisdictions this happens as a matter of course; in others, it may require a court order. In any case, be aware that if you are conducting such an examination you may have nonmedical people standing over your shoulder during the process. You should take care to write your report as clearly and explicitly as possible since the other side will always request a copy. Always make sure that you specify exactly what reports or other documents helped you formulate your opinion. State clearly those parts of these other reports with which you agree and disagree.

The request for admission is another important major discovery device, frequently underutilized by lawyers. It is, however, important that you be familiar with it because its use can save you a great deal of time and effort when preparing your actual testimony and help you avoid many problems of admissibility under the Rules of Evidence. In Part II, we will discuss many ways in which pretrial use of the request for admission can be useful.

FRCP Rule 36. Requests for Admission

(a) Request for Admission.

A party may serve upon any other party a written request for the admission, for purposes of the pending action only, of the truth of any matters within the scope of Rule 26(b)(1) set forth in the request that relate to statements or opinions of fact or of the application of law to fact, including the genuineness of any documents described in the request. Copies of documents shall be served with the request unless they have been or are otherwise furnished or made available for inspection and copying........

Each matter of which an admission is requested shall be separately set forth. The matter is admitted unless, within 30 days after service of the request, or within such shorter or longer time as the court may allow ... the party to whom the request is directed serves upon the party requesting the admission a written answer or objection addressed to the matter, signed by the party or by the party's attorney. If objection is made, the reasons therefore shall be stated. The answer shall specifically deny the matter or set forth in detail the reasons why the answering party cannot truthfully admit or deny the matter. A denial shall fairly meet the substance of the requested admission, and when good faith requires that a party qualify an answer or deny only a part of the matter of which an admission is requested, the party shall specify so much of it as is true and qualify or deny the remainder. An answering party may not give lack of information or knowledge as a reason for failure to admit or deny unless the party states that the party has made reasonable inquiry and that the information known or readily obtainable by the party is insufficient to enable the party to admit or deny....

The provisions of Rule 37(a)(4) apply to the award of expenses incurred in relation to the motion.

(b) Effect of Admission.

Any matter admitted under this rule is conclusively established unless the court on motion permits withdrawal or amendment of the admission. Subject to the provision of Rule 16 governing amendment of a pretrial order, the court may permit withdrawal or amendment when the presentation of the merits of the action will be subserved thereby and the party who obtained the admission fails to satisfy the court that withdrawal or amendment will prejudice that party in maintaining the action or defense on the merits. Any admission made by a party under this rule is for the purpose of the pending action only and is not an admission for any other purpose nor may it be used against the party in any other proceeding.

The request for admission under Rule 36 is an exceptionally powerful tool. If the other side unreasonably refuses to make the admission and you eventually prove the matter, then the other side can be compelled to pay all costs you incurred in the process of proving the matter, as Rule 37(c)(2) states:

FRCP Rule 37. Failure to Make or Cooperate in Discovery: Sanctions

*   *   *

(c) Failure to Disclose, False or Misleading Disclosure; Refusal to Admit.

*   *   *

(2) If a party fails to admit the genuineness of any document or the truth of any matter as requested under Rule 36, and if the party requesting the admissions thereafter proves the genuineness of the document or the truth of the matter, the requesting party may apply to the court for an order requiring the other party to pay the reasonable expenses incurred in making that proof, including reasonable attorney's fees. The court shall make the order unless it finds that (A) the request was held objectionable pursuant to

Rule 36(a), or (B) the admission sought was of no substantial importance, or (C) the party failing to admit had reasonable ground to believe that the party might prevail on the matter, or (D) there was other good reason for the failure to admit.

The expenses for failure to make an admission may be substantial, as the following case demonstrates:

MARCHAND V. MERCY MEDICAL CENTER, 22 F.3D 935 (9 CIR. 1994)

A jury awarded Kevin Marchand $4.2 million in a medical malpractice action. He then petitioned to recover attorneys' fees and costs under Fed.R.Civ.P. 37(c), because three defendants failed to admit key requests for admission that he proved at trial. The district court ordered Dr. Neil Farris to pay Marchand's reasonable expenses. Farris appeals this award and we affirm.

Background

Kevin Marchand was seriously injured in an industrial accident. To prevent movement of his neck, paramedics placed him on a back board with a cervical neck collar, sandbags on both sides of his head, and tape stretched across his forehead between the sandbags. The immobilization devices were used to prevent movement of his neck. An ambulance rushed him to Mercy Medical Center. Several physicians treated him in the emergency room, the radiology department, and the intensive care unit (ICU).

Farris provided care to Marchand in the emergency room and radiology department. He and the other doctors agreed to order a full set of cervical spine x-rays. While in the radiology department, Farris removed Marchand's cervical collar. He said this was necessary because Marchand was experiencing respiratory distress and Farris needed to examine his patient's jugular vein. No other person at Mercy Medical Center, nor any medical report from the hospital confirmed the occurrence of a serious respiratory problem in radiology.

Farris did not complete the full set of x-rays he and the other doctors originally contemplated. Five x-rays were taken of Marchand's chest and neck. Farris delivered Marchand to the ICU because of his respiratory distress, and testified that the sandbags were in place, but probably not the collar. But it is undisputed that both were absent shortly after admission. Then he claims to have consulted with a radiologist, Dr. Walker, who confirmed Farris's view that the cervical spine was within normal limits. Walker did not recall consulting with Farris.

Marchand arrived in ICU about 5:30 p.m. Dr. Blome became his primary care provider, and radiologist Truksa reviewed the x-rays and issued a written report. About 1:50 p.m. the next afternoon, Marchand became paralyzed and is now a quadriplegic. The doctors had missed a fracture of the cervical spine. The fracture appeared on three of the chest x-rays, but was not pictured on the lateral cervical spine x-ray.

Marchand sued five doctors and the Mercy Medical Center. After a lengthy trial the jury found Farris, Blome, and Truksa negligent, and apportioned each 33% of the fault. In a posttrial petition, Marchand asked for an award of attorneys' fees under Fed.R.Civ.P. 37(c). He claimed that the negligent doctors had improperly failed to admit some requests for admission that he proved at trial. The requests asked the doctors to admit negligence, to admit that Marchand's immobilization devices were removed at the hospital, and to admit causation. The court imposed fees and costs of $205,798.34 against Farris alone.

*　　*　　*

A. Standard of Care

Request for admission 26 asked Farris to

"[a]dmit that the care and treatment provided to Kevin Marchand at the Mercy Medical Center on March 13, 1987, and March 14, 1987, by Neil K. Farris, D.O., failed to comply with the applicable standard of care which existed for that person on that date."

He responded, "denied."

Farris argues that Rule 37(c) sanctions should not have been imposed because he had "reasonable ground to believe" that he might prevail on the negligence issue. Fed.R.Civ.P. 37(c)(3). He notes accurately "that the true test under Rule 37(c) is not whether a party prevailed at trial but whether he acted reasonably in believing that he might prevail." Fed.R.Civ.P. 37(c), Advisory Committee Notes on 1970 Amendment. This reasonable ground, he urges, was supported by expert testimony that he complied with the standard of care. See Dyer v. United States, 633 F.Supp. 750, 759 (D.Or.1985), aff'd on other grounds, 832 F.2d 1062 (9th Cir. 1987) (defendant entitled to rely on expert testimony to deny difficult request for factual admission).

Dr. Carlson testified as an expert on behalf of Farris. He said that Farris satisfied the standard of care in all respects. Other experts testified that the number and type of x-rays taken complied with the standard of care.

Despite this evidence, we cannot accept a per se rule that reliance on an expert opinion provides a reasonable ground for a party to believe he would prevail at trial. The district court had ample evidence to discredit the expert testimony, as well as that of Farris. Critical to both were the trial statements of Farris that he removed the cervical collar supporting Marchand's neck due to respiratory distress, and that he cleared Marchand's cervical spine as being within normal limits based on the x-rays and consultation with radiologist Dr. Walker. Scant trial testimony or evidence corroborated either assertion.

Moreover, Carlson's trial testimony was contradicted by his deposition statement that no event after Marchand was intubated warranted removal of the neck immobilization devices. And Farris testified in his deposition that an emergency room physician should not remove the cervical collar before obtaining a series of cervical spine x-rays.

Perhaps most damaging was Farris's belated admission that he removed the cervical collar. In his deposition he said that "[t]he patient went to the intensive care unit, to the best of my recollection, with the cervical collar and sandbags." At trial he conceded that he removed the cervical collar in the radiology department before a complete series of cervical spine x-rays was obtained.

The district court concluded that Farris, knowing he removed the cervical collar before obtaining a full series of cervical spine x-rays, could not under the circumstances have reasonably denied his negligence. It applied the correct legal standard, and did not abuse its discretion.

*   *   *

C. Causation

Requests for admission 1-6 asked Farris to admit that Marchand's quadriplegia was caused by movement of his spine that could have been avoided if proper immobilization had been maintained after he was admitted. Farris answered similarly to each question. In response to request for admission 1 he said:

Defendants object to this Request for Admission on the grounds that it is compound, ambiguous, and because the use of the phrase "avoidable movement" is vague and undefined. Without waiving such objections, the Request for Admission, couched in its present form, must be denied.

The district court reasoned that Farris could not deny that the quadriplegia would have been avoided had Marchand's spine been immobilized, when Farris obviously knew he had removed the collar.

Farris seeks to excuse his failure to admit because he objected to the requests as compound, ambiguous, and vague. Fed.R.Civ.P. 37(c)(4). He argues that Marchand's failure to move for an order concerning the objection, "should bar him from subsequently recovering expenses." Note, Proposed 1967 Amendments to the Federal Discovery Rules, 68 Col.L.Rev. 271, 294 n. 169 (1968). See also 8 Charles A. Wright and Arthur R. Miller, Federal Practice and Procedure Sec. 2290 at 804 n. 87 (1970) ("court[s] should consider [an objection] a 'good reason' for failure to admit and hold that it falls within condition (4) of Rule 37(c)"). We disagree.

Counsel routinely object to discovery requests. It would be unduly burdensome to require each and every objection to be challenged in order for sanctions to issue. And to aid the quest for relevant information, parties should not seek to evade disclosure by quibbling and objection. They should admit to the fullest extent possible, and explain in detail why other portions of a request may not be admitted.

Farris could have provided frank answers to these requests, which were clearly designed to establish causation. Or he could have "set forth in detail the reasons why [he could not] truthfully admit or deny the matter." Fed.R.Civ.P. 36(a). He did neither, relying on unfounded objections to the wording, instead of admitting the uncontestable question: Were Marchand's injuries caused by movement of the spine that could have been avoided had proper immobilization been maintained?

The record shows he had no reasonable basis to deny that question. Marchand's expert testified at trial that paralysis would not have occurred if he had been properly immobilized. Farris did not cross-examine the expert, and presented no experts to challenge causation.

He relies on the deposition of another expert to establish a reasonable belief that he might prevail on the causation issue. But that witness agreed with Marchand that there was a greater than 50% chance that Marchand would not have become paralyzed had he been properly immobilized before the onset of paralysis at the hospital. And Farris presents no other evidence that could reasonably support his denial of causation. The district court did not err.

D. Fee and Cost Calculation

When Farris refused to admit, Marchand was put to the expense of proving negligence and causation. He may recover "the reasonable expenses incurred in making that proof." Fed.R.Civ.P. 37(c). Ordinarily we would remand for a recalculation of the expenses that flowed directly from the improper answers to the negligence and causation requests. This calculation would exclude those expenses claimed for the proper admission that the neck support was removed. But the removal request is subsumed in the negligence request. Any work done to discover who, when, where, and why the neck support was removed, would also have been done to prove that Farris was negligent. So all claimed expenses for the removal of the collar also flowed directly from the denial of negligence. No remand is necessary.

Farris argues that Marchand failed to establish sufficient causal nexus between the awarded expenses and his failure to admit. He primarily asserts that no additional expenses flowed from his answers because Marchand would have had to prove these issues against the other defendants.

But the claims against other defendants do not protect Farris from sanctions for his unreasonable conduct. More importantly, had Farris admitted negligence and causation, Marchand would have been relieved of proving a significant portion of this case, but not all of it. Accordingly, his petition sought only one half to one third of the hours that were only partially dedicated to Farris.

The court's calculation was reasonable. The hours requested comprised 25% of the total hours spent on the case, which is appropriate in light of the pivotal nature of the requests for admission on negligence, causation, and whether the immobilization devices were removed. The request was not rubber stamped. The district judge reduced the requested hourly fee, which lowered the fee award from $350,000 to $156,360. The calculation of $49,438.34 in costs was well supported. The award of $205,798.34 in fees and costs was well within the discretion of the district court.

The judgment is affirmed.

CHAPTER 5

Failure to Cooperate in Discovery

Rule 37 specifies the process for "forcing" an answer if the other side fails to answer interrogatories or otherwise does not respond to a request for discovery.

FRCP Rule 37. Failure to Make or Cooperate in Discovery; Sanctions

(a) Motion for Order Compelling Disclosure or Discovery.

A party, upon reasonable notice to other parties and all persons affected thereby, may apply for an order compelling disclosure or discovery as follows:

(1) Appropriate Court.

An application for an order to a party shall be made to the court in which the action is pending. An application for an order to a person who is not a party shall be made to the court in the district where the discovery is being, or is to be, taken.

(2) Motion.

(A) If a party fails to make a disclosure required by Rule 26(a), any other party may move to compel disclosure and for appropriate sanctions. The motion must include a certification that the movant has in good faith conferred or attempted to confer with the party not making the disclosure in an effort to secure the disclosure without court action.

(B) If a deponent fails to answer a question propounded or submitted under Rules 30 or 31, or a corporation or other entity fails to make a designation under Rule 30(b)(6) or 31(a), or a party fails to answer an interrogatory submitted under Rule 33, or if a party, in response to a request for inspection submitted under Rule 34, fails to respond that inspection will be permitted as requested or fails to permit inspection as requested, the discovering party may move for an order compelling answer, or a designation, or an order compelling inspection in accordance with the request. The motion must include a certification that the movant has in good faith conferred or attempted to confer with the person or party failing to make the discovery in an effort to secure the information or material without court action. When taking a deposition on oral examination, the proponent of the question may complete or adjourn the examination before applying for an order.

(3) Evasive or Incomplete Disclosure, Answer, or Response.

For purposes of this subdivision an evasive or incomplete disclosure, answer, or response is to be treated as a failure to disclose, answer, or respond.

(4) Expenses and Sanctions.

(A) If the motion is granted or if the disclosure or requested discovery is provided after the motion was filed, the court shall, after affording an opportunity to be heard, require the party or deponent whose conduct necessitated the motion or the party or attorney advising such conduct or both of them to pay to the moving party the reasonable expenses incurred in making the motion, including attorney's fees, unless the court finds that the motion was filed without the movant's first making a good faith effort to obtain the disclosure or discovery without court action, or that the opposing party's nondisclosure, response, or objection was substantially justified, or that other circumstances make an award of expenses unjust.

(B) If the motion is denied, the court may enter any protective order authorized under Rule 26(c) and shall, after affording an opportunity to be heard, require the moving party or the attorney filing the motion or both of them to pay to the party or deponent who opposed the motion the reasonable expenses incurred in opposing the motion, including attorney's fees, unless the court finds that the making of the motion was substantially justified or that other circumstances make an award of expenses unjust.

Several points about this part of Rule 37 are noteworthy. As the following case illustrates, if you really want to secure the information you are requesting in discovery, you must apply to the court for an order compelling the other side to cooperate.

MASTERS V. CITY OF HIGHLAND PARK, 294 N.W.2D 246 (CT. APP. MICH. 1980)

On December 8, 1972, the plaintiff, Bruno M. Masters, filed suit against the City of Highland Park, the Civil Service Board of the City of Highland Park, and Highland Park General Hospital, alleging that his discharge, after 22 years of service with the Highland Park Hospital maintenance department, was wrongful. He had been discharged for alleged noncompliance with the city's residence requirements. The discharge was first upheld by the Highland Park Civil Service Commission and then by the Wayne County Circuit Court in an order dated December 26, 1975. This Court reversed and ordered the plaintiff reinstated with accrued back wages. The Michigan Supreme Court's order of affirmance remanded the matter to the trial court for a determination of the amount of back pay to be awarded to the plaintiff. This order gave the defendants an opportunity to establish that the plaintiff had not properly mitigated his damages.

On August 25, 1978, plaintiff was deposed by the defendants regarding his income and attempts to find employment following discharge. The defendants submitted a set of interrogatories to plaintiff on December 13, 1978, which were not answered. On December 28, 1978, the plaintiff moved for entry of judgment. The city objected to any entry of a judgment based on the plaintiff's failure to respond to the interrogatories and its own desire to depose the former personnel director of Highland Park. On February 2, 1979, the trial court rejected defendants' arguments and rendered judgment for plaintiff in the amount of $242,281.91. The city now appeals, claiming that the trial court reversibly erred by not allowing them to adequately explore the mitigation of damages issue.

Discovery was designed to clarify the factual and legal questions to be litigated at trial. Through this mechanism, complete and honest disclosure of the underlying issues can occur, preventing surprise at trial. To this end, the discovery rules are to be liberally construed. However, these disclosure considerations must be balanced against the necessity for expeditious disposition of litigation. It is up to the trial judge to balance these ofttimes competing concerns so as to ensure both parties' right to a fair trial.

Defendants objected to the entry of judgment prior to answers being submitted on the December interrogatories. Despite the ready mechanism available under GCR 1963, 313.1, defendants failed to move for an order compelling a response to the interrogatories. We believe that their failure constituted a waiver and we will not review defendants' claim absent manifest injustice.

Determining the relevancy of interrogatories is a decision within a trial judge's discretion which will not be reversed on appeal absent an abuse of discretion. We agree with the trial judge that most of defendants' interrogatories had either already been answered at plaintiff's deposition or were irrelevant to the mitigation issue. Since most of the questions were of this nature, the interrogatories were not submitted until late in the litigation, the defendant did not move to compel answers, and the burden of mitigation was on defendants, no manifest injustice results if we do not review defendants' claim.

Defendants further argue that the trial court erred in not allowing them time to depose an out-of-state witness, the former personnel director of Highland Park.

The granting or denial of discovery is within the trial judge's discretion. An underlying consideration must be whether the granting or extension of discovery will facilitate rather than impede the litigation. Factors such as the timeliness of the request, the duration of the litigation, and possible prejudice to the litigants should be considered. Unless it will create manifest injustice, after a reasonable length of time a judge should be able to terminate discovery and proceed with trial.

In the instant case, defendants had 10 months between the Supreme Court's remand order and the entry of judgment. Yet, it was only when plaintiff moved for judgment that the defendants indicated any dire need for the witness's testimony. We believe that a reasonable time for discovery had elapsed so that it was proper for the trial judge to refuse to extend defendants' investigation.

In summary, we hold that the failure to utilize the discovery sanctions listed in GCR 1963, 313, will waive the issue of noncompliance on appeal, absent manifest injustice. Parties should only be allowed a reasonable time prior to trial in which to pursue discovery methods such as depositions or interrogatories or discovery sanctions such as orders and default judgments. After that period, the trial judge should be able to terminate discovery and to proceed to trial or the entry of judgment. His decision to do so will not be reversed by this Court unless manifest injustice has resulted to the appealing party.

Affirmed.

As this case shows, if a motion to compel discovery is not made, the discovery is considered to be unimportant and the request is considered to be dropped.

As the courts have become more accustomed to dealing with computers and computer storage practices, it has become necessary to provide an "out" for information that was destroyed with no intent to hinder the progress of the current litigation, and Rule 37 (f) so provides.

FRCP Rule 37 (Cont'd.)

(f) Electronically Stored Information.

Absent exceptional circumstances, a court may not impose sanctions under these rules on a party for failing to provide electronically stored information lost as a result of the routine, good-faith operation of an electronic information system.

Note also that Rule 37(a)(3) treats an incomplete or evasive answer as equivalent to a failure to answer. Rule 37(a)(4) is a deliberate exception to the "American Rule" that each party to a lawsuit bears its own costs of participation. By adopting the "British Rule" that the winner can obtain costs from the loser, the rule makers hoped to encourage cooperation and the settlement of discovery disputes without resort to the courts. If after one side obtained a court order to compel discovery the other side still refuses to comply, the courts have a variety of instruments available to force compliance, as enumerated in Rule 37(b).

FRCP Rule 37 (Cont'd.)

(b) Failure to Comply with Order.

(1) Sanctions by Court in District Where Deposition is Taken.

If a deponent fails to be sworn or to answer a question after being directed to do so by the court in the district in which the deposition is being taken, the failure may be considered a contempt of that court.

(2) Sanctions by Court in Which Action is Pending.

If a party or an officer, director, or managing agent of a party or a person designated under Rule 30(b)(6) or 31(a) to testify on behalf of a party fails to obey an order to provide or permit discovery, including an order made under subdivision (a) of this rule or Rule 35, or if a party fails to obey an order entered under Rule 26(f), the court in which the action is pending may make such orders in regard to the failure as are just, and among others the following:

(A) An order that the matters regarding which the order was made or any other designated facts shall be taken to be established for the purposes of the action in accordance with the claim of the party obtaining the order;

(B) An order refusing to allow the disobedient party to support or oppose designated claims or defenses, or prohibiting that party from introducing designated matters in evidence;

(C) An order striking out pleadings or parts thereof, or staying further proceedings until the order is obeyed, or dismissing the action or proceeding or any part thereof, or rendering a judgment by default against the disobedient party;

(D) In lieu of any of the foregoing orders or in addition thereto, an order treating as a contempt of court the failure to obey any orders except an order to submit to a physical or mental examination;

(E) Where a party has failed to comply with an order under Rule 35(a) requiring that party to produce another for examination, such orders as are listed in paragraphs (A), (B), and (C) of this subdivision, unless the party failing to comply shows that that party is unable to produce such person for examination.

In lieu of any of the foregoing orders or in addition thereto, the court shall require the party failing to obey the order or the attorney advising that party or both to pay the reasonable expenses, including attorney's fees, caused by the failure, unless the court finds that the failure was substantially justified or that other circumstances make an award of expenses unjust.

Note that this is a varied list of what a court can do and that, once again, the "British Rule" regarding cost applies. As this next case shows, as specified in Rule 37(b)(2)(C), the most extreme action a court can take is rendering a judgment by default.

G-K PROPERTIES V. REDEVELOPMENT AUTHORITY, 577 F.2D 645 (9 CIR. 1978)

G-K Properties and Genesco, Inc. appeal from the trial court's order dismissing their action with prejudice, by reason of failure to comply with the court's discovery orders. Appellants argue that dismissal of their case was an abuse of the trial court's discretion and was a taking of property without due process of law. G-K Properties argues in addition that dismissal was improper as to it because that company does not have custody, control, or possession of the records which were ordered to be produced. We affirm the district court's dismissal as to both parties.

G-K Properties and Genesco commenced this action in the district court on April 1, 1974. It was a proceeding for inverse condemnation. The complaint alleged that property on which an S.H. Kress store was formerly located became unusable as a retail store location as a result of a redevelopment project of the City of San Jose, which unreasonably interfered with appellants' ownership. When the suit was filed, the property was owned by G-K Properties, an employee trust for Genesco employees. Genesco was a tenant of G-K Properties and it operated the property through its S.H. Kress division.

From the earliest stages of this action the parties and the court below perceived one of the key factual issues to be whether the San Jose Kress store was closed as a result of the alleged inverse condemnation or rather because it was, for other reasons, an unprofitable enterprise. In a set of interrogatories issued August 20, 1975, appellees asked for "the written reports, including the annual reports, since 1964 of the Kress Store division made to the Genesco Board of Directors." The response to that question was that "(a)t the present time, no reports are known to exist." Thereafter, appellees requested, inter alia, the following items by way of a motion to produce: "All reports of any kind in writing, including annual reports, concerning the nature and extent of the Kress operation and profit and loss performance, goals, purposes, and the like in the files of Kress stores since 1960." On October 28, 1975, the court issued an order to produce those documents, stating its order in the words of appellees' motion. It was for failure to comply with the October 28 order that the court eventually dismissed this action.

In response to the court's order, plaintiffs' counsel supplied annual reports for Kress from 1960 through 1968, and annual reports to the Securities and Exchange Commission from 1964 through 1966. However, no reports of the financial condition of Kress on an annual or monthly basis after 1969 were forthcoming. After continuing the trial date because of delays in complying with discovery orders, the court directed appellants at least twice to produce the documents included in the October 28 order or to file an affidavit of a responsible officer stating that such documents did not exist and advising appellees what, if any, documents did contain the financial information they sought. The opinion of the court below also indicates that this directive was repeated at conferences held in chambers and that it was clearly explained that the discovery order was intended to comprise records showing profit and loss for the Kress division. Appellants neither supplied the documents nor filed affidavits concerning them. On February 10, 1976, appellees moved for dismissal as a sanction for appellants' failure to comply with the October 28 discovery order. The hearing on this motion was set for March 4. On March 1, appellants submitted an affidavit revealing that an unaudited financial statement for Kress did exist for 1969, and that, after 1969, periodic internal operating statements were prepared for Kress, as for all Genesco operating companies.

At the hearing on the motion to dismiss, the court obtained from appellants' counsel a clear statement that compilations of periodic financial data for Kress did in fact exist;

however, the court rejected appellants' tender of those documents. The court found that an additional continuance of the trial date would not be an effective sanction, and that to impose a fine would merely "introduce into litigation a sporting chance theory encouraging parties to withhold vital information from the other side with the hope that the withholding may not be discovered and, if so, that it would only result in a fine." Accordingly, the court dismissed the case to protect the integrity of its orders.

Where it is determined that counsel or a party has acted willfully or in bad faith in failing to comply with rules of discovery or with court orders enforcing the rules or in flagrant disregard of those rules or orders, it is within the discretion of the trial court to dismiss the action or to render judgment by default against the party responsible for noncompliance. Fed.R.Civ.P. 37(b). Here the court dismissed the plaintiffs' action with prejudice. It acted properly in so doing. We encourage such orders. Litigants who are willful in halting the discovery process act in opposition to the authority of the court and cause impermissible prejudice to their opponents. It is even more important to note, in this era of crowded dockets, that they also deprive other litigants of an opportunity to use the courts as a serious dispute-settlement mechanism. Here the appellants' last-minute tender of relevant documents could not cure the problem they had previously created. As the Supreme Court stated in upholding a dismissal for failure to comply with a discovery order,

> "[Although] it might well be that these [litigants] would faithfully comply with all future discovery orders entered by the District Court in this case ... [if the order of dismissal were overturned] other parties to other lawsuits would feel freer than we think Rule 37 contemplates they should feel to flout other discovery orders of other district courts." National Hockey League v. Metropolitan Hockey Club, Inc., 427 U.S. 639, 643.

Appellants contend the noncompliance with the October 28 order was not willful because they did not understand that the order referred to anything other than Kress annual reports. The court below, however, did find that appellants acted willfully when they refused to cooperate. At the hearing when the dismissal was ordered, the trial judge stated in a colloquy with appellants' counsel:

"I do not think there's a human being that could have sat through conferences in chambers and Court who can have misconstrued the thrust of the Court's comments that your client having brought the lawsuit was directed to produce accounting records such as the annual profit and loss statements from the Kress Division, and if they did not exist as was represented over and over that an Affidavit had to be filed by a responsible Court (sic) official."

On the facts of this case we do not think that the court below could have done other than to conclude that appellants' refusal to cooperate was in direct disobedience to the authority of the court.

* * *

Affirmed.

Dismissal of a case (rendering a judgment by default) is the ultimate sanction to which a court can resort to ensure compliance with its orders. Note, however, that the Appellate Court in the preceding case stated, "We encourage such orders," a clear indication that courts do not like the parties to "play games" during the discovery process.

CHAPTER 6

Pretrial Conferences

After the discovery is complete, the lawyers and the judge meet for a pretrial conference. Those present discuss a variety of matters, and the judge attempts to simplify the trial. The provisions for a pretrial conference are set forth in Rule 16.

FRCP Rule 16. Pretrial Conferences; Scheduling; Management

(a) Pretrial Conferences; Objectives.

In any action, the court may in its discretion direct the attorneys for the parties and any unrepresented parties to appear before it for a conference or conferences before trial for such purposes as

(1) expediting the disposition of the action;

(2) establishing early and continuing control so that the case will not be protracted because of lack of management;

(3) discouraging wasteful pretrial activities;

(4) improving the quality of the trial through more thorough preparation, and;

(5) facilitating the settlement of the case.

(b) Scheduling and Planning.

Except in categories of actions exempted by district court rule... [the court] shall...after consulting with the attorneys for the parties and any unrepresented parties by a scheduling conference, telephone, mail, or other suitable means, enter a scheduling order that limits the time

(1) to join other parties and to amend the pleadings;

(2) to file motions; and

(3) to complete discovery.

The scheduling order may also include

(4) modifications of the times for disclosures under Rules 26(a) and 26(e)(1) and of the extent of discovery to be permitted;

(5) the date or dates for conferences before trial, a final pretrial conference, and trial; and

(6) any other matters appropriate in the circumstances of the case.

The order shall issue as soon as practicable but in any event within 90 days after the appearance of a defendant and within 120 days after the complaint has been served on a defendant. A schedule shall not be modified except upon a showing of good cause and by leave of the district judge or, when authorized by local rule, by a magistrate judge.

(c) Subjects for Consideration at Pretrial Conferences.

At any conference under this rule consideration may be given, and the court may take appropriate action, with respect to

(1) the formulation and simplification of the issues, including the elimination of frivolous claims or defenses;

(2) the necessity or desirability of amendments to the pleadings;

(3) the possibility of obtaining admissions of fact and of documents which will avoid unnecessary proof, stipulations regarding the authenticity of documents, and advance rulings from the court on the admissibility of evidence;

(4) the avoidance of unnecessary proof and of cumulative evidence, and limitations or restrictions on the use of testimony under Rule 702 of the Federal Rules of Evidence;

(5) the appropriateness and timing of summary adjudication under Rule 56;

(6) the control and scheduling of discovery, including orders affecting disclosures and discovery pursuant to Rule 26 and Rules 27 through 37;

(7) the identification of witnesses and documents, the need and schedule for filing and exchanging pretrial briefs, and the date or dates for further conferences and for trial;

(8) the advisability of referring matters to a magistrate judge or master;

(9) settlement and the use of special procedures to assist in resolving the dispute when authorized by statute or local rule;

(10) the form and substance of the pretrial order;

(11) the disposition of pending motions;

(12) the need for adopting special procedures for managing potentially difficult or protracted actions that may involve complex issues, multiple parties, difficult legal questions, or unusual proof problems;

(13) an order for a separate trial pursuant to Rule 42(b) with respect to a claim, counterclaim, cross-claim, or third-party claim, or with respect to any particular issue in the case;

(14) an order directing a party or parties to present evidence early in the trial with respect to a manageable issue that could, on the evidence, be the basis for a judgment as a matter of law under Rule 50(a) or a judgment on partial findings under Rule 52(c);

(15) an order establishing a reasonable limit on the time allowed for presenting evidence; and

(16) such other matters as may facilitate the just, speedy, and inexpensive disposition of the action.

At least one of the attorneys for each party participating in any conference before trial shall have authority to enter into stipulations and to make admissions regarding all matters that the participants may reasonably anticipate may be discussed. If appropriate, the court may require that a party or its representatives be present or reasonably available by telephone in order to consider possible settlement of the dispute.

(d) Final Pretrial Conference.

Any final pretrial conference shall be held as close to the time of trial as reasonable under the circumstances. The participants at any such conference shall formulate a plan for trial, including a program for facilitating the admission of evidence. The conference shall be attended by at least one of the attorneys who will conduct the trial for each of the parties and by any unrepresented parties.

(e) Pretrial Orders.

After any conference held pursuant to this rule, an order shall be entered reciting the action taken. This order shall control the subsequent course of the action unless modified by a subsequent order. The order following a final pretrial conference shall be modified only to prevent manifest injustice.

(f) Sanctions.

If a party or party's attorney fails to obey a scheduling or pretrial order, or if no appearance is made on behalf of a party at a scheduling or pretrial conference, or if a party or party's attorney is substantially unprepared to participate in the conference, or if a party or party's attorney fails to participate in good faith, the judge, upon motion or the judge's own initiative, may make such orders with regard thereto as are just, and among others any of the orders provided in Rule 37(b)(2)(B), (C), (D). In lieu of or in addition to any other sanction, the judge shall require the party or the attorney representing the party or both to pay the reasonable expenses incurred because of any noncompliance with this rule, including attorney's fees, unless the judge finds that the noncompliance was substantially justified or that other circumstances make an award of expenses unjust.

As Rule 16 states, the judge schedules a final pretrial conference, usually within 30 days of the date the case will actually go to trial, although sometimes it may be earlier. At this point, as the list in subsection C shows, the lawyers and the judge agree on many points to simplify the way the case will be tried. The judge frequently pressures the lawyers to settle their disagreements about parts of the case. Because the lawyers will continue to practice before the same judge, this pressure is frequently effective.

To ensure that your lawyer does not give away information vital to your expert opinion in the case, I strongly suggest that you ask your lawyer for the date and time of the pretrial conference. When the lawyer tells you the pretrial conference is scheduled for, say, next Thursday at 4:00 p.m., you should tell the lawyer where you can be reached by telephone at that time. Also tell the lawyer that, before he or she concedes anything in any way connected with your testimony, he or she should call you at the telephone number you provided.

If the judge then pressures the lawyer to agree to something, you have provided the lawyer an "out." Your lawyer can say, "Your honor, that sounds reasonable to me, but I would like to check it out with my expert before I agree; may I use a telephone and call my expert?" At that point, your lawyer will call you and you can say, "Sure, fine, let's agree to it," or you can say something like, "Oh, no, you can't possibly agree to that, that would blow us totally out of the water." In either case, however, you have "let your lawyer off the hook" because your lawyer does not have to make a snap judgment about something the judge is pushing him or her to agree to.

The Rules of Evidence

CHAPTER 7

Fundamental Concepts

Before we examine any of the rules of evidence in detail, I want to define some fundamental concepts.

"BURDEN OF PROOF"

The subtitle of this section is set in quotation marks because, although the term "burden of proof" is frequently used by lawyers, judges, and laypeople, it is not a term favored by academic legal commentators. Those of us who consider ourselves legal scholars prefer to subdivide the phrase into two parts: the burden of persuasion and the burden of going forward with evidence.

Burden of Persuasion

The reason for dividing "burden of proof" into two parts is very simple: the one term covers two different things. The most common usage of the term, which is frequently totally unambiguous, is that the burden of proof means the burden of persuasion. Burden of persuasion means the degree to which the finder of facts must be persuaded by the evidence that the fact is true. There are many different burdens of persuasion, and we shall examine a few of them now.

Beyond a Reasonable Doubt

Readers are undoubtedly familiar with the fact that in a criminal case the prosecution is required to prove that the defendant is guilty beyond a reasonable doubt. This means that if the finder of fact (whether judge or jury) is in any doubt as to whether the defendant is guilty, it cannot find him guilty because of reasonable doubt. If one pictures the scales of justice, beyond a reasonable doubt means one side of the scale has to be low to the ground while the other side of the scale has to be high in the air.

Preponderance of the Evidence

The major burden of persuasion in civil cases is a preponderance of the evidence. This means before the finder of fact can decide that a given statement is true or a given event occurred, it must find that to be true by a preponderance of the evidence. Again, if we picture the scales of justice, a preponderance means the scales merely have to tip slightly, more than halfway, toward the side that asserts the fact or event.

Clear and Convincing Evidence

Clear and convincing evidence is more than a preponderance but still less than beyond a reasonable doubt. Picturing, again, the scales of justice, the two sides should be significantly out of balance but need not be overwhelmingly tilted either way. The most common use of this burden of persuasion is in civil cases alleging fraud. The general rule is that civil fraud must be proved by clear and convincing evidence.

Substantial Evidence

Another test for the burden of persuasion is the test of substantial evidence. This means that if there is substantial evidence, which can be less than preponderance, then the finder of fact can find in favor of that side. Substantial evidence is a burden of persuasion that requires not that the finder of fact be convinced, but that he or she not be unconvinced that a given event occurred or a given fact is true.

Who Bears the Burden

As implied in the preceding paragraphs, the burden of persuasion or, as it is sometimes called, the risk of nonpersuasion, rests upon the party asserting that a given event occurred or that a given fact is true. In the typical criminal case, for example, the burden of persuasion, beyond a reasonable doubt, is on the prosecution to prove the defendant guilty. In the typical civil case the burden of persuasion, preponderance of the evidence, is on the plaintiff to establish that the plaintiff is entitled to the relief requested in the complaint.

This is not, however, always true, especially in the civil case. Think back to the hypothetical automobile collision that we discussed in Chapter 1. In that case, when the defendant alleged in her answer to the complaint that she had to pull out to clear the way for an emergency vehicle, the burden of persuasion is on the defendant as to whether or not the emergency vehicle was present and that she needed to give way to it. The defendant bears the burden of persuasion because the defendant is the party seeking to establish that a given fact is true or that a given event occurred.

Burden of Going Forward

As the above discussion indicates, the burden of persuasion is set at the beginning of the trial based on the pleadings, and it never changes during the course of the trial. The burden of going forward, however, does shift back and forth between the parties during the course of the trial.

The burden of going forward is initially on the person who has the burden of persuasion. It is that party's responsibility to produce some evidence to support its argument that its version of events is correct. After that party has presented enough evidence that a jury or judge could find for that party, the burden of going forward shifts to the other party, which then has the burden of coming forward with evidence to convince the judge or jury that the event did not occur or that the fact is not true.

In most situations, the party who has the burden of going forward has the right to just stop and not go forward on any given issue. The fact that one side does not present evidence controverting the other side's evidence does not automatically mean that the first side will lose on that issue. The first side can still argue that the evidence presented by the other side is weak or is presented by prejudiced witnesses and therefore should not be believed. It is not incumbent upon a party to go forward merely because the burden has shifted to that party.

If, however, a party does go forward and present evidence to controvert the evidence presented by the other party, the burden of going forward then shifts once again, to the first party. That party now has the obligation of coming forward with whatever evidence regarding the issue it might have, which it had not presented previously. It is very rare that we reach this stage, because it is generally not advisable not to present all your evidence at the first opportunity, since if the other party does nothing you will not have a second opportunity. Nevertheless, this shifting back of the burden is possible; indeed, the burden could shift back and forth again and again, at the discretion of the judge in deciding to admit new evidence on an issue that has already been discussed.

Presumptions

The way in which the law changes the burden of persuasion and/or the burden of going forward is with presumptions. A presumption means it is presumed, as a matter of law, that a given fact is true or that a given type of event occurred. This does not, of course, mean that anybody actually believes that the fact is true or the event occurred, merely that, for legal purposes, we will presume that.

One of the most common burden-shifting presumptions in law is res ipsa loquiter, which translates as "the thing speaks for itself." It is generally stated along the lines of "if a party is injured and the injury occurred totally beyond the control of the injured party and the injured party has no evidence as to what occurred and is unable to obtain any, then it is presumed that the injury was due to the action of the defendant." The classic example of res ipsa loquiter is a situation like the following:

A person goes into the hospital for an operation on the right foot. Upon recovering from anesthesia, the person discovers that the left foot was operated upon. Since anesthesia rendered the person totally unconscious, there is no way for the person to know what really happened and why the other foot was operated upon. There is an injury, since the wrong foot was operated upon, so the presumption of res ipsa loquiter comes into play. It is up to the hospital and physicians to come forward with evidence and perhaps bear the burden of persuasion as to why this untoward event occurred.

ORIGINS OF THE LAW OF EVIDENCE

The law of evidence is a peculiarly common law area, which has developed over the centuries through court decisions and which has remained relatively unaffected by legislative enactments. The rules of evidence throughout the common law world, from Australia to Zimbabwe, are relatively similar. The standard text-book on the law of evidence is *A Treatise on the Law of Evidence in Anglo-Saxon Jurisdictions*. As the title implies, this book covers the law of evidence in all common law countries.

In the late 1960s, the U.S. Supreme Court appointed a panel of lawyers, law professors, and judges to "codify" the law of evidence for the federal courts. The resulting document, the "Federal Rules of Evidence (FRE)," is nothing more than a uniform compilation of the preexisting law of evidence in the courts throughout the United States. Although many states have followed the lead of the U.S. Supreme Court and developed state rules of evidence, even in those states that do not have such a compilation, the evidentiary principles are the same as those we will discuss in Part II of this book.

It is vital for a witness to know those rules of evidence that can impact upon his or her testimony. If, for example, part of an expert's opinion is based upon hearsay, it is important for the witness to have an idea as to whether that hearsay information can be admitted into evidence. Obviously, when you face a tricky problem in preparing your testimony, you should consult your lawyer about whether something will or will not be admissible. Part II will help you to make a preliminary assessment and to understand what the lawyer is talking about when you discuss the matter with him or her.

WEIGHT AND ADMISSIBILITY

As a preliminary matter, you must understand the difference between what lawyers call weight of evidence and admissibility of evidence. Weight refers to whether the decision maker (whether judge or jury) will believe the information being presented and decide in accordance with the views of the witness. Admissi-bility refers to whether the decision maker will even have the opportunity to hear about the piece of information. The rules of evidence deal only with issues of admissibility (with one exception we will discuss later), not with weight. A frequent response of judges when deciding a question of admissibility is, "We will admit that, and the issues you have raised, Ms. Attorney, will be considered as going to the weight."

THE FUNDAMENTAL RULE OF EVIDENCE

FRE Rule 402. Relevant Evidence Generally Admissible; Irrelevant Evidence Inadmissible

All relevant evidence is admissible, except as otherwise provided by the Constitution of the United States, by Act of Congress, by these rules, or by other rules prescribed by the Supreme Court pursuant to statutory authority. Evidence which is not relevant is not admissible.

Rule 401 defines relevant evidence.

FRE Rule 401. Definition of "Relevant Evidence"

"Relevant evidence" means evidence having any tendency to make the existence of any fact that is of consequence to the determination of the action more probable or less probable than it would be without the evidence.

Rule 402 is the most basic of all evidentiary rules — "If it's relevant, it's admissible." All other rules are, then, exclusionary rules, which tell us why something that is relevant will, nevertheless, not be admitted into evidence. Of course, as we will see, the exclusionary rules have specific exceptions that allow something to be admitted, and the exceptions have exceptions that again exclude it, ad infinitum. Our first question about any prospective bit of evidence, then, must be: "Is it relevant?"

The next rule gives a general set of reasons for excluding from evidence something that is relevant, but which is not excluded by a more specific rule. This "catch-all" exclusion is very rarely invoked by courts.

FRE Rule 403. Exclusion of Relevant Evidence on Grounds of Prejudice, Confusion, or Waste of Time

Although relevant, evidence may be excluded if its probative value is substantially outweighed by the danger of unfair prejudice, confusion of the issues, or misleading the jury, or by considerations of undue delay, waste of time, or needless presentation of cumulative evidence.

Part II of the book will differ slightly from Part I. Some rules, such as Rule 403, have no cases illustrating them, as they are relatively easy to apply. Other rules may have more than one case illustrating them, either because the rule is complicated or because several of its points need to be illustrated.

Some cases presented in Part II illustrate more than one issue or rule. Sometimes this may be a review of a topic previously discussed. Other times more than one point might be new. When necessary, different parts of the same case may appear in different places to be near the point illustrated. When that occurs, a cross reference will be supplied for the other part of the case.

CHAPTER **8**

Who Is an Expert and When Can One Testify

Legal terminology distinguishes between "lay" (as in clergy and laity) and "expert" witnesses. The difference between the two is expressed very simply in Rule 701.

FRE Rule 701. Opinion Testimony by Lay Witnesses

If the witness is not testifying as an expert, the witness' testimony in the form of opinions or inferences is limited to those opinions or inferences which are (a) rationally based on the perception of the witness and (b) helpful to a clear understanding of the witness' testimony or the determination of a fact in issue.

The lay witness cannot say "I think," "I believe," or "It is my opinion that" unless the phrase that follows is clearly based on the witness' perception. Here is a simple example:

Q. How hot was it on the afternoon of July 17?
A. I'd say it was about 90.

The witness is giving an opinion. She was not asked what temperature the thermometer showed, as she apparently did not look at a thermometer, so her testimony is an opinion. But this opinion is based on her perception, as she was there and felt it, thus satisfying part (a) of the rule. It is almost impossible to think of any other way in which the witness could give an answer that would be as helpful to the fact finder. Statements such as "It was hot," "It was really hot," and "It was sweltering" do not convey as much information as the opinion, "It was about 90." This satisfies part (b) of the rule. In all other circumstances lay witnesses are limited to testifying about what they saw, heard, felt, smelled, tasted, etc.

FRE Rule 702. Testimony by Experts

If scientific, technical, or other specialized knowledge will assist the trier of
fact to understand the evidence or to determine a fact in issue, ...

Most courts believe experts may have an undue influence on a jury. Thus experts
are not permitted to testify on matters that are believed to be "within the common
knowledge of the jury," as this case illustrates.

COLLINS V. ZEDIKER, 218 A.2D 776 (PA. 1966)

How fast does a man walk? A woman? A child? An aged person? If in a hurry?
If not in a hurry? The answer to these questions would inevitably be: It depends on
the circumstances. That is what this case is about.

Mrs. Catharine Collins, while crossing from the western to the eastern side of a
road 18 feet wide, was about two thirds of the way to her goal when an automobile
traveling in a northward direction struck her. The jury returned a verdict for the
defendants and the plaintiff seeks a new trial, asserting that the Trial Court erred in
allowing an expert witness to estimate the speed of a pedestrian's pace.

William P. Greenough, an engineer, testified that a person walking at a slow rate
would take 6 seconds to advance 18 feet, moving at a moderate rate of speed he
would occupy 5 seconds to traverse that distance, and if he walked at a fast rate,
4 seconds would carry him to his destination. This same engineer had testified that
if the defendant's automobile was moving at 50 miles per hour, it would take
13.3 seconds to cover the unobstructed clear vision south of the plaintiff.

It could well be that the jurors, having accepted as scientific fact the engineer's
testimony as to the time required for an automobile to travel a certain distance
(a subject not necessarily within the general knowledge of the average layman),
concluded that the engineer must have been equally expert on walking speed and
that if he had worked it out mathematically and engineeringly that the plaintiff
deliberately walked into a collision, they had no further responsibility in the case.
On that basis of reasoning, if it occurred, and we cannot say by the record that it
did not occur, since the verdict included the possibility of that conclusion, that
plaintiff was done an injustice, since it was the jury's responsibility to determine
the speed of the plaintiff's walking, not the engineer's.

Phenomena and situations which are matters of common knowledge may not be
made the subject for expert testimony. In Burton v. Horn and Hardart Baking Co., 371
Pa. 60, 88 A.2d 873, 63 A.R.S.2d 731, this Court said: "Expert testimony is inadmissible when the matter can be described to the jury and the condition evaluated by them
without the assistance of one claiming to possess special knowledge upon the subject."

No experience could be more ordinary and within the range of a jury's comprehension than the speed of a walker. Everybody walks. Every normal person has a
pair of legs. Not every person, however, owns an automobile, and even if one does,
he may not be able to calculate with accuracy the distance an automobile travels
moving at a certain velocity.

The speed of a person in a 100-yard dash, of a football player making a 90-yard run, of a pugilist rising from the resin to achieve perpendicularity to receive another fusillade of blows of the kind which had floored him before, may be a matter of stop-watch calculation, but determination of the time involved in a pedestrian's reaching a spot only 18 feet away not only does not require the services of a mechanical computer, an IBM machine or a graduate engineer, but the fact is that none of these can work out the correct answer as satisfactorily as a layman. The function of walking embraces imponderables and variables which a machine or an engineer does not compute, as for instance, agility of footwork, acuity of eyesight, surface of terrain underfoot, noises of distraction, intrusion of visual objects, nervous tension of the walker, state of his reflexes, vigor of concentration, the nature of the clothing worn, the weight of the shoes on his feet. Where fractions of seconds are involved, all these factors contribute to the speed with which a pedestrian moves between two points especially when those termini are not far apart.

The tangle of inaccuracy and unreliability into which testimony such as that given by Greenough may lead a jury is made additionally manifest in the fact that he testified to the speed of a pedestrian traveling 18 feet, the width of the road, whereas the evidence indicated that the plaintiff had gotten only two thirds of the way across when she was struck, which of course would mean that she had not traveled 18 feet.

Moreover, there was no unanimity of view as to the gait the plaintiff employed in undertaking the passage of the road before her. The defendant testified that Mrs. Collins "came at a fast walk." The defendant's sister testified that the plaintiff "looked up and smiled and then sort of hurried across the road more than what she had done before." Did the expert witness take into consideration the smiling of the plaintiff? The plaintiff could not have smiled if the defendant's car was about to crush her beneath its wheels. The quoted testimony would suggest that the defendant's car was far enough away, when the plaintiff smiled, that she was assured she could negotiate the road in safety. It cannot be argued that she was smiling in anticipation of what was to happen to her because in the next few moments she was knocked unconscious, her hip smashed, her face and head bleeding from wounds.

We are convinced from the record that the engineer's formidable testimony of a pedestrian's speed in walking, presented in more or less of a professional and scientific fashion from the witness stand, could well have unduly influenced the jury on behalf of the side which had called him, regardless of inherent merit involved. Jurors are humans and are impressed by scientific talk even though, upon profound reflection, they could realize that in the particular field under discussion they are as much at home as the scientist. The jury should be insulated, to the extent that it is possible, from undue persuasion from the witness stand based upon externals removed from the intrinsic problem to be solved. The trial court here should have refused expert testimony on a situation so obviously within the jury's comprehension, its concluding potentialities, and the scope of its responsibilities as judges of the facts. Allowing expert testimony in the circumstances here related on the speed of walking was as much error as if the judge had allowed expert testimony on the speed with which the average person consumes a hamburger sandwich, wraps spaghetti around his fork or drinks a glass of California wine. As this Court said in Dooner

v. Delaware & H. Canal Co., 164 Pa. 17, 30 A. 269: "The jury still have some duties to perform. Inferences drawn from the ordinary affairs of life ought to be drawn for them, and turned over under oath from the witness stand."

Reversed.

After the judge has decided that expert testimony is proper, it is necessary to establish one's qualifications as an expert, as the last clause of Rule 702 requires:

FRE Rule 702 (Cont'd.)

[A] witness qualified as an expert by knowledge, skill, experience, training, or education, may testify thereto in the form of an opinion or otherwise.

Note that this clause is written in the disjunctive. Although the typical expert will have all of these qualifications (knowledge, skill, experience, training, and education), only one of these qualifications is required to qualify as an expert. Later on we will review several cases in which the expert may have only one or two of these attributes.

The first set of questions asked of an expert are those that establish the qualifications. The usual outline for presenting them is as follows:

Name   Employer (if any)
Home Address   Address
                                                             Job Title

Education:
   Degree, College, major, year
   Graduate or professional degree[s], University, major, year[s]
   Residency or other training, where, years

Employment History:
   First relevant job after graduation
   Next relevant job
      ...
      ...
   Job before present one

Professional Licenses and Organizations:
   State licenses
   Board certifications (for physicians)
   Membership in professional societies
   Offices in professional societies (if any)

Number of publications in professional lifetime, X; in last 10 years, Y

Number of times an expert witness, X; in last 4 y

The next sheet starts the publication list; all of them for the past ten years and relevant ones from before then. After that come the cases in which you have testified as an expert, giving party names and the court in which it occurred.

At this point in your testimony a voir dire examination may occur. The term voir dire, translated literally from the French, means "see speak" or, as we might render it, "show and tell." At a voir dire the judge hears the witness' qualifications and arguments regarding the validity of the evidence, then rules whether the testimony will be allowed. Nowadays voir dire is very rare because such issues are usually settled at the pretrial conference.

This next case illustrates the two parts of Rule 702 that have been covered so far. First the court reviews the qualifications of the proposed expert witness, then the judge discusses whether an expert was needed to discuss the issue of proper design of golf courses.

JOHNSON V. CITY OF DETROIT, 261 N.W. 2D 295 (CT. APP. MICH. 1978)

On May 12, 1972, while waiting on the fairway to hit his second shot on the eighth hole of Detroit's Rouge Park Golf Course, plaintiff-appellant, Roland R. Johnson, was struck in the eye by a golf ball, hit and hooked to the left by Robert H. Scheuer, from the tee area for the seventh hole.

Plaintiff seeks damages against defendant City of Detroit for personal injuries, including loss of vision in one eye, claiming defendant City maintained and operated an unsafe and dangerous golf course. Plaintiff's opening statement says that while the initial design of the golf course was satisfactory when it was built about 1928, that changes in the golf balls, the golf clubs, and the ability of golfers make placing of the parallel adjoining fairways for the seventh and eighth holes, which are separated by rough of a width of only about 15 feet, dangerous and unsafe. Plaintiff claims defendant should have taken steps to correct this condition either by redesigning the two holes, by planting shrubs and trees which would grow into a natural barrier, by erecting a protective screen as an additional barrier between the two fairways, or by placing warning signs, or by all of these measures.

After a two-day trial in July, 1976, a jury found no cause for action in favor of defendant City. Plaintiff appeals as of right. We reverse and remand for a new trial for the following reasons.

Plaintiff's first issue is that the trial court erred when it declined to allow plaintiff's expert to testify. The expert testimony was offered in the following context. After paying the usual green fees, plaintiff began to play a round of golf at Rouge Park Golf Course which is operated by defendant. At the eighth tee, plaintiff's drive came to rest about 250 yards down the fairway and off to the left. Then, while waiting to take his second shot, plaintiff was struck on the head by a ball hit from the seventh tee.

Although running in opposite directions, the seventh and eighth holes have contiguous fairways; 10 to 15 feet of rough separated the two fairways at the point where plaintiff was struck. In addition, testimony was offered to show that the layout of the seventh fairway would encourage golfers to play down the left side even though it is claimed that the common tendency of golfers is to slice to the right. Since the left side of the seventh fairway was the portion closest to the eighth fairway, playing down that side would increase the possibility of overlap between the areas in which drives would land from the respective tees.

The design and maintenance of these two fairways form the basis of plaintiff's allegations of defendant's negligence. Plaintiff sought to introduce expert testimony to show negligence both in the design of the two fairways, as applied to present-day golfing conditions, and in the failure of defendant, while maintaining the course, to provide protective screening or shrubbery between the two fairways.

The expert offered by plaintiff was William Newcomb of Ann Arbor. Extensive credentials were presented for Mr. Newcomb in regard to both his academic achievements and his actual experience with golfing, golf courses, and golf course design. Among other things, the evidence indicated that he had a Bachelor of Arts degree in architecture and a Master of Arts degree in landscape architecture from the University of Michigan. Golf course design was the subject of his master's thesis and of the courses he taught at both Michigan State University and the University of Michigan. As a golfer himself, Mr. Newcomb won the Michigan State amateur championship in 1967 and coached the University of Michigan golf team. In addition, as a golf course architect and contractor since 1965, he had designed over 50 golf courses and had redesigned some 20 more. It is clear that in golfing circles, Mr. Newcomb is a well-known and well-respected member.

The defendant opposed introduction of Mr. Newcomb's testimony on the ground that the absence of commonly accepted standards in the field precluded Mr. Newcomb from being considered an "expert." The defendant also argued that the testimony was unnecessary because the person who actually hit the drive had given a deposition in which he said that he was not trying to hit down the left side of the fairway and that he was not influenced by the layout of the seventh fairway in any of the ways that plaintiff alleged. Finally, the defendant argued that the testimony was unnecessary because both the alleged negligence and the proposed remedies were well within the understanding of the jury without such assistance.

Before, during, and after plaintiff's offer of proof, the trial court ruled that the expert testimony would not be admissible. The plaintiff's evidence, therefore, consisted of his own testimony and that of various employees of defendant whom he called under the adverse party statute. The defendant introduced some of the deposition of the person who had hit the drive. The jury then returned its verdict of no cause of action.

In general, it is true that it is within a trial court's discretion to admit or exclude expert testimony and that an exercise of that discretion will not be reversed except where it is clearly abused. The uncontroverted evidence indicates that by education and experience, Mr. Newcomb qualifies as an expert in the design and construction of golf courses. To the extent, if any, that the trial judge's various rulings may be interpreted to hold otherwise, they are in error and constitute an abuse of his discretion.

*   *   *

However, this Court has not hesitated to reverse when abuse of discretion has resulted in a denial of substantial justice. In particular, when competent, material, and relevant evidence on an essential issue has been excluded, when the party offering the evidence has received an adverse factual determination of that issue, and when consideration of the excluded testimony might have resulted in a different finding, this Court has held the exclusion to be reversible error.

In the context of expert testimony, the special test is that three criteria must be satisfied: (1) there must be an expert; (2) there must be facts in evidence which require or are subject to examination and analysis by a competent expert; and (3) there must be knowledge in a particular area that belongs more to an expert than to the common man.

Here, the offered expert testified that, although there were no published standards regarding the internal design of golf courses, there were, he thought, "some common accepted standards." In addition, he testified:

Q. (by Mr. Brochert, plaintiff's attorney) "Are these standards, these unwritten standards, are they generally accepted throughout the community of design or people within the field of golf course design?"

A. "I think they accept certain numbers or certain widths that are acceptable or unacceptable."

Q. "And that is in the layout what we are talking about here, specifically the separation of fairways?"

A. "Yes."

Mr. Newcomb, in the context of his credentials and these standards, satisfies the first requirement, that there be an expert. The second requirement, that there be facts in evidence which are subject to an expert's analysis, is also satisfied both in the offer of proof regarding Mr. Newcomb, and in the other testimony concerning the golf course in question. Finally, the last requirement regarding the need for the expert testimony is satisfied in this case. It is true, as asserted by defendant, that the remedies proposed by the expert appear in large part to be based upon common sense. However, we also note that an answer or solution often appears obvious after it has been pointed out. We also note that, in this case, the record indicates that six of the jurors had no golfing experience. Finally, we note that at least one of the suggested remedies, that of changing the design of the holes, was exactly in the area of the offered expertise. In addition, since it is dependent upon such factors as golfers' average driving distance, etc., it is a remedy that cannot be said to relate solely to common sense and knowledge. Thus, we conclude that there was knowledge which belonged more to the offered expert than to the common man.

With the test satisfied, [we then] look to the actual jury verdict and to the effect the excluded testimony might have had. Neither consideration requires extended discussion. The jury verdict was adverse and the excluded testimony, as presented in the offer of proof, might well have changed the result.

Having reviewed all the considerations for examining an exercise of judicial discretion in excluding evidence, we hold that the trial court committed reversible error when it declined to allow plaintiff's offered expert to testify. We, therefore, reverse and remand for a new trial.

Reversed and Remanded.

This next case uses the same principles to deny expert status to certain witnesses and grant it to others.

STATE OF MONTANA V. BARNES, 443 P.2D 16 (MONT. 1968)

This is an appeal by the State of Montana, acting by and through its State Highway Commission, from a judgment entered pursuant to a verdict in the district court of Lewis and Clark County, the Hon. James Freebourn, district judge, presiding with a jury.

John and Margaret Barnes are the owners of 52.69 acres of land condemned by the plaintiff State for the purpose of constructing Interstate Highway No. 15 between Helena and Great Falls. The land is located approximately 1 mile north of Craig, in Lewis and Clark County. The jury awarded $14,403 for the land taken and $29,976.83 for depreciation to the remainder.

The Barnes ranch, before the taking, consisted of a unit of 3164 acres, the shape of which was roughly square with the Missouri River forming the east boundary. The land condemned for the highway is a strip which goes through the ranch from north to south close to the river. The Great Northern Railway had already severed the ranch in this area and the new highway approximately parallels the railroad right-of-way.

Of the land taken, 46.20 acres was for the highway and the remainder for the relocation of access roads to the ranch. To the south, it was necessary to relocate access to the ranch from Craig. The old access road going south to Craig was on bottom land close to the river and the railroad and is now covered by the Interstate. The new access road built by the State is on higher ground to the west of the Interstate. Unlike the old road, there are some rather steep grades on the new road. Evidence was introduced as to whether or not more work was necessary to make the new road safe in all types of weather; however, early in the negotiations concerning the taking the Barneses insisted that the access road to Craig, as now built by the State, go over the area the road now covers as against the State's suggestion of another roadway.

It was also necessary to relocate access to the ranch from the north. The State constructed a new road and paid for the land it required but after construction a slide occurred and for a time this road was impassable. The State guaranteed to either repair the slide area or change the road to the Barnes' satisfaction. During the trial the court allowed testimony as to whether or not additional items were needed to make both the north and south access roads safe and passable in all seasons.

A domestic water well used by the defendants was located in the path of the new highway and was destroyed in the taking. The State drilled a new well for defendants' use to the west of the old well. The new well is in the farmyard close to the doors of a garage and machine shop; defendants claim that this location causes them inconvenience in getting machinery in and out of the shop. There was a dispute as to whether or not certain additional items were needed to make the well usable and it was agreed that a sand filter should be installed.

The new highway necessitated several other changes in the operation of the ranch. Direct access to water for animals was severed. A drainage culvert was placed under the Interstate to provide normal drainage but free access by cattle to the river is prevented. A sleeve was placed under the highway so that the landowners can pump water to the ranch side of the highway, if they wish. Another intrafarm road was severed and there was conflict in the testimony as to whether or not it had been restored.

Prior to the taking the defendants had 21 acres of irrigated land east of the railroad which was used for feeding cattle and raising pigs. There was also a "holding pen" for bulls on this land. This parcel of land was .4 of a mile from the residence before the taking, now it is necessary for the defendants to drive to the Craig interchange, cross the Interstate, and then double back to the land, a distance of $3^3/_4$ miles. Defendants claim this makes it impractical to use the parcel of land for pasture, bull pens, or pig raising.

A calf pasture and calving lot needed relocating because the Interstate covered most of the level land on which they were located. A shelter for cows and calves, which before the taking was within sight of the residence, was eliminated by the taking.

Approximately 2 acres lying $1/_2$ mile north of the residence is now completely landlocked with the new highway on one side, the railroad and the river on the other; most of this land is sloped rather steeply and is of limited value.

There were only two qualified witnesses testifying as to the value of the land and improvements. The State's witness, Mr. Neil, appraised the taking at $5,869 while Mr. Steele, the Barnes' witness, appraised the taking at $9,586. The jury awarded $14,403, some $4,817 above the highest value testified to by either witness.

The State has set forth 21 issues complaining of errors made during the course of the trial. For our consideration and discussion these issues will be grouped as follows: Whether or not the court erred in admitting testimony of the owner, Barnes, and his neighbors concerning value.

* * *

The issues grouped under No. 1 concern the admission of testimony by Mr. and Mrs. Barnes and their neighbors as to values. We find the court erred in allowing much of the testimony given over the objection of the State and on these grounds alone a new trial is necessary.

* * *

Mr. Barnes was a value witness, who put the before taking value at $204,590 and testified that he should be given $92,000 compensation for the taking and depreciation of his ranch. It is to this testimony on depreciation that the error goes, due to the failure to lay any foundation that Mr. Barnes testified from "some peculiar means of forming an intelligent and correct judgment as to the value of the property" or facts within his knowledge as to the values he testified to. In addition he did not use accepted procedures in arriving at the value figures. His value testimony would have been acceptable had he used as a basis for his testimony "market values," "the animal unit method," or had he shown how he arrived at his figures.

His testimony was clearly unacceptable because the basis of his rationale was how he was "personally affected" by the changes and on that basis it became not only conjecture but highly speculative. This type of testimony has been condemned repeatedly by this Court and should not have been admitted.

When coupled with the testimony of his neighbors whose testimony likewise failed to live up to accepted evidentiary standards on values, the record clearly shows the necessity for retrial.

One neighbor, Mr. Frank Sterling, a very successful rancher, was allowed to testify on values based on his "personal opinion" even though he admitted that his testimony was not founded on market values based on sales of comparative property, or any other accepted method of arriving at value. While he most certainly is a highly qualified rancher, he still must show some basis for his valuations, other than his "personal opinion" based on his "experience."

The Peterson case recognizes that a witness might be so familiar with sales and market values he could have an intelligent and correct judgment of market value of land, even though he is not a technical expert. But here Mr. Sterling admitted that he had no knowledge of sales of any sort. In fact, he stated they were of no import and it was his "personal opinion" that controlled insofar as his testimony was concerned. Under these facts and circumstances the court should have sustained the State's objection to his testimony.

Another neighboring rancher, Clyde Lahti, was called to give value testimony. When the State requested permission to voir dire on his qualifications as an expert, the trial judge refused and he testified that the values were his "personal opinion"; that he had no knowledge of sales and had made no inquiry into the ranch lands carrying capacity. The State moved to strike Mr. Lahti's testimony but the motion was overruled. The rule has long been in this State that an expert witness giving an opinion upon facts of his own knowledge or based upon his own observations first testify to the facts upon which his opinion is based. The trial court erred in not allowing voir dire of witness Lahti.

Yet another neighbor, John H. Warhime, was called as "an expert" value witness; again the trial court refused the State's request to voir dire. He too relied on "personal opinion" as to before and after values. The court erred in refusing the State's voir dire examination of witness Warhime.

In the course of getting their case to the jury, the defendants had a Mr. C.R. Steele appear as their expert appraiser. Mr. Steele is by profession a real estate consultant and appraiser with considerable experience in the western states, appearing both in

State and Federal courts. He had been hired by Mr. and Mrs. Barnes to make the appraisal on November 1, 1966, just a few weeks before trial and he had not seen the ranch for the purposes of appraisal prior to the highway construction. He testified at length as to the methods he used in arriving at the fair market value of the ranch prior to the taking and the methods used to determine the depreciation of the fair market value of the ranch after the taking. The methods used were the acceptable methods used by other appraisers, including the "market data" approach, the "cost of reproduction less depreciation," and the "income" approach. His testimony set the cost to the State for the land and improvements taken for right-of-way at $9,586 and $52,094 for depreciation to the remainder.

The State moved to strike the Steele testimony on the following basis: "that the appraisal testimony be stricken under Rules of Court, because he is not qualified to give an appraisal of the before value when he never saw it. How can he inspect it?"

We find no error in the court's overruling of the State's motion to strike the Steele testimony, for to compel a landowner to hire professional appraisers at the outset of every eminent domain case would be both costly and in many cases restrictive to negotiated proceedings between the parties involved in the taking. However, in view of the fact this matter is being returned to the district court for a new trial, it should be noted that Steele's testimony concerning certain access road problems should have been restricted as no proper foundation was laid for this testimony.

*   *   *

Reversed and remanded for a new trial.

Note, however, that the neighbor, Mr. Sterling, was by implication recognized by the Court as qualified to give expert testimony on ranch operations. The point here is that it would be difficult to show formal education in ranching operations. As the Court here recognizes, such expertise can only be acquired through experience.

So far we have discussed the two basic principles for the admission of expert testimony. The topic must be outside the ordinary experience of a jury such that specialized knowledge would enable the jury to better understand and resolve the case, and the proposed witness must have sufficient qualifications to convince the judge that he or she has the necessary knowledge, however it might have been obtained. There is, however, a third segment of the rule.

FRE Rule 702 (Cont'd.)

if (1) the testimony is based upon sufficient facts or data, (2) the testimony is the product of reliable principles and methods, and (3) the witness has applied the principles and methods reliably to the facts of the case.

The problem that arises here is whether the expert will be allowed to testify because of the substance of what she has to say. In 1993 the Supreme Court decided the landmark case Daubert v. Merrell Dow Pharmaceuticals, Inc., 509 U.S. 579, in which it held that, in federal courts, the expert's opinion must be based on recognized scientific principles, not unsupported speculation. The duty of determining this rests with the trial court.

Notice the main qualification in that last statement; Daubert and the subsequent Supreme Court decisions on the same issue [General Electric Co. v. Joiner, 522 U.S. 136 (1997) and Kumho Tire Co. v. Carmichael. 526 U.S. 137 (1999)] are the rule only in the federal courts and in those states that choose to follow the same reasoning. Twenty-seven states follow the Daubert rule (AK, AR, CO, CT, DE, ID, IN, IW, KT, LA, ME, MS, MT, NE, NM, NC, OH, OK, OR, RI, SC, SD, TN, TX, VT, WV, WY), 17 states and the District of Columbia have rejected it (AZ, CA, DC, FL, GA, IL, KS, MD, MI, MN, MO, NY, ND, PA, UT, VA, WA, WI), and six states have gone part way to adopting it (AL, HI, MA, NV, NH, NJ).[1] These decisions are not binding on all courts in the country since they are procedural (concerned with how trials should be conducted), not substantive (dealing with the legal rights of parties).

The test the Supreme Court enunciated in the cases requires the trial judge to look at the following factors: (a) If it is a theory, has it been, or can it be, tested; (b) Has it been subject to peer review; (c) Has it been published in the appropriate specialized literature; (d) For tests and techniques, has an error rate been determined; (e) Are there existing standards for the test; and (f) Is there general acceptance of the theory, test, or technique in the relevant scientific community. The expert's testimony does not have to meet all these criteria, just enough of them to satisfy the judge that it should be admitted.

The test used by the courts in the 18 jurisdictions that do not follow Daubert is simply the last of these; is there general acceptance in the scientific community? And the other six states add one or two of these factors to the general acceptance criteria, most frequently peer review and publication. The most recent research on the issue, however, tends to the conclusion that it does not matter which test is used; the same evidence is admitted in either case.[2]

All of this, of course, is the lawyer's problem, not yours, as she will have to convince the judge if the issue arises. But the expert can help by writing the report in such a way that it demonstrates that the conclusions reached rely on recognized principles. You should, for example, cite refereed literature that utilizes the concepts, principles, and tests you rely upon. In these matters, it is most helpful to consult with your attorney before writing your report.

It is also possible for the judge to appoint an expert witness totally unconnected with either side of the case, as Rule 706 provides:

FRE Rule 706. Court Appointed Experts

(a) Appointment.
The court may on its own motion or on the motion of either party enter an order to show cause why expert witnesses should not be appointed, and

may request the parties to submit nominations. The court may appoint any expert witnesses agreed upon by the parties, and may appoint expert witnesses of its own selection. An expert witness shall not be appointed by the court unless the witness consents to act. A witness so appointed shall be informed of the witness duties by the court in writing, a copy of which shall be filed with the clerk, or at a conference in which the parties shall have opportunity to participate. A witness so appointed shall advise the parties of the witness' findings, if any; the witness' deposition may be taken by any party; and the witness may be called to testify by the court or any party. The witness shall be subject to cross-examination by each party, including a party calling the witness.

(b) Compensation.

Expert witnesses so appointed are entitled to reasonable compensation in whatever sum the court may allow. The compensation thus fixed is payable from funds which may be provided by law in criminal cases and civil actions and proceedings involving just compensation under the fifth amendment. In other civil actions and proceedings the compensation shall be paid by the parties in such proportion and at such time as the court directs, and therefore charged in like manner as other costs.

(c) Disclosure of Appointment.

In the exercise of its discretion, the court may authorize disclosure to the jury of the fact that the court appointed the expert witness.

(d) Parties' Experts of Own Selection.

Nothing in this rule limits the parties in calling expert witnesses of their own selection.

Although the rules provide for court-appointed experts, such occurrences are rare. I have never participated in a case where the judge considered it worthwhile to appoint an expert. If, however, you are asked to serve in this capacity, do not think that you are home free. All provisions of the law of evidence still apply to your testimony. You receive no special preferences simply because you were appointed by the judge rather than hired by one side. In fact, you may be in a more troublesome position, since both sides, rather than just one, will have the opportunity to cross-examine you.

REFERENCES

1. Gross, M.L. and Kellogg, J., Fifty-State and Federal Court Survey of the Standards Governing the Admissibility of Expert Testimony, ABA Section of Litigation Annual Conference, 2005.
2. See, e.g., Cheng, E.K. and Yoon, A.H., Does Frye or Daubert matter? A study of scientific admissibility standards, *Va. L. Rev.,* 91, 471, 2005; Vickers, A.L., Daubert, critique and interpretation: What empirical studies tell us about the application of Daubert, *U.S.F.L. Rev.,* 40, 109, 2005.

CHAPTER 9

The Form of Questions to an Expert

An expert may be asked to present an opinion in two basic ways. The first way is generally called "narrative testimony," in which the expert, after being qualified, proceeds to present his or her opinion in his or her own words with minimal prompting from the lawyer. We will discuss how to organize and present narrative testimony in Part III. The second way in which expert testimony is presented is by response to hypothetical questions. Because hypothetical questions can easily be misused by lawyers there is a body of law regarding what these questions may and may not include. Most of these legal rules are "court-made" in the common law tradition. Only the following brief paragraph of the codified Rules of Evidence addresses this issue.

FRE Rule 703. Bases of Opinion Testimony by Experts

The facts or data in the particular case upon which an expert bases an opinion or inference may be those perceived by or made known to the expert at or before the hearing. If of a type reasonably relied upon by experts in a particular field in forming opinions or inferences upon the subject, the facts or data need not be admissible in evidence.

The most important part of this rule is the second sentence. If, for example, you are a physician being asked why you reached certain decisions regarding the treatment of your patient, it is perfectly acceptable to discuss the reports you received from consultants such as radiologists, clinical laboratories, neurologists, etc. Even if these consultants themselves do not appear to testify, so their reports might be hearsay (see Chapter 14), you may discuss them, since that is the usual way you, as a physician, practice your profession.

You need to be aware of the rules regarding formulation of hypothetical questions because it is part of your job as expert witness to help the lawyer prepare the question you will answer. The first such rule is stated clearly and simply in the last paragraph of this next case: You can only include in the hypothetical question facts that have some basis in the evidence.

BARNETT v. WORKMEN'S COMPENSATION COMM'R, 172 S.E.2d 698 (W.Va.1970)

Garcie Barnett was employed by the Gauley Coal and Coke Company as foreman of a three-man "moving crew" and as a result of circumstances that will be related in detail hereinafter, occurring about three hours after his shift began, he was admitted to the Sacred Heart Hospital during the early morning hours of April 10, 1968. His attending physician saw him after his admission to the hospital and diagnosed his condition as "a coronary occlusion." The patient died on April 12 of what his physician diagnosed as a recurrence of the heart attack which he had suffered two days previously. The widow and minor dependent children of the deceased filed application for workmen's compensation benefits upon the theory that the deceased's death was due to an injury received in the course of and resulting from his employment. These parties will hereinafter be referred to as appellees and the coal company as the appellant. The commissioner originally denied benefits to appellees upon the ground that "deceased husband's death was not due to the injury received in the course of and as a result of his employment." There was a protest and after three hearings the commissioner set aside his former ruling, held the claim compensable, and made an award to each of the appellees. On November 21, 1969, the Workmen's Compensation Appeal Board affirmed the commissioner's ruling by a two to one vote. The view of the majority is expressed in an opinion accompanying and explaining the reasons for their order in this language:

> [T]he claimant, at the time of his death, was engaged in a strenuous under-taking to unfoul a heavy belt. This Board further takes cognizance of the evidence that the employee had been performing extra work as requested by his employer. Further, that the claimant, at the time of sustaining his heart attack, was helping in the unfouling of the belt all of which could have caused an extra strain on his heart.

> Under the circumstances, this Board is of the opinion that this was a fortuitous event; that it did result from his employment; that the coronary occlusion was suffered under unusual strains and exertions and it was as a result of the claimant's employment.

This Court granted an appeal from that decision and the case was submitted upon extensive briefing by counsel for the parties but without oral argument.

The only medical witness who testified in this case was Dr. James Richard Glasscock of Richwood, West Virginia, who stated that he first saw Mr. Barnett as a patient after he was admitted to the Sacred Heart Hospital in Richwood "on the 10th about 8:15 a.m." The lay evidence showed that after the deceased became ill inside the mine, he was taken to the "head" on a belt and that he insisted on walking the remaining distance to the mine entrance which was about 500 or 600 feet. There is a hiatus in the testimony as to what occurred between the time he started walking out of the mine and was admitted to the hospital. To continue with Dr. Glasscock's testimony, he said when he first saw Barnett, "He was in quite a degree of shock and complained of rather intense internal chest pain which he claimed was radiating down his left arm." As heretofore stated, the witness diagnosed his patient's condition as coronary occlusion followed by a "myocarditis infarction" which the witness described as "the death" of the area of the heart which the blocked or occluded artery had served. These are questions asked of and answers made by the medical witness:

Q. Doctor, would unusual exertion on the part of the patient result in a hemorrhage of a vein?
A. Well, it could result in a hemorrhage of the vein or the breaking of it, or these little plaques that form with the aging of the arteries could be displaced and cause a blockage.
Q. What are these plaques that you speak of?
Q. They're principally cholesterol or a form of cholesterol plaques.
Q. Do I understand your testimony to be that unusual exertion might displace this plaque and cause a blockage of the vein?
A. Those little plaques will come on with age and tend to weaken the artery to create some blockage. At times they just break loose on their own after most any form of exertion.

At the August 5, 1968, hearing, this witness was asked a hypothetical question but, because an emergency arose, it was necessary for him to leave the hearing without answering the question. The trial examiner had sustained an objection to it, but for the purposes of the record he was to give his answer. At the May 21, 1969, hearing the hypothetical question was repeated. Another trial examiner overruled the objection to it and the witness answered. The witness was first asked if he took a history from Barnett and this was his answer:

A. From his wife, because he was not able to speak. He was in very bad condition.
Q. What was the history that you obtained from his wife?
A. That he complained to her of feeling rather poorly for the previous few days and had complained of considerable shortness of breath after exertion, and that she had tried to keep him from going to work that day but that he went ahead.

Then the hypothetical question asked at the former hearing was repeated and this is the question in its entirety:

Q. Now, in a prior hearing, just to refresh your recollection and I am going to read this question Mr. Barber says from Page 9 of the record of November 12, 1968: "All right, Doctor, if you will assume that Garcie Barnett had no prior medical history of a heart condition, that he had not experienced any chest pains nor any complaint prior to his attack while working, that until his attack he had worked regularly six days per week, approximately eight to 12 hours per day, that he suffered an attack while helping to drag a conveyor belt because it was too heavy to be lifted by the work crew, Doctor, assuming those facts as being correct, would this be sufficient exertion in your opinion within a reasonable degree of medical certainty to cause this attack?"
[Y]ou said, "I think it would be."
Upon cross-examination he was asked this question and made this answer:
Q. This type of condition can even happen when a person is home in bed, is that correct?
A. It has.

*   *   *

It is the view of this Court upon a careful examination of the testimony of the lay witnesses that the question was utterly unsupported by the evidence and for that reason the doctor should not have been allowed to answer the question or, having answered it, that his answer should not have been considered by the commissioner or the appeal board in arriving at a decision in this case. The witness was asked to assume that the deceased "suffered an attack while helping to drag a conveyor belt because it was too heavy to be lifted by the work crew." There was no evidence upon which to base that factual assumption....

"A hypothetical question which assumes facts unsupported by the evidence should not be submitted to an expert witness." The statutory provisions as to the informality of proceedings before the commissioner do not warrant such a departure from the ordinary rules of evidence.

Reversed.

The next case illustrates the remaining two important rules regarding the content of hypothetical questions: (1) hypothetical question should fairly reflect the proven facts, and (2) hypothetical question may include only a part of the facts in evidence as an expert witness can ignore any facts which he or she does not believe either relevant or true.

HAWKINS CONSTRUCTION CO. v. MATTHEWS CO., 209 N.W.2d 643 (Neb. 1973)

This is an action for property damage sustained by plaintiff Hawkins Construction Company as a result of the collapse of a scaffold manufactured by the defendant Waco

Scaffold and Shoring Company and leased to the plaintiff by the defendant Matthews Company, Inc. The jury returned a verdict for the plaintiff and against both defendants in the amount of $32,635.48. We affirm the judgment of the District Court.

The purpose of the scaffolding involved in the collapse was the support of the roof deck cement pour. The plaintiff's men first consulted soil compact tests made by a local laboratory in an effort to determine whether the foundation upon which the scaffold would be erected was firm. Under the supervision of Thomas Flynn, the plaintiff's carpenter foreman, "mud sills" were then placed on the ground to support the structure. These sills consisted of 2×12 inch boards laid flat on the ground, and their purpose was to prevent sinkage by distributing the weight of the scaffold and its load more evenly over the base soil. Screw jack base plates, permitting vertical adjustment of the panels, were then nailed to the mud sills, and levels were taken at each stage of this assembly to insure that the base scaffold structure was perfectly horizontal. The tubular frame panels forming the bottom section of the structure were then fitted into the base plates.

The roof deck construction required the scaffolding to reach to a height of 20 feet and, since each scaffold panel is only 6 feet high, the job thus required panels to be stacked on top of each other until the desired height was reached. In order to accomplish this, the plaintiff had ordered tubular connectors, manufactured by the defendant Waco, from the defendant Matthews Company. These connectors are merely hollow tubes with an interior diameter slightly larger than the tubular feet of a scaffold panel. Connectors are fitted over the tubular supports of the bottom panel, and the upper panel is then stacked on top by fitting its feet into the connectors.

Originally, these connectors were manufactured by simply welding a reinforcing ring washer to the outside center of a solid length of pipe. More recently, however, the connectors have been formed by hydraulically pressing two smaller lengths of pipe together with an amount of pressure greater than their yield value, so that the two pieces deform at the center to form an exterior ridge as they join. All this is accomplished without heating the connector components, and the procedure is correspondingly known as a "cold form process." It was the latter type of connector which Matthews Company provided for the plaintiff's use on the Swift job, and the effect of the cold form process on the stability of these connectors is actively disputed.

Once the panels have been stacked to reach the desired height they are topped off with "shore heads," U-shaped holders designed to cradle some of the supportive lumber bracing which will underlie the plywood pour base. More specifically, the shore heads cradle the "ledgers," which consist of a minimum of three and sometimes four 2×12s nailed together front to back and fitted into the shore heads on edge. That is, if three 2×12s are used, the ledger when installed would be 6 inches wide in the shore head and would stand 12 inches above it. The ledgers, in turn, support the "joists." Joists are lengths of lumber placed on edge on top of the ledgers and at right angles to them. It is the joists that provide direct structural support to the plywood pour base above, and, in this case, they were placed 16 inches apart on center.

In the construction of these joists the plaintiff departed from the plans supplied to it. The variances involved the size of lumber used for joists and the type of structural bracing supporting them. It is undisputed that the Waco plans called for the joists to be made from 2×10s and that the plaintiff used 2×12s instead; thus, the joists supporting the plywood pour base stood 12 inches off the ledgers rather than the recommended 10 inches. The plaintiff's job sponsor admitted that one of the reasons 2 × 12s were used was that they are more versatile, and could be reused, either as joists or as ledgers, on other jobs.

The Waco plans also called for the joists to be supported by cross-bracing, and the plaintiff used horizontal bracing. Cross-bracing involves the placement of an "X"-shaped set of cross beams at specified intervals between the joists; horizontal bracing consists of running lengths of 1 × 4s along the bottom edges of the joists at specified intervals and securing them to the joist edges with double head eight-penny nails. The joists themselves are then secured to the plywood pour base above the seven-penny block nails. The ends of both the ledgers and the joists are rested against the outer wall of the plant structure in order to add stability to the form system. Cross-bracing is more expensive and time consuming to employ, but is somewhat stronger than horizontal bracing, particularly where lateral force is involved. Horizontal bracing is commonly used in the construction industry, however, and had been used by the plaintiff on many prior projects. The supportive effectiveness of the larger joists, buttressed by horizontal rather than cross-bracing, is also actively disputed.

On October 22, 1968, the plaintiff's workmen were engaged in a cement pour on a portion of the roof deck. Edward Pechar, the "pour watcher," was stationed underneath the deck to make sure the tower legs did not settle as a result of the cement being placed on the plywood pour base. This he did by tying red indicator ribbons at premarked points on the scaffold and then sighting on them with a construction level throughout the pour. He observed nothing unusual. Thomas Flynn, the carpenter foreman, had routinely checked the connectors, shore headings and footings before the pour, and he, too, had found nothing unusual. Jack Moore, the concrete superintendent, and Stan Siedlik, the labor foreman, were both up on the pour deck, and had just waved off an empty bucket which had dumped a load of wet cement onto the plywood base.

Without warning of any kind a portion of the roof deck on which the men were working suddenly gave way. Siedlik went down with the collapse to the ground and cement and debris came down on top of him, but he miraculously escaped with only minor injuries. Pechar, who had turned away from the pour temporarily, heard a loud noise and turned to see the roof collapsing less than 10 feet away. Moore was standing just beyond the area of collapse, and was not injured. All three men agreed that prior to the collapse there was no vibration, noise, or any other unusual symptom of trouble, and that the only noise accompanying the accident was the single loud report as the roof fell.

After the collapse, Lang inspected the scene and determined that the damage had taken place in a square area approximately 48 feet on a side. The ground was covered with debris, including at least a dozen broken connectors. Flynn, the carpenter foreman, testified that all the broken connectors he observed after the accident were fractured in the middle, where the deformed ring is located. The area was also strewn with splintered lumber, bent scaffolding sections, and other debris.

At the threshold of this case is the question of causation. The plaintiff contends that the collapse was proximately caused by the failure of defectively manufactured connectors. The defendant Waco contends that the collapse was caused by insufficient bridging applied to unstable joists, permitting the joists to roll over and thus give way. As to this point, the trial involved a conflict of expert testimony.

James Hossack, a professor of civil engineering at the University of Nebraska at Omaha, was employed by the plaintiff on December 26, 1968, to investigate the collapse. After studying the plans, interviewing persons who witnessed the accident, and consulting relevant literature, Hossack proceeded to conduct experimental tests at the University in the summer and fall of 1969, with a view toward determining the cause of the collapse....

[*We will look at the tests Professor Hossack conducted in Chapter 10.*]

The defendants' expert was Fred C. Kosmach, the senior engineer for Waco and the designer of the scaffolding plans for the Swift job. He and the Waco Company had been notified of the collapse by Hawkins, and he flew to Omaha from the home office in Illinois the same day. Upon arriving at the site, Kosmach began an inspection of the debris and the remaining structure. He observed the deviations which the plaintiff made from his plans, and he also observed that some of the plywood which had fallen did not appear to have been nailed to the joists. He testified that an instantaneous collapse could occur if one or two joists which were not nailed down suddenly rolled. He further testified, based on his experience in testing over 100 Waco scaffolding configurations to failure, that the Swift system failed because of the deviations from the Waco plans and a resulting rollover of joist supports. He computed the "leg load" on this job at 7,100 pounds, and testified that the Waco equipment could withstand a load of 22,500 pounds per leg before collapse if properly constructed. Furthermore, he testified that a connector has never failed in use before.

A strenuous attack is made upon the competency of Hossack's testimony for the plaintiff....that the hypothetical question which elicited the opinion did not fairly reflect the proven facts.

[*The objections to the tests are also discussed in Chapter 10.*]

* * *

In an overlapping argument the defendants assail the form of the hypothetical question and particularly because it omitted the testimony of Pechar, who observed the collapse. A hypothetical question should fairly reflect the proven facts. Great latitude is allowed the trial judge in ruling on admissibility of such a question. A hypothetical question is not improper simply because it includes only a part of the facts testified to. An expert witness in giving an opinion has a right to confine the facts that he recites to those which are believed to be true, or which are believed to be material to the issue. The question of what facts are relevant to the determination is one of the basic ones upon which experts in any given field may differ. Again the disregarding of Pechar's lack of evidence on the bending is an argument directly on the merits to the jury in an attack upon the credibility of Hossack's testimony, and does not affect its admissibility.

We have examined the other contentions made by the defendant Matthews Company in this area and for the same reasons find them to be without merit....

Affirmed.

There was a time in the U.S. when it was considered improper for experts to testify regarding the ultimate fact at issue in a suit. The rationale underlying this position was the same rationale that refuses to admit expert testimony unless that testimony is needed to help the fact finder understand the issue — fear that the fact finder will be overawed by the expert. This rule was under attack and gradually being discarded by most courts when FRE was adopted, thus eliminating this objection in Federal courts. The vast majority of states also have abandoned the "ultimate issue" rule.

FRE Rule 704. Opinion on Ultimate Issues

...[T]estimony in the form of an opinion or inference otherwise admissible is not objectionable because it embraces an ultimate issue to be decided by the trier of fact.

As a point of interest, it is perfectly permissible for an expert, after being qualified as an expert, to be asked only a single question: "What is your opinion?" There is no rule that the expert must give the basis for his opinion. Lawyers occasionally use this type of expert testimony, viewing it as a "trial tactics" trap for the opposing lawyer. The strategy is to prompt the other side's lawyer to ask for the basis of the expert's opinion so that it appears less rehearsed. I consider this method worse than useless and do not recommend it, but, as an expert witness, you need to be aware of it.

FRE Rule 705. Disclosure of Facts or Data Underlying Expert Opinion

The expert may testify in terms of opinion or inference and give reasons therefor without first testifying to the underlying facts or data, unless the court requires otherwise. The expert may in any event be required to disclose the underlying facts or data on cross-examination.

The next case, which predates FRE, indicates that FRE Rule 705 merely restates the existing common law evidentiary rule.

ARKANSAS STATE HIGHWAY COMMISSION v. JOHNS,
367 S.W.2d 436 (Ark. 1963)

In this eminent domain proceeding the appellant seeks to acquire about half of a twelve-acre tract owned by the appellees. The circuit court, sitting without a jury, awarded the landowners $3,500 as compensation for the property taken. For reversal the appellant contends that the court erred in refusing to strike the testimony of certain witnesses for the landowners.

Two of the witnesses, Bob Gelly and Joe Snelly, were real estate dealers in Crawford County. After having first stated that they were familiar with land values in the vicinity of the Johns property and that they had inspected the property, both of these witnesses expressed their opinion as to the fair market value of the appellees' property before the taking. The appellant made an unsuccessful attempt to have this testimony stricken, on the ground that neither witness stated the facts and reasons forming the basis for his opinion....

We think counsel have misconstrued the intent of our cases. It is true that a non-expert witness, such as a layman testifying about a testator's mental capacity, must state the facts upon which his opinion is based before giving that opinion. But there is no similar condition to the admissibility of an expert's opinion.

An expert witness, after having established his qualifications and his familiarity with the subject matter of the inquiry, is ordinarily in a position to state his opinion. For example, a physician might testify that he had examined a certain patient and found him to be afflicted with malaria. That testimony would unquestionably be admissible. Yet if this physician, on cross-examination, were forced to admit that he had found no recognized symptom of malaria and had based his conclusion solely upon the fact that the patient had been bitten by a mosquito, then, under the rule...the witness' opinion would no longer constitute substantial evidence.

It was incumbent upon counsel for the appellant to support their motion to strike by showing that the landowner's expert witnesses had no reasonable basis for their opinions. Counsel actually made no effort in that direction, the motion to strike Snelly's testimony having been made without any cross-examination at all.

* * *

Affirmed.

CHAPTER 10

Tests, Experiments, and the Chain of Custody

TESTS AND EXPERIMENTS

To a lawyer, the terms "test" and "experiment" are not equivalent. The legal mind makes an extremely important technical distinction between the two terms. A test is something done to, at, or with a thing (or the equivalent thereof) involved in the original event or happening. An experiment is an attempt to duplicate, as closely as possible, the original event or occurrence. It is much better to perform a test rather than an experiment because the phrase "as closely as possible" leaves a lot of room for lawyers to argue. Let us now read the remainder of the *Hawkins* case that we previously discussed in Chapter 9. [See pp. 86–90 for the facts of this case.]

HAWKINS CONSTRUCTION CO. v. MATTHEWS CO. (Cont'd.)

These tests were conducted under the supervision of Flynn, the carpenter fore-man; Jack Folker, the job superintendent; and Thomas Lang, the job sponsor; all of whom assisted in constructing the scaffolding for the tests.

The tests were divided into two parts. The first series of experiments involved outdoor testing of various portions of the scaffold configuration. The first two tests examined the effect of lateral force on the wood shoring system, the first test involving horizontal bracing and the second involving the recommended cross-bracing. In both cases the ultimate failure of the structure was slow — in the case of the horizontal bracing the joists held the load for 15 to 20 minutes before significant relaxation — and in both cases the failure was clearly audible before the collapse. When the horizontal bracing was tested, for example, the system held the simulated load up to the point where 5 inches of joist deflection was reached, and the deformation of wood and nailing could be heard after the 2-inch deflection point was reached. Hossack testified that "(w)ood systems literally groan and you can hear them quite loud under load." This is the result when the joist system rolls. It is to be contrasted with the testimony of the witnesses who said that the collapse was sudden and inaudible prior to the failure.

A third outdoor test was conducted to determine if the wood joist system would interact with the steel scaffolding system to produce a failure, and the result was that no collapse was produced, and no joists rolled, but 10 connectors were either partially or completely fractured at the center.

Indoor tests were conducted on the connectors to determine whether they contained a defective weakness. The tests were conducted on a Tinus Olson Axial Load simulator, which has the capability to apply either tension or compression forces to a given component subject. Two of the tests involved bending the connectors until failure, and both resulted in breakage of the connector along the seam line at the center. A third test involved what Hossack called 'straight tension,' i.e., a pulling apart to determine whether the connector contained a weak spot. In a fourth test, in which compression force was applied, a connector withstood approximately 15,000 pounds of pressure, at which point the pin couplings attaching it to the stimulator failed.

In addition, Hossack cut two connectors along the longitudinal axis in order to examine their interior structure. One of these connectors was found to be incompletely joined at the center, which Hossack attributed to insufficient pressure in the manufacturing process.

Over objection, Hossack was permitted to offer his opinion as to the cause of the collapse, based on his examination of photographs taken at the scene, his testing of the scaffolding system and its components, and the testimony of the witnesses who heard no noise prior to the sudden collapse. In his opinion the accident was not caused by a failure of the wood shoring system, but by a defect in the steel scaffolding, to wit: A plane of imperfection in the center of the connectors.

*   *   *

A strenuous attack is made upon the competency of Hossack's testimony for the plaintiff. The defendant Waco argues that his tests were conducted improperly, that his opinion was based on assumptions and speculation, and that the hypothetical question which elicited the opinion did not fairly reflect the proven facts. This court has repeatedly held that a trial court has wide latitude in the admission of experimental tests. We have said that the difficulties attending an offer of evidence of illustrative experiments require that in such cases a wide latitude or discretion be conferred upon the trial court and that unless there is a clear abuse of discretion a judgment will not be reversed on account of the admission or rejection of such testimony. More precisely we have said that the proponent of such expert testimony based upon the experiment must demonstrate 'that the person who makes the experiment is competent to do so, that the apparatus used was of the kind and in the condition suitable for the experiment, and that the experiment was honestly and fairly made.' Most of the defendants' argument in this area appears to be an argument on the merits to the jury and not an argument as to admissibility or competency. Waco argues that Pechar, the employee charged with the observation of the scaffolding, had not observed, prior to the collapse, any bending or change of position of any of the scaffolding towers. It also argues that Hossack, the plaintiff's expert, failed adequately to explain why the connectors had not failed in the two-month period prior to the collapse. Of course, it would be completely impossible to absolutely duplicate the actual conditions and repeat the scaffolding collapse. A review of the evidence we have given demonstrates that a jury could reasonably find Hossack had conducted an experiment that was reasonably if not almost a duplicate of the conditions existing in this rather complex accident situation. The defendant Waco cites no authority that would support the proposition that the observer Pechar was required to testify to the element of bending in the tower. Pechar testified that his job was to watch for tower settlement, not bending. Hossack, plaintiff's expert, testified that the bending which occurs under this type of stress is slight — perhaps no more than 5/8 of an inch — and thus almost invisible to the naked eye. We hold that there was no abuse of discretion by the trial judge in admitting the results of these experiments, as testified to by Hossack, into evidence.

The defendant Waco generally contends that Hossack's opinion is based on mere speculation. From what we have said it is clear that Hossack exhaustively outlined the nature and the scope of his tests, and their results. It appears that he carefully and clearly explained the reasons for his conclusions. We point out that the defendants' expert constructed a model also and conducted an experiment, all of which was admitted into evidence. But the jury accepted Hossack's and not the defendants'. The argument that the scaffold had not collapsed previously is directed toward the merits, and is insufficient to sustain an attack upon the admissibility of Hossack's expert opinion.

* * *

[As shown on p. 93, the judgment was affirmed.]

In this case, Professor Hossack conducted a test by obtaining connectors of the type used to create the original scaffold (but not the ones from the original scaffold, because those were destroyed in the original event), taking them into his laboratory, and determining the torsion, shear strength, etc. This is a test because the connectors were equivalent to those used in the original, mass-produced by the same company using the same equipment, etc. Professor Hossack's taking of micrographs of the shear faces of the connectors that were involved in the original event was also clearly a test.

On the other hand, it was clearly an experiment when Professor Hossack built a scaffold supposedly like the original that collapsed and then took high speed photographs of it while loading weights onto it. This was an attempt to duplicate, as closely as possible, the original event. In this case, the court saw no problem, that "as closely as possible" had been met. Nevertheless, it is a good idea, if in doubt whether what you have done is a test or an experiment, to call it a test. When a lawyer hears the word "experiment," the lawyer's ears will "pick up" and he or she will come charging out ready to fight the question of whether you duplicated the original events as closely as possible.

CHAIN OF CUSTODY

Lawyers frequently question whether an adequate "chain of custody" has been demonstrated for the items an expert tested. The purpose is to ensure that the item tested is indeed what it purports to be and that it was not changed, intentionally or unintentionally, before it was tested. Lawyers who raise objections, however, frequently lose sight of this original purpose. They object in the hope that the whole matter will be thrown out of court because of a technicality, but this rarely occurs.

BEGLEY v. FORD MOTOR CO., 476 F.2d 1276 (2d Cir. 1973)

Plaintiffs John H. Begley and Lawrence J. Sinnott commenced this diversity action in the southern district of New York to recover damages for personal injuries sustained as the result of an automobile collision on the Connecticut Turnpike on April 22, 1966. Plaintiffs claimed that the 1965 Lincoln Continental in which they were riding home from work (Begley driving, Sinnott a front seat passenger) collided with the rear of another automobile, both proceeding eastbound, at the Greenwich Toll Station when the Lincoln's brakes failed to operate. The brake failure allegedly was caused by defective brake fluid supplied by defendant Ford Motor Company (Ford) through one of its dealers, Eastman Motors of Greenwich (Eastman Motors), the brakes having been tested a month prior to the accident by defendant Empire Lincoln-Mercury, Inc. (Empire). Plaintiffs' claims against Ford were based on negligence and breach of warranty in the manufacture of the brake fluid.

After a five-day jury trial before Lloyd F. Macmahon, District Judge, verdicts in favor of Begley and Sinnott in amounts of $25,000 and $14,000, respectively, were returned against Ford. The jury also returned a defendant's verdict in favor of Empire. Only Ford has appealed. The issues raised on appeal are simple and straightforward. They involve the sufficiency of the evidence, the admissibility of certain expert testimony, and the propriety of portions of the jury charge. Finding no reversible error, we affirm.

There was evidence at the trial from which the jury could have found as follows. The Lincoln involved in the accident was owned by Great Lakes Carbon Corporation, of which Sinnott was an officer and Begley an employee. The vehicle was assigned to Sinnott for his use. It had been purchased from Eastman Motors in April 1965. Shortly after the purchase, Sinnott on several occasions complained to the service department of Eastman Motors that the brakes would not function until the pedal was close to the floorboard. On October 19, 1965, Eastman Motors made certain modifications to the braking system of the vehicle. This was done pursuant to a general sales bulletin, referred to as "campaign 165-07," which Ford issued in September 1965 to its dealers and sales representatives. Sinnott took the vehicle back to Eastman Motors on January 11, 1966, at which time he complained that the brakes "were catching too close to the floor." On the morning of March 21, 1966 — one month before the accident here involved — the vehicle experienced total brake failure on the East River Drive while in bumper to bumper traffic. It was taken to Empire's service station in mid-Manhattan where the braking system was checked and some new brake fluid which had been furnished by Ford was added to the existing fluid.

Employees of both Eastman Motors and Empire testified at the trial that they had received numerous complaints concerning the braking mechanism — particularly "a low brake pedal" — on other 1965 Lincoln Continentals.

Plaintiffs' principal witness at the trial was Roger Harvey, an expert in chemical engineering. Harvey had inspected the vehicle on May 25, May 27, and August 31, 1966, and had tested a specimen of brake fluid taken from the vehicle. He determined that the brake fluid contained 4.4% water by volume which in his opinion indicated that the fluid was in a defective condition. He testified that, due to an excess of water, the boiling point of the brake fluid was only 250–280°F rather than the normal 550°F. This meant, according to Harvey, that when the brakes became heated the water in the fluid would boil, thus creating a vapor lock in the hydraulic system, and the vapor lock would prevent the brakes from operating properly.

*   *   *

Plaintiffs adduced substantial evidence, through the testimony of Harvey, that the brake fluid which he tested was defective and not fit for the purpose of stopping the vehicle. Ford argues that, since brake fluid is hygroscopic (absorbs water), the water content of the fluid could have been increased after it left Ford's possession, through no negligence of Ford, and before it was tested by Harvey.

Viewing the evidence in the light most favorable to plaintiffs, as we must at this stage, plaintiffs adduced sufficient evidence to indicate that such absorption did not occur after the accident. Following the accident, the vehicle was kept inside a Greenwich garage. The sample tested by Harvey was first removed from the vehicle with a clean, dry battery syringe. An insurance investigator delivered the fluid to an attorney who, after marking it for identification, delivered it to Harvey in a clean, dry glass bottle sealed with a metallic cap.

There also was evidence that it was the inherent characteristics of the fluid itself, and not water absorption, which caused the fluid to be defective. Harvey testified that in his opinion a substantial amount of water could not be absorbed; and that the water in the fluid came from a breakdown under heat and pressure of the ethers which made up the chemical composition of the fluid. There also was evidence of prior difficulties with this vehicle, as well as with other 1965 Lincoln Continentals, which were symptomatic of defective brake fluid. Such evidence goes a considerable distance toward establishing that the fluid sold by Ford was defective.

We are satisfied that there was sufficient evidence in support of each of the essential elements of plaintiffs' case to warrant its submission to the jury.

Ford next contends that the trial judge should have stricken the testimony of plaintiffs' expert witness, Harvey, on the ground that no proper foundation had been laid for his testimony. We find no merit in this claim.

Ford's essential argument here is that there was insufficient evidence that the brake fluid tested by Harvey was the same fluid which was in the vehicle at the time of the accident. As we have stated, there was evidence that the fluid tested was that removed from the vehicle. Moreover, there was evidence that the fluid was removed and transported in a manner which would not allow substantial absorption of water. While there was some conflicting evidence as to the chain of possession of the jar and as to the cleanliness of the equipment used, that goes to the weight rather than the admissibility of the evidence.

* * *

Affirmed.

The next case illustrates the same point as *Begley v. Ford*, but in the context of a somewhat more complicated sampling effort.

GOVERNMENT SUPPLIERS CONSOLIDATING SERV. v. BAYH, 753 F. Supp. 739 (S.D. Ind. 1990)

Introduction

In 1978 the U.S. Supreme Court applied the dormant commerce clause to dispose of a New Jersey law banning the importation of out-of-state trash. In his majority opinion Justice Potter Stewart observed as follows:

"Today, cities in Pennsylvania and New York find it expedient or necessary to send their waste into New Jersey for disposal, and New Jersey claims the right to close its borders to such traffic. Tomorrow, cities in New Jersey may find it expedient or necessary to send their waste into Pennsylvania or New York for disposal, and those states might then claim the right to close their borders. The commerce clause will protect New Jersey in the future, just as it protects her neighbors now, from efforts by one state to isolate itself in the stream of interstate commerce from a problem shared by all."

City of Philadelphia v. New Jersey, 437 U.S. 617, 629 (1978). The day foretold in *City of Philadelphia* has arrived.

Today cities in New Jersey and other eastern states find it necessary, or at least expedient, to ship their waste hundreds of miles to the State of Indiana. This case involves an attempt by Indiana to regulate the influx of that out-of-state waste. In a broader sense, however, this case involves the collision of local concerns with a national problem.

The citizens of the State of Indiana are in the unenviable position of residing in a state which is an economically favorable dumping ground for the refuse of the eastern states. Besides the deposit of undesirable materials from other states into Indiana soil, the status of being a trash "receiving" state means that the space available to her for the disposal of Indiana waste is diminishing due to the inflow of non-Indiana trash.

Indiana's problem is not unique. The reported cases reflect that out-of-state trash is the object of nationwide concern, as well as disdain. Congress itself, however, has not yet deigned to touch the subject in a comprehensive manner. Thus, as the states become fed up, or filled up, with out-of-state waste, the harmony of each state's regulations with the dormant commerce clause is likely to be considered on a case by case basis.

[The three parts of the Indiana statute at issue in this case would: (1) charge Indiana-generated waste a "tipping fee" of $0.50/ton and non-Indiana-generated waste a fee equal to that of the landfill nearest the location the waste was generated; (2) require all non-Indiana-generated waste to be accompanied by a certificate from a health officer in the generating state that the waste is neither "hazardous or infectious as defined by Federal Law"; and (3) require all haulers to certify the state of origin of the greatest part of each load of waste "tipped" in Indiana.]

* * *

The plaintiffs broker the hauling of loads of solid waste from sites in the eastern portion of the United States to locations primarily in the Midwest. The trash that the plaintiffs broker originates in the states of New York, New Jersey, and Pennsylvania. Landfill space is at a premium in those states, particularly in the more urban areas. Consequently, despite the cost of transporting the trash hundreds of miles to Indiana, it is still far less expensive to dump the waste here where landfill space is more plentiful. For example, a Long Island [sic] landfill named Fresh Kills charges $125.00 per ton to dump municipal waste. In most Indiana landfills, the typical charge is $12.00 per ton. The hauling cost per ton is approximately $33.00 to $35.00 per ton.

The business of matching trash collectors with less expensive Midwestern landfill operators, known as "trash-brokering," can be profitable. The revenue obtained by trash-brokering results from putting the disposal deal together rather than performing any part of the disposal transaction. Thus, the plaintiffs do not haul the trash themselves nor do they own the vehicles in which it is hauled. Typically, they arrange verbally to have haulers pick up trash at particular municipal solid waste and recycling stations in New York, New Jersey, and Pennsylvania after having arranged for the dumping of this waste in Midwestern landfills. As brokers, the plaintiffs use their contacts to link the waste from an Eastern trash collection source with the independent haulers who then transport the trash to the Midwestern landfills.

* * *

Enforcement of the three provisions of the Act at issue in this suit will tend to diminish the amount of trash that comes into the State of Indiana from outside the state. Similarly, enforcement of the three provisions in question will have an adverse effect on the amount of the plaintiffs' business that could be conducted within Indiana. Jack Castenova indicated that the enforcement of the statutes at issue would be disastrous to his business. Jack Lynch of Government Suppliers indicated that enforcement of these statutes would wreak havoc on that business and would, in his words, "send it down the tubes." The tipping fee provision would completely prevent

Castenova and Government Suppliers from conducting their business in the State of Indiana because the cost of dumping the trash, combined with the cost of transporting it to Indiana, would exceed their profits.

* * *

IDEM [Indiana Dept. of Environmental Management] directed the inspection of several loads of trash at landfills on May 24, 1990, and on June 5, 1990. On May 24, 1990, John Hale, an Environmental Scientist at IDEM, was part of a three-person inspection team at Talley Hunt landfill near Wabash, Indiana. The loads inspected contained baled trash which in Hale's opinion came from outside the State of Indiana. The bales were broken open on the landfill surface by a bulldozer and the contents spread out in a roughly square area approximately fifteen feet by fifteen feet. The waste square was approximately one foot deep. The inspection was difficult work, requiring three workers to be suited up in heavy protective gear on a hot day. The workers raked through the trash and looked for items that were not supposed to be deposited in a sanitary landfill. When a team member spotted an item that was suspicious, the other members would be called over to the spot. If the members thought that the item appeared to be a prohibited item, it would be collected and placed in a sealed container. Hale's group collected various items, including a rubber glove with what appeared to be blood in it and four or five used syringes. Hale delivered these items to the Indiana State Police laboratory on the next day.

On June 14, 1990, Hale participated in a four-person inspection team under similar circumstances at the Center Point landfill. On this occasion, Hale's group again discovered various items, including a syringe and some medical tubing. Again, it was Hale's opinion that the loads inspected came from outside Indiana. To some degree, this opinion was corroborated when one of the Hale team members discovered a piece of paper during the inspection that bore the identification of Mount Sinai Hospital which is located in New York. Hale also delivered these objects, sealed in containers, to the Indiana State Police laboratory.

On May 24, 1990, Jerome Rud of IDEM worked as part of a four-person team on similar inspections at the Center Point landfill. The trash inspected, in the opinion of Rud, originated outside of Indiana. The inspection technique was much the same as the one used by Hale's group. The Rud group discovered various items of concern, including objects he described as respirator tubing, an evacuator bag, several vials containing a reddish liquid and a hypodermic needle. Martin Harmless, Assistant Commissioner for Solid and Hazardous Waste at IDEM, also participated in the inspection at the Center Point landfill. His principal role was to collect any items found by the workers and to transport those items to the Indiana State Police laboratory for examination. He accomplished this by placing the items in sealed containers, transporting them to the lab and depositing them there in substantially the same condition in which he received them from the others on the inspection team.

James Romack, a chemist at the Indiana State Police laboratory, examined the various items collected by the Hale and Rud teams. In connection with the Hale team examination at Halley Hunt landfill on May 24, 1990, Romack found dried human blood on various plastic devices and a bandage and liquid blood on two syringes and a glove. Examination of the results of the Rud team inspection disclosed the presence of human blood on two vacutainers, a wound suction evacuator, an alcohol preparation pad, paper materials, and gauze pads. The June 14, 1990, inspection results showed dried human blood on a plastic device with attached tubing. None of the items collected were tested for the presence of hazardous materials, infectious qualities, or to determine whether they had been treated.

Although the defense contends that these searches were part of stepped-up enforcement efforts, there was no evidence to show that they were part of routine enforcement practices. The inspections appeared to be an effort to gather information for this litigation, or for some similar purpose, and were ordered well after the enactment of the legislation and the initiation of this litigation. In general, the inspections were conducted in a reasonably professional manner. Neither Rud nor Hale were accurate in all details as to the number and description of the items; none of those examined match the Rud and Hale descriptions "on all fours." However, the collection and preservation processes were sufficiently reliable to permit the admission of the results of the inspections into evidence.

*   *   *

State IDEM inspectors discovered infectious medical waste deposited in Indiana landfills from out-of-state.* While this evidence may establish that the federal act is less than 100% effective in preventing the illegal dumping of infectious waste, it does not address the effectiveness of Indiana's statute. Thus, this court cannot draw the inference that the state wants it to draw — i.e., that Indiana trash is inherently safer than out-of-state trash. Moreover, this court doubts that a state can, under the commerce clause, justify discrimination against interstate commerce on the sole grounds that the regulatory scheme developed by the state appears to be more stringent than other states' regulations. The *City of Philadelphia* Court spoke in terms that suggest that there must be an *inherent* difference between in-state and out-of-state trash to justify a discriminatory state regulation. Regulatory differences are not enough to justify the discriminatory treatment of out-of-state waste, without sufficient evidence that the effect of the regulation actually results in "cleaner" in-state waste.

*   *   *

---

* This court took under advisement the plaintiffs' objections to the admissibility of the defendant's evidence of medical waste found at Indiana sanitary landfills. Specifically, the plaintiffs objected to the evidence on the grounds of failure to lay an adequate foundation, insufficient chain of custody and irrelevancy. This court now overrules the plaintiffs' objections and admits the evidence of medical waste. While it is clear that the defendant did not present a complete chain of custody, the cases establish that any breaks in the chain of custody impact the weight of the evidence and not its admissibility, as long as the court makes a threshold determination that such evidence has not been changed in any important respect. A trial court also is entitled to assume that public officials who had custody of evidence did not tamper with the evidence. In this case, this court finds no hint that the defendant and his agents did anything to compromise the authenticity of the proffered evidence.

Conclusions

Today Indiana joins the list of states whose statutes have not fully survived constitutional scrutiny. This case may thus be closed, although the weighty concerns it represents persist.

The attempt to regulate the out-of-state waste coming into Indiana through these three regulations fails to clear the constitutional hurdles posed by the commerce clause. By no means, however, does this prevent Indiana from regulating the trash that is brought here. Indiana has full authority to regulate out-of-state refuse in all ways that it regulates in-state refuse, including imposing and enforcing stringent regulations on infectious or hazardous waste. Similarly, this opinion does not restrict future legislative or regulatory efforts to address the problems caused by the influx of out-of-state waste, assuming that the evenhandedness required by the commerce clause is present.

*   *   *

Therefore, IT IS FURTHER ORDERED that the defendant, the Honorable Evan Bayh, Governor of the State of Indiana, is hereby PERMANENTLY ENJOINED from enforcing these statutory provisions.

The most important evidentiary rules in this case are found in the footnote cited, where the court says that breaks in the chain of custody go to the weight, not the admissibility, of the evidence. For those readers who work for government agencies, there is also, in the same footnote, the aside that public officials do not tamper with evidence. These last two cases should encourage you in the correct belief that courts no longer lay down a detailed list of requirements for the chain of custody and, if these requirements are not met, throw out the resulting test.

For those who might be in a jurisdiction that is "strictly old-fashioned," the rules laid down in this next case can be generalized to account for a sufficient chain of custody in almost any jurisdiction.

ROSE v. PAPER MILLS TRUCKING CO., 209 N.W. 2d 305 (Ct. App. Mich. 1973)

In this case the court stated a nine-part test for determining the admissibility of a blood sample:

"[T]he party seeking introduction must show (1) that the blood was timely taken (2) from a particular identified body (3) by an authorized licensed physician, medical technologist, or registered nurse designated by a licensed physician, (4) that the instruments used were sterile, (5) that the blood taken was properly preserved or kept, (6) and labeled, and (7) if transported or sent, the method and procedures used therein, (8) the method and procedures used in conducting the test, and (9) that the identity of the person or persons under whose supervision the tests were conducted be established."

These rules can be generalized as follows: (1) when and (2) where the sample was taken; (3) that it was taken by a properly trained person; and (4) that it was not contaminated while being taken. The remaining criteria of the *Rose* case are as applicable to other types of samples as they are to blood samples.

The issue of samples is one example where the request for admission, discussed in Chapter 4, can very properly and powerfully be used. After the test is conducted, a request for admission can be attached to the report of the test and sent to the other parties, asking them to admit that this report accurately represents the condition of what was sampled at the time the sample was taken. This type of request eliminates any disputes about the chain of custody as the parties agree the report represents the actual condition of what was sampled. They agree to the representativeness of the sample and to the lack of tampering and deterioration of the sample. If another party then refuses to admit, your side can collect the costs of proving the facts.

CHAPTER 11

Common Knowledge and Routine Practice

Two rules of evidence are exceptionally useful for all witnesses, experts and otherwise. The first is the rule that allows the court to take judicial notice of facts. The great virtue of judicial notice is that, after judicial notice is taken, such facts are, from that point on in the case, assumed to be true. If there is a jury, the judge will turn to its members and say something like: "Ladies and gentlemen of the jury, I am telling you that in your deliberations in this case you must assume that the following fact is true."

FRE Rule 201. Judicial Notice of Adjudicative Facts

(a) Scope of rule.

This rule governs only judicial notice of adjudicative facts.

(b) Kinds of facts.

A judicially noticed fact must be one not subject to reasonable dispute in that it is either (1) generally known within the territorial jurisdiction of the trial court or (2) capable of accurate and ready determination by resort to sources whose accuracy cannot reasonably be questioned.

(c) When discretionary.

A court may take judicial notice, whether requested or not.

(d) When mandatory.

A court shall take judicial notice if requested by a party and supplied with the necessary information.

(e) Opportunity to be heard.

A party is entitled upon timely request to an opportunity to be heard as to the propriety of taking judicial notice and the tenor of the matter noticed.

In the absence of prior notification, the request may be made after judicial notice has been taken.

(f) Time of taking notice.

Judicial notice may be taken at any stage of the proceeding.

(g) Instructing jury.

In a civil action or proceeding, the court shall instruct the jury to accept as conclusive any fact judicially noticed. In a criminal case, the court shall instruct the jury that it may, but is not required to, accept as conclusive any fact judicially noticed.

The most likely use of Rule 201 for expert witnesses is part (b)(2). Part (b)(1) deals with such matters as street directions ("Pine Street runs north and south"), one-way streets ("Pine Street is one-way northbound"), locations of rivers, bridges, etc. Part (b)(2), on the other hand, is very useful for almost any type of scientific or technical information you might look up in a reference book. As such, it is closely related to one of the hearsay exceptions we will examine later (see Chapter 17). If you are asked, "How do you know that the LD_{50} for this chemical is 3 mg/kg?" you can answer, "I looked it up in the *Merck Manual*." If they continue to question you on the validity of this data, you are perfectly correct to ask the judge, "Your honor, could you take judicial notice of this?"

Habit is one of the most important factors that determines individual behavior, as Rule 406 demonstrates.

FRE Rule 406. Habit; Routine Practice

Evidence of the habit of a person or of the routine practice of an organization, whether corroborated or not and regardless of the presence of eyewitnesses, is relevant to prove that the conduct of the person or organization on a particular occasion was in conformity with the habit or routine practice.

Note that Rule 406 states "whether corroborated or not." This means it is only necessary for the witness to say "I always do it this way" or "That's the way our organization does things." It would, however, be desirable to provide some sort of corroboration, especially in cases before a jury. This is why it is particularly useful to have a written procedures manual for your organization, which provides corroboration for typical practices and procedures.

Remember that, unlike judicial notice, habit and routine practice merely make the evidence admissible but do not conclusively establish that the activity occurred in that way on this occasion. A wonderful example of how this works can be found in the last case cited in this book, *In Re Swine Flu Immunization* (see Chapter 20), where the court found, based on testimony regarding the routine practice of the health department in administering vaccinations, that the plaintiff had received a certain piece of paper, although she denied receiving it and the health department was unable to produce her signed receipt.

CHAPTER 12

Real Evidence

"Real" evidence is what lawyers sometimes call objects and papers that will be admitted into evidence. The distinction here is between physical things and testimony (oral) evidence. Sometimes an additional distinction is made between "real" physical things and "testimonial" documents, but, for our purposes, we will treat them the same way. The most important point about real evidence is that it is possible for the jury, if there is one, to request that the real evidence be made available in the jury room while jury members are deliberating.

Since the jury is not allowed to have a transcript of testimony in the jury room but must, instead, rely on its collective memory of what was said, real evidence is potentially much more likely to sway the jury. For this reason, there are several rather strict rules concerning the admission of real evidence, which are really only relevant in a jury trial because the law operates under the assumption that judges are capable of deciding how much weight to give such things without imposing severe restrictions. For this reason, in a judge trial, it is much simpler to use exhibits and demonstrations, which we will discuss in Chapter 13.

This first case illustrates the simplest type of real evidence.

WESTERN COTTONOIL CO. v. ADKISSON, 276 S.W.2d 411
(Civ. App. Tex. 1955)

Suit was brought by Louis Adkisson and wife against Western Cottonoil Company for damages. It was alleged that such damages were caused and resulted from odors from soap stock stored by Western Cottonoil Company in an earthen pit near the home of plaintiffs. The trial was before a jury which found that the storing of the soap stock constituted a nuisance and plaintiffs were awarded judgment for damages. Western Cottonoil Company has appealed.

During the trial of the case the court admitted in evidence over appellant's objections, plaintiffs' Exhibit No. 1 which was a jar containing soap stock from appellant's earthen pit. In the only point presented by appellant it is contended that such action of the court was reversible error.

The witness Patterson testified that he went to the pit during the time complained of, and put some of the soap stock from appellant's earthen pit in jars; that plaintiffs' exhibit No. 1 was one of the jars and that it contained soap stock taken from the pit; that he smelled the odor from the pit and it was an awful odor; that he had never in his life smelled anything that compared with it. He testified that the odor from the jar which was introduced in evidence was the same odor as that which came from the pit except that the odor from the jar was not as strong as that from the pit because there was not as much of it.

The admission of real or demonstrative evidence is largely within the discretion of the trial court....

The soap stock in the jar in question was identified as a sample taken from appellant's earthen pit during the period of time complained of. The purpose of the evidence was to show the odor which appellees claimed to have come from appellant's pit. The sample was shown to have been in the continuous custody and possession of the witness, to be in the same condition as when taken from the pit and to have the same odor as that which came from the pit. The court did not abuse its discretion in admitting the exhibit in evidence.

The judgment of the trial court is affirmed.

Two points about this simple case are important. First, the issues of chain of custody and representativeness, which we discussed in Chapter 10, apply equally to real evidence. Second, it is necessary to authenticate and verify the evidence is a proper example of what it purports to be. In this case, a live witness testified that the smell was the same smell as the smell from the pit in dispute. Authentication can also be achieved by a certificate from authorized persons as, for example, certified copies of land titles from the county clerk or driver's license records from the DMV.

The next case demonstrates the need for authentication and verification.

RHOADES v. VIRGINIA-FLORIDA CORP., 476 F.2d 82 (5th Cir. 1973)

This case concerns erosion damage to the Florida residential beachfront property of plaintiffs, caused or substantially contributed to by the construction of a seawall for a beachfront high-rise apartment complex. The property faces the Atlantic Ocean in the golden beach area of South Florida, at or near the intersection of the beach with the Dade-Broward county line. Defendants are the corporate lessee, builder, mortgage assignee, and indenture trustees of the apartment complex. Plaintiffs are the owners of residential lots lying successively to the south of the apartment complex, the lot of the most northerly plaintiff being adjacent to the south boundary of the apartment property.

Plaintiffs brought this diversity suit for an injunction, damages, and an order requiring removal of the seawall. Following a nonjury trial the district judge found that defendants were entitled to judgment although the seawall substantially contributed to the erosion of plaintiffs' properties. His premise was that the defendants were not liable if they had built the wall on property owned by them, that is, landward (west) of the mean high water mark (MHWM), which is the boundary between the privately owned apartment property and the state sovereignty soil seaward thereof. He found that the wall was built landward (west) of the MHWM, and, accordingly, denied relief to plaintiffs.

The central issue at the trial was the location of the seawall vis-à-vis the MHWM. The case must be reversed because the finding that it was located landward of the MHWM was based in part upon the content of three drawings which could not be utilized by the court for that factual determination because they had not been verified. The three documents are defendants' exhibits 38, 40, and 49 (D.38, D.40, and D.49). D.38 and 40 purport to be surveys of the apartment complex property by Maurice E. Berry, a registered surveyor, the former drawing purporting to show along the beach side of the property the actual location of the MHWM, the latter purporting to show along the beach side a proposed location for a seawall. D.49 is labeled as a tentative layout drawing (dated 1953) of a proposed city bulkhead line, made by a named firm of engineers and surveyors and containing a line labeled as mean high water mark.

(1) Use of the drawings as evidence.

D.38, 40, and 49 were offered into evidence without any stated limitation on the purposes for which offered. Plaintiffs had acknowledged their authenticity but pointed out that authentication only identified the documents as having been prepared by the purported authors. Plaintiffs repeatedly objected to admission on the ground that there had been no testimony by the authors or by persons participating in the preparation of the surveys concerning what the drawings purported to show. Plaintiffs urged that without such testimony the documents were meaningless, and that they were entitled to cross-examine the authors.

The court admitted the drawings without any stated limitation on their use and without any testimony from their authors, and, as we have said, utilized their content in its dispositive finding that the seawall was located landward of the MHWM.

The error was critical because plaintiffs introduced without objection P.31, the McGill survey, made by a state-employed surveyor for an agency of the state of Florida, which located the MHWM considerably landward of the locations which the court believed were shown by D.38, 40, and 49.

Since rule 43(a) FED.R.CIV.P. requires evidence to be admitted in a diversity case if admissible under federal statutes, federal equity practice, or state statutes, rules or common law, we necessarily have engaged in a search of the authorities much broader in scope than the nominal assistance afforded us by the parties.

As urged by plaintiffs at the trial, authentication of the documents merely established their authorship, the proof of some human's "personal connection with a corporal object." Before the documents could be admitted for "testimonial use," that is, where the documents themselves would "testify" as direct evidence on a material disputed issue of fact, they were required to be verified. "Whenever such a document is offered as proving a thing to be as therein represented, then it is offered testimonially, and it must be associated with a testifier." Verification required at the minimum a showing by the testimony of some competent witness that the lines of the drawings were correct representations of the actual physical character-istics of the land and objects which they purported to show. The significance of verification is demonstrated by what we do not know in this case. There was not even generalized testimony that the drawings accurately depict the property or the description and locations of monuments presumably used as starting points, and there is no evidence of the competency of the surveyor or of the manner in which the drawings were prepared. There is no evidence that lines, calls, and monuments portrayed on the drawings were based on or tied into, or derived from, an official survey or the oldest private survey. We do not know that on-the-ground measurements were made, and, if they were, when made and by whom and whether accurately done, and whether measured data was correctly transferred onto the drawings.

Generally, when a survey is to be used as direct evidence the author appears, establishes his competency, and testifies to the accuracy and the manner of his work. Neither Berry, the author of D.38 and 40, nor the unidentified author of D.49, appeared and testified. One who participated in the survey and can attest to its accuracy may be able to verify it if the author is acknowledged to have been competent. No participant in the work underlying D.38, 40, or 49 so testified. We set out in a footnote some of the cases in which there have been efforts at verification, but the efforts have been held insufficient in degree to make maps or drawings admissible as documents which themselves "testify."

It is possible, through exceptions to the hearsay rule, for a survey to receive requisite verification without in-court appearance by a person whose testimony would verify it. None of the exceptions have been shown in the trial court or in this court to be applicable to D.38, 40, and 49. Defendants' drawings were made by private persons acting in a private capacity and thus were not within the official written statements exception to the hearsay rule.

Two of the three documents bore what purported to be a certificate of Berry, as a registered Florida land surveyor. We have found no basis for concluding — and defendants have referred us to none — that the certificates themselves gave to the documents an official character or otherwise verified their contents. The certification itself lacked the necessary verification to be admissible as a hearsay exception. Without statutory authorization it could not provide verification for the document on which it appeared.

Defendants have not claimed that the three drawings were admissible under federal or state business record statutes, 28 U.S.C. 1732, FLA.STAT.ANN. 92.36, and in our opinion they were not admissible under either.

Since D.38, 40, and 49 were not admissible for testimonial purposes, that is to "testify" themselves concerning the location of the seawall vis-à-vis the MHWM, the allowable range of discretion permitted the trial court under rule 43(a), FED.R.CIV.P., did not permit it to admit them and then employ them for a testimonial — and, in this instance, dispositive — purpose.

The defendants seek the sanctuary of authorities allowing the use of documents to explain and illustrate the testimony of witnesses who refer to them. Authenticated documents can be employed in such a limited and ancillary manner. However, as the Supreme Court of Alabama explained in *Crocker v. Lee*, 261 ALA. 439, 74 SO.2D 429 (1954):

> "the use of a map, drawing or plat for purposes of illustration must be distinguished from its admission in evidence. In the latter case the instrument possesses within itself evidential characteristics tending to establish a particular fact. In the former case the testimony of the witness is the evidence and the map or diagram is merely an aid to its understanding." 74 SO.2D at 435. In the case before us the three drawings were not offered, admitted or utilized for the limited and ancillary purpose of explaining oral testimony of witnesses who referred to them....

Reversed and remanded.

We will return, in Chapter 13, to the issue of documents used to "illustrate the testimony of witnesses who refer to them" mentioned in the next-to-last paragraph of the preceding case. Since the issue of authentication and verification is so important, however, and since you may wish to learn what happened next in the *Virginia-Florida* case, we will first look at the "next round" of that case.

RHOADES v. VIRGINIA-FLORIDA CORP., 549 F.2d 985 (5th Cir. 1977)

This diversity suit charges negligence and nuisance in the construction and maintenance of a seawall by defendants, causing or contributing to erosion damages to plaintiffs' residential beachfront properties located in Florida. In the original nonjury trial the court found that the seawall substantially contributed to the erosion of plaintiffs' properties. The trial court proceeded on the premise of law that the defendants were not liable if they had built the wall on property owned by them, that is, landward (west) of the mean high water mark (MHWM), which is the boundary between privately owned property and the state sovereignty soil seaward thereof. The court found that the wall was built landward (west) of the MHWM, and, accordingly, denied relief to plaintiffs.

On appeal we reversed and remanded because surveys relied upon by the court, D.38, 40, and 49, were not properly verified. 476 F.2d 82. On remand the defendants presented additional testimony in an attempt to verify the surveys erroneously admitted into evidence at the first trial. The court held D.38, 40, and 49 were admissible. Based on the evidence at the first and second trials, the court held that defendants' seawall was constructed landward of the MHWM and again found for defendants. The decision must again be reversed.

First, as to verification. M.E. Berry, Jr., a registered surveyor, testified that D.38 and 40 were survey drawings prepared by his office based on field notes compiled by Frank Harrison, chief of the survey party which made the actual physical measurements represented on the drawings. He further testified that he checked the completed drawings against Harrison's field notes. Harrison himself testified as to his participation in and on-site direction of the actual survey.

Berry's and Harrison's testimony was sufficient to trace the reliability of D.38 and 40 with respect to the making of measurements by the crew, the recording of field data in field notes, and the conversion of that data into line drawings. D.38 and 40 were admissible. The difficulty is that the purported ground location of the MHWM, which was measured and then recorded in field notes and exemplified in the drawing, was nothing more than a rough estimate. No established monuments showed its location, which was not determined by measurements from any point whose location was established, nor was it established by mathematical calculation. Harrison testified that he "estimated or eyeballed" the location of the MHWM by observing "where the high water is from the seaweed and debris that is washed up on the shore," and by looking at "the varying points...where the high water has been." He recognized that he could have located the MHWM by an alternative method of "establishing an elevation." Thus, according to the testimony, D.38 and 40 reflect measurements made by the crew but they do not reflect the true location of the MHWM with any more accuracy than the original "eyeball estimate" made on a single occasion on one day.

* * *

Harrison testified that he received no special instructions but was told just to make a survey. After describing the manner in which he established the line by visual observation, he testified as follows:

Q. Is that a scientific way of doing it? Are there other ways of doing it?
A. Yes. There is another way to do it.
Q. What is the other way to do it?
A. By establishing an elevation.
Q. Now, did you do that?
A. No. I didn't.

Another witness, Reeves, who made another survey, testified that normally his surveying firm would not use the visual observation method to establish the mean high water mark but would "arrive at it by means of an elevation."

* * *

The above-quoted finding must be vacated, and on remand the district court can reconsider the matter of the landowner's right to rely upon a survey vis-à-vis his obligations to other landowners.

Vacated in part, reversed in part, and remanded.

Here the plaintiffs were correct to challenge the admissibility of the surveys at issue. It was not a case of a lawyer raising silly technical issues; the surveys were not accurate with regard to the mean high water location.

One way to avoid problems like this is to use the request for admission during the discovery phase of the case. The defendant in this case could easily have served a simple request that the opponent admit that the attached survey accurately represents the location of the MHWM. Of course, the plaintiff would have refused to admit that, and would have been right to so refuse, but nevertheless that would have simplified the issue considerably. In the more typical case, where the disputed real evidence would not be dispositive of the entire proceeding, the request for admission may save considerable time and effort.

CHAPTER 13

Exhibits and Demonstrations

In Chapter 12, we examined how "things" are introduced into evidence. In this chapter, we will look at the issue of materials used to help the decision maker better understand an issue, but that are not introduced into evidence. Like the law on introducing "things" into evidence, there are no provisions in FRE regarding this issue; it is all common law found in court decisions.

The fundamental rule is that materials used only for illustrative purposes need not be verified. All that is necessary is that you, as the expert witness, state that a particular material will be useful to the jury for understanding your testimony. The line of questioning typically runs: "Expert, do you have something with you that would better enable the jury to understand this part of your testimony?" Answer: "Yes. It is a chart of X." This is all that you need to do to use something for illustrative purposes. The next case shows a use of x-rays of persons totally unconnected to this actual case (as well as other issues).

ROGERS V. RAYMARK IND., 922 F.2D 1426 (9TH CIR. 1991)

This is an asbestos case. The appeal raises questions about the extent of a trial judge's discretion to exclude expert and percipient witness opinion testimony under Fed.R.Evid. 403 and to permit use of third-party x-rays for demonstrative purposes even though they had not been identified in the pretrial order.

Hester Rogers ("plaintiff"), widow of Clinton Rogers ("Rogers"), sued Fibreboard Corporation and Keene Corporation, two asbestos manufacturers ("defendants"), following her husband's death from lung cancer [that allegedly] could be traced in part to his exposure to asbestos as a shipyard worker at the Kaiser Shipyard #1 in Richmond, California, during World War II. Defendants countered that Rogers developed lung cancer solely from cigarette smoking. Mrs. Rogers appeals from the judgment entered on a special jury verdict in favor of defendants, challenging the district court's evidentiary rulings. We affirm.

*   *   *

Rogers smoked between half a pack and two packs of cigarettes a day for 45 years. He smoked during the period he worked at Kaiser. Rogers died of lung cancer in 1982.

Both sides agree that cigarette smoking was the primary cause of Rogers' lung cancer. Plaintiff claimed, however, that asbestos also contributed significantly to her husband's cancer.

Her experts testified that when a person smokes cigarettes and inhales asbestos at the same time, the two substances work together to increase the absorption of carcinogens. Opinions were in conflict about what evidence is needed to link asbestos to a particular person's cancer. Some experts thought epidemiological evidence alone was enough. Others required epidemiological evidence along with the presence of asbestosis or some other disease specifically linked to asbestos. Still others required epidemiological studies combined with the presence of pleural plaques.

Epidemiological studies showed that workers in asbestos production plants have the highest cancer rates. Workers who install insulation — for example, the pipe insulators at shipyards like Kaiser — also develop cancer at an increased rate but not as frequently as plant workers. Shipyard workers do not develop cancer at a greatly increased rate; but welders do show some increased cancer rates. Finally, there was evidence that workers exposed to asbestos during World War II have developed cancer at rates higher than similar workers before and after the war.

Plaintiff argued that Rogers should not be considered a shipyard worker for the purpose of determining his cancer risk because that group included people with jobs and exposure levels unlike Rogers'. Instead she urged that Rogers' exposure level was closer to that of insulation workers because the frenzied pace of work during World War II forced him to spend much time working alongside insulators. There was evidence that Rogers' additional task of instructing workers in installation and removal of asbestos increased his level of exposure beyond that experienced by an ordinary welder. Defendants countered that Rogers' risk could not be compared to that of insulators because he only spent a small portion of his time around insulation work, and that any increased risk of cancer could not be traced to asbestos because welders are exposed to a variety of other carcinogens, including nickel and cadmium.

The parties likewise disagreed about whether Rogers' lungs evidenced significant exposure to asbestos. It was undisputed that he did not have asbestosis or any other disease specifically associated with asbestos. Yet plaintiff claimed that Rogers had one pleural plaque, and that the presence of this plaque indicated asbestos exposure. Pleural plaques are bulges in the lining of the lung. They do not cause pain or inhibit breathing and they are not malignant, but there was evidence that plaques are frequently seen in people who have been exposed to significant doses of asbestos and may serve as markers of that exposure. Some experts opined that if a patient had true asbestos-related plaques there would be more than one plaque, and the plaques would be found on both sides of the chest cavity. Defendants' experts testified that the abnormality in Rogers' lung was not a plaque but rather was a change related either to the lung cancer or to a previous respiratory illness, and that, even if there were a plaque, it was irrelevant because true asbestos plaques are multiple and bilateral. Finally, the defense claimed that Rogers' lungs showed the types of abnormalities and diseases specifically associated with cigarettes.

The jury returned a special verdict, finding that defendants' products contained a design defect, that defendants knew of the defect when it left their possession, and that the defect did not cause Rogers' lung cancer. Mrs. Rogers contends that the district court erred by (1) excluding testimony proffered by Buddy Ay, one of plaintiff's expert witnesses, which would have explained how asbestos was installed on liberty ships; (2) excluding testimony of Harry Dutton, a percipient witness, offered to show that the level of dust at Kaiser was greater than the level of dust at certain asbestos production factories for which no epidemiological studies existed; and (3) permitting defendants' expert physician to use x-rays of an unidentified person to demonstrate what a supposedly true pleural plaque would look like, when these x-rays had not been identified in the pretrial order.

*　*　*

A. Exclusion of Expert Testimony

Plaintiff offered Buddy Ay as an expert in marine asbestos insulation techniques. Ay has worked in the field of asbestos insulation for 30 years. He worked as an insulator for the Navy from 1960 through 1981. He also served as an asbestos safety consultant for the National Cancer Society from 1977 through 1979. Ay retired from the Navy in 1981 and now runs his own insulation business. Ay has testified frequently as an expert in asbestos cases.

Rogers spent some of his time in a canvas enclosure teaching various skills, including the use of a pneumatic chipping gun to remove asbestos insulation. Plaintiff's order of proof indicates that Ay would have explained the job of chipping and the amount of dust that would have been created in the canvas enclosure. He would have shown samples of asbestos products to the jury. Finally, Ay would have described the types of insulation that were used on World War II liberty ships and how they were installed. He would also have identified what type of asbestos dust would become airborne in a given worksetting and the type of worksettings that existed in 1945.

Ay's knowledge of shipyard conditions during the war came from discussions with insulators of that period, including his father and his father's friends. In addition, although Ay did not himself build World War II liberty ships, he did repair work on these ships in later years. By other witnesses plaintiff proposed to show that insulation practices during the war were the same as those used through the 1960s.

*　*　*

The district court found that the probative value of Ay's testimony was not strong for three reasons: (1) it was only tangentially related to the issues at trial; (2) plaintiff had presented testimony bearing on the same point through other witnesses; and (3) the proffered testimony had the potential of confusing the jury by unduly emphasizing a narrow issue. This ruling was well within the court's discretion.

Ay's testimony had minimal probative value. His description of shipyard insulation techniques would have been relevant only to that portion of Rogers' work experience which put him in close proximity to insulators...

Against that level of probative value, the district court correctly balanced prejudicial effect. The jury might well have been confused into equating Ay's description of life as an insulator with life as a welder and have been misled by Ay's videotapes and samples of asbestos products into supposing that these were the dispositive items upon which to focus.

The district court also properly considered the fact that plaintiff's other witnesses already had presented most of the relevant testimony Ay had to offer. Clark, a welder at Kaiser during World War II, described the process of insulation in detail and explained how it affected working conditions for the welders ... Plaintiff also introduced the videotaped deposition of Harry Dutton, a contractor who supplied insulation workers and materials to Kaiser during World War II, who testified about the process of installing insulation and about the conditions at Kaiser which placed welders in close proximity to insulators. One of plaintiff's epidemiological experts, Dr. Smith, compared conditions at shipyards and compared the extent of asbestos exposure for each. Finally, plaintiff showed a 1943 Department of Education training tape depicting the process of insulating pipes.

Plaintiff contends that she particularly needed Ay's testimony because he would make an articulate, eloquent, and clear presentation. In this connection she notes that many of her husband's coworkers had died and that others had forgotten the details or were too unsophisticated to describe their former working conditions articulately. Nevertheless, a party is not entitled to have an expert testify solely because that witness can eloquently summarize the evidence. That job belongs to counsel.

*   *   *

B. Exclusion of Testimony on Dust Levels

Plaintiff sought to introduce portions of a videotaped deposition of Harry Dutton, a contractor who supplied insulation workers and materials to Kaiser during World War II, to link asbestos dust levels at the Kaiser shipyards to asbestos dust levels at insulation factories. In those portions Dutton testified that he had visited several plants where defendants manufactured asbestos, and that the level of visible asbestos dust aboard ships at Kaiser was equal to or greater than the level of dust normally found at defendants' manufacturing facilities. Dutton's comparison was based on his personal observations rather than a scientific sampling. It was offered to establish that (1) Dutton observed dust levels at Kaiser; (2) Dutton observed dust levels at defendants' plants; (3) epidemiological studies at the plants of other manufacturers showed the asbestos exposure level for their workers to be X; (4) the dust level Dutton saw at defendants' plants was similar to the dust level he saw at the shipyard; therefore (5) the exposure level at Kaiser for Rogers was also X.

The district court excluded Dutton's comparison of the dust levels under Rule 403 because it found such evidence to be more misleading than probative. This exclusion was correct, because the plants Dutton visited were not part of any epidemiological study introduced at trial and there was no evidence of similarity between those plants and the plants subject to epidemiological study. The only relevance of the proffer was to show that the dust levels at Kaiser exposed Rogers to a risk similar to that of workers in those asbestos factories for which there were epidemiological studies ... The jury could have been confused by the comparison between Kaiser and asbestos manufacturing plants and misled into making the leap from defendants' plants to the plants for which there were studies, without foundation in the evidence.

* * *

C. Use of Unidentified X-Rays as Demonstrative Evidence

The district court allowed defense witness Dr. Norman Moscow to show the jury four x-rays for illustrative purposes; the x-rays were not formally admitted into evidence, however. The x-rays were of an unknown patient and purported to show pleural plaques. They were not listed in the pretrial order despite the fact that the court told the parties to list all items to be used at trial, regardless of whether they would be admitted into evidence.

Dr. Moscow used the x-rays to support his opinion that Rogers did not have a pleural plaque. He testified that plaques are round, like a rock, and can be seen from all x-ray angles, whereas Rogers' abnormality could only be seen from one view. The x-rays were used to demonstrate this difference.

* * *

Even if the district court did err in allowing use of the x-rays, an evidentiary error is not reversible unless refusing to reverse would cause substantial injustice. In this case, injury to the plaintiff was limited. The x-rays did not introduce new evidence; they were simply a more graphic version of what Dr. Moscow had said already. Plaintiff does not suggest that they were inaccurate or misleading. Since the x-rays did not introduce any new evidence, and plaintiff did not show that they were inaccurate, the error, if any, is harmless.

* * *

Affirmed.

This case shows the use of illustrative materials. You can also perform demonstrations in court. It was not at all uncommon in the early days of blood typing in paternity actions for the actual blood test to be performed in the courtroom. (This was at the time when only A, B, AB, or O blood type had to be determined.) The expert came in, took blood from the three people, applied the reagents, and read aloud the results in the courtroom — a powerful and memorable demonstration for the jury.

I strongly encourage you to use illustrative materials and demonstrations whenever possible in the course of your testimony. It is very clear that people remember longer whatever they both see and hear. What is only heard certainly fades from memory more rapidly, and makes less of an impression, than what is seen and heard. Remember that the use of materials for illustrative purposes is limited only by your imagination.

It is particularly useful when dealing with large data sets to reduce them to a visual presentation. Most Americans are, as we are constantly told by science and mathematics educators, completely innumerate. Thus, presenting the information visually can be a great aid to understanding.[1]

I do not, however, recommend that you use documents as illustrative materials. Documents are inherently boring, so people tend to dismiss them from their minds. When using a document in any way, I strongly suggest that, when quoting from it, you cite it specifically, to "Preserve the Record for Appeal." An appellate court only has a transcript of the testimony and a copy of the document in front of it. The judges have no great desire to thumb through a 600-page report to find the five paragraphs you quoted in the course of your testimony. If you say "I would like to read the paragraphs beginning in the middle of page 213 and running through the middle of page 215," the appellate court can immediately find the place to which you refer.

I also have some personal preferences regarding what you should do with maps, charts, photographs, etc. If you intend to point out things on your charts then you should ensure, when using them, you put a mark at the place you are discussing. If you have a map, for example, and you want to talk about the point where Highway 13 crosses Elm Creek, you would say, "This is the location I am talking about, and I am putting an 'A' on the map to mark it." You then take your felt-tipped pen and put a big red "A" at that location on the map. You can use the same method to compare the mass-spectrometer printout of an unknown about which you are testifying with the mass-spectrometer printout of the known standard. You would say something along the lines of, "Now you can see that the graphs at Point A and B are identical and they are also identical at Points C and D." Label Points A, B, C, and D as you discuss them.

Much can be accomplished with illustrative evidence and demonstrations. The only real limitation is your imagination and the risk that your illustrative evidence will distract your audience (the judge and/or jury) or detract from the substance of your testimony. Of importance here is the type of courtroom you will be in (Figure 13.1).

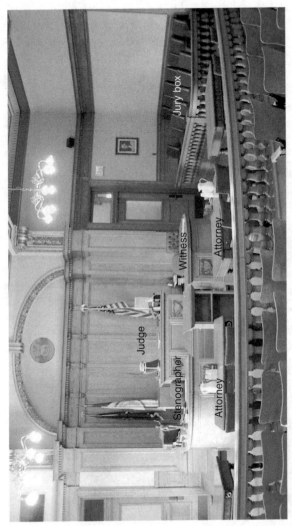

Figure 13.1 A traditional courtroom with some retrofitting. Notice monitors only for Judge and clerk/stenographer. Ingham County Circuit Court, Mason, Michigan (photograph by author).

Figure 13.2 A modern courtroom. Notice large video behind witness chair and the plentitude of monitors everywhere, especially in the jury box. Also notice that, in a nonjury trial, the witness can turn and address the Judge directly. Ingham County Circuit Court, Lansing, Michigan (photograph by author).

As you can see, it is not really set up for using visual aids. There are no screens and there are no electrical outlets in the action arena. For this reason I am reluctant to use slides, moving pictures, and videotapes in such a courtroom. The audience members become so distracted by the time and effort required to set up the necessary equipment that they lose track of what you are really discussing. If you and the attorney really think that you should be using such things, she will probably attempt to schedule your testimony first thing in the morning or immediately after lunch, so the equipment can be set up and tested without interrupting the flow of the case.

Furthermore, since these devices are used for illustrative purposes only, they are not crucial to your case. However, I know lawyers who advocate showing a videotape of the way in which detailed analytic chemistry is performed with a GC-MS, if merely to overwhelm the jury with the sophistication of the equipment; I do not recommend using such a videotape. You could use photographs of a midnight dumper turning the stopcocks of a toxic waste truck, or of a supposedly injured person playing basketball, but such photographs would not be for illustrative purposes only; they would be part of your direct case.

On the other hand, look at Figure 13.2.

This is a modern courtroom and is obviously designed for the use of demonstrative aids. There are monitors everywhere, including the jury box and it is fully wired for computer and video input. The judge has an override control that she can use at any time, and so is less likely to worry about inadmissible material sneaking into evidence. If you are in such a courtroom, the only thing you need worry about is overwhelming the merits of your case with the technology.[2]

Computer animations and simulations are a newer category of illustrative materials. All are agreed that they can be most useful, but they can also be deceptive and are expensive to create. Thus, before embarking on the production of one it would be best to consult the attorney who, in turn, might need to consult the Judge.

As with items to be introduced into evidence, it may sometimes be helpful to use the request for admission with illustrative materials; it is not, however, necessary. As a matter of law, the only necessary criterion is that you testify that the item will help in understanding your testimony. Demonstrations should be discussed by your lawyer with the judge at the pretrial conference and not "sprung" on the judge at trial. The only factors that limit what you may do during your testimony are your imagination and what the particular judge presiding at the trial will allow.

REFERENCES

1. Any of Tufte's books can help you create such a presentation. The classic, reissued in 2001, is *The Visual Display of Quantitative Information.*
2. The standard reference for lawyers in this area, now a bit dated, is Siemer et al., *Effective Use of Courtroom Technology,* Notre Dame, IN, 2002.

CHAPTER 14

The Rule Against Hearsay

The most famous of all common law rules of evidence is the rule against hearsay. The text of Rule 802 is simple:

FRE Rule 802. Hearsay Rule

Hearsay is not admissible except as provided by these rules or by other rules prescribed by the Supreme Court pursuant to statutory authority or by Act of Congress.

What is sometimes more complicated is defining and understanding exactly what constitutes hearsay. For that, we first have to look at the definitions Rule 801 provides.

FRE Rule 801. Definitions

The following definitions apply under this article:
    (a) Statement.
    A "statement" is (1) an oral or written assertion or (2) nonverbal conduct of a person, if it is intended by the person as an assertion.
    (b) Declarant.
    A "declarant" is a person who makes a statement.
    (c) Hearsay.
    "Hearsay" is a statement, other than one made by the declarant while testifying at the trial or hearing, offered in evidence to prove the truth of the matter asserted.

(d) Statements which are not hearsay.

A statement is not hearsay if —

(1) Prior statement by witness.

The declarant testifies at the trial or hearing and is subject to cross-examination concerning the statement, and the statement is (A) inconsistent with the declarant's testimony, and was given under oath subject to the penalty of perjury at a trial, hearing, or other proceeding, or in a deposition, or (B) consistent with the declarant's testimony and is offered to rebut an express or implied charge against the declarant of recent fabrication or improper influence or motive, or (C) one of identification of a person made after perceiving the person; or

(2) Admission by party-opponent.

The statement is offered against a party and is (A) the party's own statement, in either an individual or a representative capacity or (B) a statement of which the party has manifested an adoption or belief in its truth, or (C) a statement by a person authorized by the party to make a statement concerning the subject, or (D) a statement by the party's agent or servant concerning a matter within the scope of the agency or employment, made during the existence of the relationship, or (E) a statement by a coconspirator of a party during the course and in furtherance of the conspiracy.

At least two people are necessary before there can be a hearsay problem. The person who made the out-of-court statement is the declarant and the person on the witness stand telling us what the declarant said is the witness. If the witness is also the declarant then there is no hearsay problem under Rule 801(c). The interesting problem is the part of Rule 801(c) that discusses "offered in evidence to prove the truth of the matter asserted."

The next case, in addition to reviewing issues we have already discussed, shows how statements that would be hearsay for one reason may be admitted for other purposes.

GREAT LAKES GAS TRANSMISSION CO. v. GRAYCO CONSTRUCTORS, INC., 506 F.2d 498 (6th Cir. 1974)

This is an appeal from a verdict and judgment of $1,838,544.56, recovered by plaintiff from the company to whom it had awarded a contract to construct part of its pipeline project. After the work was completed and the pipeline had been placed in service, the pipeline ruptured for substantial distances on two separate occasions, thereby causing damages which required repairs and which resulted in loss of revenue.

On this appeal, error is charged in the admission of certain opinion evidence and in the rejection by the Court of evidence which would show that plaintiff had recovered substantial benefits in its rate allowance by changing its accounting procedures whereby the loss was passed on to plaintiff's customers. Appellants also assign as error the lack of competent evidence to support the verdict on the issues of negligence and breach of warranty; that plaintiff's witness improperly construed the contract between plaintiff and its gas supplier; that the verdict is excessive; and that defendant was prejudiced by the trial court's jury charge. We find it necessary only to discuss the first two contentions.

Plaintiff is a Delaware corporation which was formed as a joint venture by two major North American natural gas distributing and pipeline companies: TransCanada Pipelines, Ltd., and American Natural Gas Company. The company was formed to build and operate a new and larger gas pipeline to extend across northern Minnesota, Wisconsin, the upper peninsula of Michigan, and through the lower peninsula to Sarnia, Michigan [sic], where it would connect with TransCanada's facility at the international boundary. The construction of the line was divided into two phases, the first of which was completed in 1967 and ran from Sarnia to Farwell, Michigan. The second phase began in 1968 and involved several pipeline construction companies, one of whom was the defendant.

Defendant Grayco entered into a contract with plaintiff in which Grayco was to build a 60-mile section of the pipeline running from eastern Wisconsin into the upper peninsula of Michigan. Grayco's obligation extended from unloading the pipe from railroad cars; clearing and excavating the land; welding pipe sections together; cleaning, priming, and coating the pipe; laying the pipe into the ground and filling in the trench; final testing and purging of the pipeline; and "all things necessary to completely construct a gas transmission facility ready to be operated * * *." The steel pipe used in the line was, under the contract, to be capable of withstanding pressures of 65,000 pounds per square inch without rupturing or being deformed.

Grayco began work in the spring of 1968 and was to complete the section by November 1, 1968. Work was substantially finished by late October, 1968, in spite of unusually wet and cold weather which began in September. As part of its testing procedures, Grayco performed a hydrostatic test of the pipeline at pressures up to 105% of the specified strength with the pressure maintained for a 24-hour period. These tests were successful at the two sites with which we are here concerned, the pipe surviving long tests in excess of 100% of the specified minimum strength. Great Lakes assumed beneficial occupancy of the Grayco section by November 1, 1968, although certain rough cleanup work continued until severe weather conditions forced a halt to this activity on November 13, 1968.

Great Lakes began gradually after November 1, 1968, to build up the pressure in its new line to the allowable maximum. In spite of some "start-up" problems in the first weeks, the pipeline was operating by mid-December so as to enable Great Lakes to meet the requirements of certain gas transmission contracts.

However, on December 27, 1968, the line suddenly ruptured at milepost 403.2 (measured as 403.2 miles from the western terminus of the line) causing approximately 850 feet of pipe to be split and violently thrown out of the ground. Great Lakes immediately began repairs using Grayco equipment which had been stored in the vicinity for the winter. By January 10, 1969, the line had been completely repaired and gas pressure was gradually increased.

Great Lakes' tranquility was to be short-lived, however. A few hours after gas transmission had resumed, the line ruptured again, this time at milepost 400.2 (nearly three miles west of the first rupture). Approximately 380 feet of pipe was split and thrown out of the ground, again completely severing the pipeline. Repairs were quickly begun, using Grayco equipment still in the area. On January 17, 1969, the line had been completely repaired and was restored to operation.

As a result of these two ruptures, the U.S. Department of Transportation ordered the operating pressure on the line to be severely limited between the nearest compressor stations on both ends of the Grayco section. Great Lakes undertook to make an internal examination, known as a Linalog survey, of the portion of the pipeline which was now suspect.

While awaiting completion of the necessary preparations for the Linalog survey, Great Lakes sought and was granted permission to raise its operating pressure, although still not near its planned capacity. After the Linalog survey had been completed, all pressure restrictions were completely removed, and the line began operating as planned on May 29, 1969.

*   *   *

The case was tried by a jury on three theories: negligence, breach of contract, and breach of implied warranty of fitness. Plaintiff submitted a total damage claim of $2,444,193.94 to the jury which returned a verdict as to all counts of $1,838,544.56, apparently reflecting a decision not to permit recovery of the revenue lost during the period of pressure restriction.

Defendant's first major ground for appeal is that the district court erred in permitting plaintiff to introduce certain opinion testimony as to the cause of the two ruptures. In this regard, defendant also charges error in permitting the Order of the Department of Transportation of January 17, 1969, to be introduced because it also is alleged to have contained an opinion as to the cause of the ruptures which is assailed as being hearsay. We do not believe that prejudicial error was committed in either instance.

The opinion testimony to which appellant refers is that of the witnesses Holstead and Etchegary. Holstead is the executive vice president and general manager of plaintiff. According to his testimony, he had been in the pipeline business for at least 20 years at the time of the ruptures. He also had nearly ten years experience in the design, engineering and supervision of construction of gas pipelines while he was employed by TransCanada. While Holstead had a bachelor's degree in civil engineering, he testified that he had acquired through his experience a working knowledge of metallurgy and fracture mechanics. Moreover, it was uncontroverted that he had visited the sites of the two ruptures within hours after their occurrences and had examined the damaged pipe before it was removed. He testified at great length as to the specific facts which he personally discovered as to the type of fracture involved and its place of origin on the pipe. It was shown that the pipe had been badly gouged at the location of both ruptures and that this gouging had been inflicted after the welded pipe had been coated and wrapped, after the pipe had been laid in the ground and the ground filled in, and after the hydrostatic testing had been completed. Both sites were lowland areas which, because of the unusually wet weather, were soft and muddy. Heavy construction equipment was seen near both sites. Several witnesses saw a bulldozer driven back and forth across the pipeline itself, apparently while engaged in rough clean-up work.

With this foundation, Holstead was asked to give an opinion as to the cause of the pipe failure. Before he was permitted to answer, the trial judge cautioned the jury as follows:

> The Court: Ladies and Gentlemen of the jury, I am going to permit the witness to answer the question.
>
> What weight and credit you give to the testimony of a person who is qualified as an expert, that is a person who has some expertise beyond that which a normal person possesses, is up to you.
>
> It depends upon his background and his own statement and knowledge and expertise in the area concerning which he purports to testify to.
>
> Experts may give opinions, but the opinions may be considered by you only to the extent that you find the witness is qualified to act as an expert in that area and only insofar as it goes concerning factual matters forming the basis for his opinion which are established by other evidence or independent evidence in the case.
>
> I will be instructing you more fully on this at the conclusion of the trial.
>
> In the meantime I will permit him to answer the question and therefore the objection is overruled.

Holstead then testified that in his opinion the gouges were inflicted by mechanical means on the pipe. He was then asked to give his opinion as to what mechanical means could or would have inflicted the gouges. Over the objection of appellants and after *voir dire* examination outside of the presence of the jury, the court permitted Holstead to answer. Before answering, the court cautioned the jury that the question as to what actually inflicted the gouge was for the jury to decide. The trial judge said:

> * * * The witness may testify from whatever expert knowledge he may have of the process as to what would or could have caused it, but the ultimate question of what caused it being one for the jury to decide.

The witness then answered that the gouging could have been inflicted by the pipe having been struck by some piece of heavy construction equipment. It is this opinion which appellant charges was prejudicial error.

In support of its contention, appellant cites decisions which it argues are controlling. In these cases the Michigan Supreme Court ruled that opinions of causation in negligence cases where the subject matter of the inquiry is of such a character that it may be presumed to lie within the ordinary experience of all men of common education, whether offered by experts or lay witnesses, are uniformly excluded as invasive of the province of the jury. It should be noted that both cases involved an opinion as to the cause of an automobile accident when there was already evidence before the jury in the nature of an eyewitness.

Putting aside the applicability of the maximum admissibility rule, Rule 43(a), Federal Rules of Civil Procedure, we think these Michigan holdings are clearly distinguishable from the case at bar and therefore are inapplicable. As previously noted, the Michigan rule arose in the context of opinions by investigating officers as to the causation of an auto accident, a subject for which many, if not all, of the causal factors lie within the ordinary experience of all men and women of common education. We do not feel that the potential sources for gouging 3/8″ thick steel pipe, specially made to the gas transmission company's specifications, can be said to lie within the ordinary experience of most potential jurors. Hence, we find no error in the admission of Holstead's opinion testimony, particularly in view of the scrupulous cautionary instruction given by the trial judge.

What we have said applies with equal vigor to the similar testimony of the witness Etchegary. In any event, appellant failed to make any objection at the time of Etchegary's testimony, thereby rendering it unavailable as grounds for appeal....

Appellants also argue that it was error to admit into evidence the January 17, 1969 order of the Department of Transportation in which the Acting Director of Pipeline Safety claimed to have met with representatives of plaintiff, the Michigan Public Service Commission and the Federal Power Commission for the purpose of deciding what regulatory measures were necessary in view of the two ruptures. The Director based his order in his letter, limiting the operating pressure in the gas pipeline of Great Lakes, on, *inter alia,* the following findings of fact:

5. Preliminary investigation indicates that this (the first) rupture resulted from external damage to the pipe during construction....

8. As in the case of the first rupture, preliminary investigation indicates that this (the second) rupture resulted from external damage to the pipe during construction.

9. During the course of construction there were five test ruptures which resulted from prior external damage to the pipe.

Appellant argues that it was error to permit the jury to have these "findings of fact" in that they are hearsay.

Plaintiff-appellee argues that the order was admissible under Rule 43(a), Federal Rules of Civil Procedure. Moreover, Great Lakes argues that the defendant told the jury in its opening statement that the order was issued because the ruptures in the pipe had been lengthier than previously experienced. Grayco then contended that the pressure reduction which had been ordered resulted only because of doubts about the particular pipe used in constructing the pipeline and not because of anything Grayco had done. Therefore, it is argued, this statement sought to attack plaintiff's damage claim for revenue lost due to the order restricting operating pressure, and Great Lakes was thus required to show that the order had been issued without any reference therein to the length of the ruptures. Plaintiff also claims it offered the order for the purpose of showing the basis on which it acted in an effort to mitigate its damages since the order left open the chance of getting the restrictions lifted.

When defendant objected to the introduction of the letter, plaintiff explained to the court that it was being offered for the purposes previously outlined. The court then instructed the jury as follows:

This is one of those pieces of hearsay evidence that I was telling you about before you were sworn as jurors, after you were impaneled, ladies and gentlemen, where an exhibit can be received for one purpose but not for another because that is hearsay. * * * This is the letter that directed (plaintiff to restrict its operating pressure). To that extent it is admissible and proper, to prove what the Department of Transportation did. It contains, however, certain findings which are to be received by you only as the understanding of the writer of the reasons, but not as proof themselves of the reasons, or as truth of the facts therein. That has to come elsewhere in this trial, if it be true at all. But I am going to allow it to be received for the purposes set forth, not for the truth of the specific factual matters. You may consider that this is what the writer himself believed as the basis for his action, but not that those facts are in fact true. * * *

The witness was then permitted to read the letter containing the order to the jury. We find no error in the admission of this letter. It bears repeating, in this context, that the hearsay rule excludes extrajudicial statements only when they are offered to prove the truth of the matter asserted. Where, as here, the trial judge has carefully instructed the jury as to the purposes for which a letter containing hearsay may be admitted, and where there is substantial evidence elsewhere in the record bearing on the subject which is contained in the hearsay, we hold there is no prejudicial error in the admission of the letter.

Affirmed.

Do not think that the judge in this case was so naive as to believe the jury would totally ignore the letter when attempting to make its decision regarding liability. The judge and the lawyers all knew that was virtually impossible. Nevertheless, the judge permitted the letter into evidence on the theory that it was to be used to prove damages, not liability. Thus you can see that, if you cannot find a hearsay exception in the next four chapters that fits your situation, you may have yet another manner in which you can have something admitted into evidence. Note, however, that this is an issue that the judge will not rule on for the first time at trial; it must be brought up at the pretrial conference so the judge can consider the matter at leisure.

CHAPTER 15

Hearsay Exceptions I — Introduction

The basic principle underlying the exceptions to the hearsay rule is that some types of hearsay are generally reliable. In the course of daily life, when we encounter such instances of hearsay we typically assume the statements are true although they are hearsay. This does not mean these statements really are true; it merely means that unless we have evidence to the contrary, we assume these statements to be true. For almost all exceptions to the hearsay rule, we can think of cases in which the statement is not true; nevertheless, these statements are true in the vast majority of instances in which we encounter such statements. The first three exceptions to the hearsay rule, which appear in Rule 803, illustrate this concept.

FRE Rule 803. Hearsay Exceptions; Availability of Declarant Immaterial

The following are not excluded by the hearsay rule, even though the declarant is available as a witness:

(1) Present sense impression.

A statement describing or explaining an event or condition made while the declarant was perceiving the event or condition, or immediately thereafter.

(2) Excited utterance.

A statement relating to a startling event or condition made while the declarant was under the stress of excitement caused by the event or condition.

(3) Then existing mental, emotional, or physical condition.

A statement of the declarant's then existing state of mind, emotion, sensation, or physical condition (such as intent, plan, motive, design, mental feeling, pain, and bodily health), but not including a statement of memory or belief to prove the fact remembered or believed unless it relates to the execution, revocation, identification, or terms of declarant's will.

Lawyers collectively refer to these three exceptions as *res gestae*, but most scholars do not approve of this term. This traditional term has been suspect since the 1920s when a famous law review article criticized it. Generations of law professors have tried unsuccessfully to eliminate it from use ever since, but lawyers still talk about the *res gestae*. Also note that for all exceptions we will examine in Rule 803 it does not matter if the declarant is available or not; these types of hearsay are admissible in either case.

The following case illustrates the application of these exceptions.

SEARS, ROEBUCK & CO. v. MURPHY, 186 F.2d 8 (6th Cir. 1953)

In the trial in the district court, without a jury, the appellee recovered a judgment of $2,333 against the appellant, Sears, Roebuck & Co., for personal injuries suffered by the appellee while shopping in the store of the appellant in Lexington, Kentucky. This appeal followed.

The trial judge found the facts substantially as follows: On August 16, 1948, in the Lexington, Kentucky, store of the appellant the appellee placed her hand upon an automobile seat cover which was being displayed to her and upon which were sharp particles of glass that caused a serious and painful injury to one finger. At some time prior, the agent of the appellant had made some changes or repairs, as a result of which glass was scattered upon the seat covers; that the appellant was negligent in not exercising ordinary care to see that all glass particles, which are very dangerous to the handling of merchandise, had been cleaned up; that this failure to exercise ordinary care was negligence and was the proximate cause of the injury sustained by the appellee. The appellant contends that the trial judge erred in admitting incompetent evidence and in ruling that the evidence was sufficient to support a finding of negligence on the part of the appellant.

The evidence complained of is an alleged statement made by Melvin Burke, division manager of the appellant. The appellee, Mrs. Murphy, testified that she went to the appellant's store in company with a friend, Mrs. Nancy French, who was shopping for automobile seat covers; that Mrs. French found a pair of seat covers which she liked and asked the appellee what she thought about them; that the appellee laid her hand on the seat covers with a gesture of rubbing, and immediately exclaimed, "Oh, my goodness. That cut me. Oh, get this out. Look, here, it's glass"; that Burke, who was displaying the seat covers, said "What's glass, lady?" and raised the end of the seat cover; that the appellee said "Oh, look, it's falling all down in the corner here"; that Burke then said, "Well, there was a repair made here" — and following an objection by the appellant, which was overruled by the Court, he continued, "There was a repair made here a few days ago," and then he said "I suppose they have failed to get it all up"; that she was given first aid treatment at the store and later in the day went to a doctor; and that it was necessary to have medical treatment for a period of several months thereafter totaling an expense of $333. Mrs. French testified to substantially the same occurrences and exclamations. Mrs. French also testified that she saw fragments of either fine glass or something that looked just like glass on the seat cover in question, and in response to a question about how many fragments there were, stated that the palm of her hand would hold it. Appellant contends that the alleged statement of Burke was both hearsay and a conclusion, and was improperly admitted. The trial judge admitted it as a part of the *res gestae*.

It is well settled that the declarations of an agent are only competent against a principal when they are a part of the *res gestae*. Appellant's first contention is that in order for such statements to be part of the *res gestae* they must be made by an actor in the transaction rather than by a bystander. The Kentucky Court of Appeals so ruled in *Louisville Railway Co. v. Johnson's Admr.*, 131 Ky. 277, 115 S.W. 207, 133, 285, and this ruling has been later followed by that Court in subsequent cases. However, the same Court recognized in *Brandenburg v. Commonwealth*, 260 Ky. 70, 74-75, 83 S.W.2d 862, that other Kentucky decisions have upheld the introduction of *res gestae* exclamations made by bystanders, and indicated, but without so holding, that such ruling was the correct one. The Kentucky Court of Appeals recognized this conflict in its rulings in *Sparks Bus Line, Inc. v. Spears*, 276 Ky. 600, 605–606, 124 S.W.2d 1031, where it stated that the rule in most jurisdictions is that an exclamation made by a bystander not a participant in the transaction may be admitted as part of the *res gestae*, and that, in any event, statements of a participant in an accident, though he is not a party litigant, are admissible as a part of the *res gestae* if the other requirements of the *res gestae* rule are met. In our opinion, Burke was such a participant in the accident as to bring him within the rule laid down in that case.

Appellant also contends that the statement of Burke was not admissible because it was a narrative of past events. In discussing the *res gestae* rule, it has generally been said that the declaration must be a spontaneous expression of thought created by or springing out of the transaction itself rather than a narrative of a transaction that has happened. However, the rule as so stated does not mean that statements concerning past events are necessarily incompetent. The distinction which the cases draw is whether the statement was made so near in point of time to the accident as to exclude the presumption that it was the result of premeditation or design. If it was so far removed from the transaction as not to constitute a spontaneous utterance, it becomes merely a narration of past events, controlled by recollection and without the necessary element of spontaneity. As stated in *Cumberland Gasoline Corp. v. Fields' Admr.*, 258 Ky. 417, 418, 80 S.W.2d 28, — "In order for a declaration to be admissible as a part of the *res gestae*, it must be the spontaneous utterance of the mind while under the influence of the transaction, the test being, it has been said, whether the declaration was the facts talking through the party, or the party talking about the facts." The opinion in that case also pointed out "The dividing line between admissibility and nonadmissibility lies between the words outcry and narration; between impulse and reflection." The same distinction was drawn by the Kentucky Court of Appeals in *Castle v. Allen*, 274 Ky. 658, 662–663, 120 S.W.2d 219, 221, where the Court pointed out that the statement of the witness "was not a spontaneous utterance while under the influence of the transaction, but was a narration of facts in response to interrogation." We think the statement of the Court in *Louisville Railway Co. v. Johnson's Admr.*, 131 Ky. 277, at 281, 115 S.W. 207, 209, 133, upon which the appellant relies, is, when properly analyzed, a similar statement of the rule. The Court there said, "but, if a declaration is so far removed in point of time from the main fact under investigation as to make it a mere narrative of a transaction that has happened, * * * the declaration is not admissible as substantive evidence or as a part of the *res gestae*." Appellant also relies upon *Cyborowski v. Kinsman Transit Co.*, 6 Cir., 179 F. 440, from this Court, where a declaration was ruled inadmissible because it was only the narrative of a past occurrence. However, that ruling was clearly based upon the conclusion of the Court that "It was not made contemporaneously with the accident, and was not, therefore, part of the *res gestae*." ... In the present case, we are of the opinion that the statement of Burke had the necessary element of spontaneity to make it admissible and was not in reality a narrative of past events within the meaning of the rule.

*   *   *

Affirmed.

The next exception to the hearsay rule clearly illustrates the basic concept that certain statements are more likely to be true than false. When we go to the doctor for treatment or diagnosis we generally tell the doctor the truth, as Rule 803(4) indicates.

FRE Rule 803 (Cont'd.)

(4) Statements for purposes of medical diagnosis or treatment.
Statements made for purposes of medical diagnosis or treatment and describing medical history, or past or present symptoms, pain, or sensations, or the inception or general character of the cause or external source thereof insofar as reasonably pertinent to diagnosis or treatment.

This rule is so obvious and straightforward that it is not necessary to present a case to illustrate it. The statement need not be made by the patient. It could be made by a person accompanying the patient, e.g., a parent talking to a pediatrician about the child's condition, how long symptoms have been present, etc.

CHAPTER 16

Hearsay Exceptions II — Writings and Records

The most commonly employed exceptions to the hearsay rule involve writings, the contents of which are offered to prove the truth of the matter asserted. There are several interrelated rules in this area, which we shall examine sequentially.

PAST RECOLLECTION RECORDED, PRESENT RECOLLECTION REVIVED

FRE Rule 803 (Cont'd.)

(5) Recorded recollection.
A memorandum or record concerning a matter about which a witness once had knowledge but now has insufficient recollection to enable the witness to testify fully and accurately, shown to have been made or adopted by the witness when the matter was fresh in the witness' memory and to reflect that knowledge correctly. If admitted, the memorandum or record may be read into evidence but may not itself be received as an exhibit unless offered by an adverse party.

Rule 803(5) does not, however, stand alone. It must be read and interpreted in conjunction with Rule 612.

FRE Rule 612. Writing Used to Refresh Memory

Except as otherwise provided in criminal proceedings by section 3500 of title 18, United States Code, if a witness uses a writing to refresh memory for the purpose of testifying, either
(1) while testifying, or
(2) before testifying, if the court in its discretion determines it is necessary in the interests of justice, an adverse party is entitled to have the writing produced at the hearing, to inspect it, to cross-examine the witness thereon, and to introduce in evidence those portions which relate to the testimony of the witness. If it is claimed that the writing contains matters not related to the subject matter of the testimony the court shall examine the writing *in camera*, excise any portions not so related and order delivery of the remainder to the party entitled thereto. Any portion withheld over objections shall be preserved and made available to the appellate court in the event of an appeal. If a writing is not produced or delivered pursuant to order under this rule, the court shall make any order justice requires, except that in criminal cases when the prosecution elects not to comply, the order shall be one striking the testimony or, if the court in its discretion determines that the interests of justice so require, declaring a mistrial.

Rules 612 and 803(5) always work together. Rule 612 must be used before Rule 803(5) can be brought into play. The questioning must run as follows:

Q. Do you remember what happened when you met with Ms. Smith on December 6?
A. No.
Q. I show you this memorandum that you wrote on December 7 regarding that meeting. Please read it and then tell me if your recollection is refreshed regarding the meeting of December 6.

[Witness reads paper.]

If the witness says that he or she now remembers the meeting, we are operating under the provisions of Rule 612, and the witness goes ahead and testifies regarding what he or she currently remembers, after having his or her recollection refreshed by reading the memo. The witness may, however, respond as follows:

A. No, I still don't remember that meeting. I can tell you what's in this memo, but I don't actually remember any details of the meeting.

In this instance, we will operate under the provisions of Rule 803(5).
This chapter section is called "Past Recollection Recorded, Present Recollection Revived" because if we use Rule 612 we have present recollection revived; if we use Rule 803(5) we have past recollection recorded. We must first attempt to revive the witness' memory before we read from the paper record. Note that under 803(5) the witness cannot have the record introduced into evidence. This is done to avoid

giving the witness with a bad memory the advantage over the witness who merely has a temporary lapse. In both cases, only the other side may introduce the writing itself into evidence.

Business Records

For many years there was general agreement among common law jurisdictions that a "business records" exception to the hearsay rule existed, but there was enormous variation among the detailed provisions of the rule. The FRE version, adopted by the Supreme Court, has gradually emerged as the common version in the United States as states adopted it or other very similar versions. The FRE version eliminates many preexisting problems. Some courts, for example, once held that the rule applied only to the records of "for profit" organizations (a narrow reading of "business"), thus excluding educational institutions, charitable organizations, and governmental agencies. Despite this general agreement, however, you should consult with your lawyer before assuming that your records will automatically be admissible. Rule 803(6) reads:

FRE Rule 803 (Cont'd.)

(6) Records of regularly conducted activity.

A memorandum, report, record, or data compilation, in any form, of acts, events, conditions, opinions, or diagnoses, made at or near the time by, or from information transmitted by, a person with knowledge, if kept in the course of a regularly conducted business activity, and if it was the regular practice of that business activity to make the memorandum, report, record, or data compilation, all as shown by the testimony of the custodian or other qualified witness, unless the source of information or the method or circumstances of preparation indicate lack of trustworthiness. The term "business" as used in this paragraph includes business, institution, association, profession, occupation, and calling of every kind, whether or not conducted for profit.

There is an obvious connection between Rule 803(6) and Rule 406 regarding habit and routine practice, as discussed in Chapter 11. Rule 406 is virtually the only way to prove that it is regular practice to make a given record. The business records rule is rarely discussed in court decisions, as the principles are well understood by lawyers and judges. This is why the following case, in which a trial judge gave the rule an extremely rigid interpretation, is very interesting.

CUNNINGHAM V. GANS, D/B/A ATLANTA ENGINEERING CO., 507 F.2D 496 (2D CIR. 1974)

George Cunningham appeals from a judgment of the Eastern District, dismissing his complaint and directing a verdict for defendants. He claims that rulings by the trial judge, refusing to admit certain pieces of evidence as business records, refusing to receive the testimony of two witnesses offered by Cunningham as experts, and refusing to allow Cunningham to examine certain witnesses as adverse witnesses, were erroneous and were unduly restrictive and that they prevented Cunningham from establishing his tort and contract claims against defendants. Since we are in basic agreement with plaintiff's position, we reverse and remand for new trial.

Cunningham was employed by M. K. Kellogg Co. (Kellogg) as a pipe fitter on a construction project at Belle, West Virginia, where an ammonia plant was being built for E. I. duPont de Nemours Co. On September 1, 1966, Cunningham helped erect a 10-inch steel pipe that connected a furnace to a boiler line. The pipe was over 40 feet long, weighed several thousand pounds, and was to be installed approximately 30 feet above the ground. In order to install the pipe it was necessary to use pipe hangers, which consisted in part of clamps that were fastened around the pipe. After Cunningham had completed the installation of one such clamp, the devices used temporarily to hold the pipe in place were released. Almost immediately thereafter the clamp that Cunningham had installed broke and the pipe fell downward. Cunningham was knocked from his perch and he was injured when he fell 30 feet to the ground.

Cunningham filed this diversity action in August 1968 against the principals of Atlanta Engineering Co. (Atlanta), the alleged seller of the clamp, and Central Iron Manufacturing Co. (Central), the alleged manufacturer of the clamp. In his complaint Cunningham claimed that the clamp that broke and caused his injury was negligently designed and manufactured and that the defendants breached an express warranty of fitness and an implied warranty of fitness and merchantability. After extensive pretrial proceedings, the case came to trial in January 1973. At the trial it became apparent that Cunningham faced several very difficult hurdles that had to be surmounted if he was to affix liability on the defendants. The problems stemmed from the fact that the clamp that broke was no longer available and could not be introduced into evidence and the fact that there was uncontroverted evidence that the clamp intended for use in hanging the pipe in question could not be found on the morning of the installation, and that another, lighter clamp had been substituted. Thus, there was no direct evidence that the clamp that broke was manufactured or sold by defendants, while there was evidence to show that a lighter, less sturdy clamp than called for in the plans had been used.

In an attempt to overcome these problems Cunningham endeavored to show that Atlanta was the only firm that had contracted to supply Kellogg with clamps, that no clamps were bought in West Virginia, and that no clamps were manufactured at the job site. If Cunningham could establish these facts, he would have shown through circumstantial evidence that it was probable that the clamp that broke was made and sold by defendants. In order to overcome the problem caused by the substitution of a lighter clamp, Cunningham attempted to show the clamp actually used, as described by the witnesses who saw it, would have held a pipe of the size involved here, if that clamp met defendants' warranted specifications.

In order to establish these contentions Cunningham offered several documents into evidence and called two witnesses as experts. After initially allowing some of the documents into evidence, the trial judge changed his mind and ruled that they were all inadmissible. In the case of one of plaintiff's experts, the judge ruled that he was not an expert. In the case of the other expert, the judge restricted the extent to which Cunningham was allowed to ask him hypothetical questions.

Exhibit 22

Exhibit 22 was a material status report on the Belle construction project, compiled by employees of Kellogg, that listed all of the purchase orders for that project. The exhibit was crucial to plaintiff's case because it apparently established that all of the clamps ordered for the project were supplied by Atlanta. Cunningham established that Mr. Connell, the Kellogg employee who had accompanied the document to the trial, was familiar with the internal records of Kellogg, that Kellogg kept records concerning the materials ordered for a project in the ordinary course of its business, and that Exhibit 22 was that record for the Belle project. Defendants attacked Exhibit 22 as not falling under the business records exception to the hearsay rule because Connell did not personally take Exhibit 22 from the company files (his superior gave it to him), was not positive that he had seen Exhibit 22 before it was handed to him, and was not employed in the records or purchasing division of Kellogg. The judge initially ruled Exhibit 22 was admissible, but the following day he changed his mind and refused to allow it into evidence. While matters such as these are usually left to the discretion of the trial judge, it appears that the judge in this case based his decision on what we feel was an erroneous reading of two cases. This fact, together with our feeling that the evidentiary rulings in this case were unduly restrictive, requires us to reverse the judgment. In *Palmer,* the Supreme Court excluded from evidence a statement made by the engineer of a train to a railroad company official following a train accident because the statement was not made in the ordinary course of the railroad's business, which the Court said was railroading, not investigating accidents. In doing so, however, the Court noted that the business records exception "should of course be liberally interpreted so as to do away with the anachronistic rules which gave rise to its need." In *Hartzog,* the Fourth Circuit refused to allow into evidence as business records the written summaries of business records prepared by a deceased government investigator in anticipation of litigation. Both of these decisions are based on a desire to exclude from the business records exception to the hearsay rule statements made or prepared with an eye toward litigation. Neither of these cases even faintly suggests that Exhibit 22 was not admissible as a business record since it clearly was prepared in the course of Kellogg's business and not for litigation.

Our recent cases also call for the admission of the exhibit. In United States v. Rosenstein, 474 F.2d 705 (1973), we held that it was not required that the witness introducing the records had personally kept the records. It was enough that "someone who is sufficiently familiar with the business practice (testifies) that (the) records were made as part of that practice." Connell testified that he was familiar with Kellogg's procedures and that Exhibit 22 was made in accordance with those procedures. There was no reason to believe that the record was unreliable and it should have been admitted.

Exhibit 23

Mr. Connell also produced a xerox copy of an isometric drawing that depicted the pipe that was being installed when the accident occurred. The drawing was an important element in Cunningham's case: he intended to use it to establish the weight of the pipe. It will be remembered that he had to establish that weight in order to show that the clamp that broke should have been able to support that weight. Connell testified that the xeroxed copy was a fair representation of the drawings that were used on the Belle project and that the copy had been made from the original which was in the files of Kellogg Co. The defendants' objections were similar to those raised against Exhibit 22. Once again, we feel, for the reasons discussed above, that Exhibit 23 should have been admitted.

Exhibit 24

Exhibit 24 consisted of documents that tended to show that Kellogg had problems with several of the clamps purchased from Atlanta. One of the documents was a laboratory report that indicated that the wrong kind of steel was used in manufacturing the clamps. Another indicated that Atlanta replaced many of the clamps because of the problems that Kellogg had with them. Cunningham sought to use these documents to establish that the clamp that broke was defective. However, the judge ruled that these documents (which were all dated within two months of Cunningham's injury) were inadmissible because they did not pertain to the specific clamp that plaintiff claimed caused his injury. Since plaintiff established that all of the clamps supplied by Atlanta had been delivered prior to the date of the accident, it seems to us that these documents, which dealt with the clamps supplied by Atlanta, were relevant and should have been admitted. Of course, Cunningham still must establish that Atlanta did supply the clamp that broke. If the jury decides that Atlanta did supply the clamp in question, they should be able to consider evidence that showed that other clamps supplied by Atlanta were defective. As expressed by McCormick: "The most acceptable test of relevancy is the question, does the evidence offered render the desired inference more probable than it would be without the evidence." C. McCormick, Evidence 185, at 437 (1972). We think that Exhibit 24 easily meets this test and should have been admitted into evidence.

John Young as an Expert Witness

Plaintiff attempted to have John Young give an expert opinion as to whether the clamp actually used should have been able to support the pipe that was being installed. In order to qualify Young as an expert in the field of pipehanger construction, plaintiff showed that Young had been a pipefitter for 33 years, had designed dies for making pipehangers, had made many thousands of hangers over a period of 16 years, had spent 17 years working exclusively as a pipefitter, and had been a general foreman in charge of pipefitting at the Belle plant. Defendants objected that these qualifications were not enough to establish Young as an expert, largely because Mr. Young was not a metallurgist and because some of his experience in the field had taken place many years ago. We do not find these objections persuasive. Indeed, the latter objection only establishes that Young had been around a long time. Moreover, in light of Young's long practical experience in the field, we do not think that his lack of metallurgic training disqualifies him as an expert witness. While we normally allow a trial judge considerable freedom in deciding whether a witness qualifies as an expert, we feel in this case that Young should have been allowed to testify as an expert. Young's extensive experience in this field certainly qualified him as a person who could aid the jury in the resolution of the question of how much weight the clamp actually used should have been able to support. See generally C. McCormick, Evidence 13 (1972). Of course, the defendants are free to cross-examine Young to develop any shortcomings in his qualifications.

Emanuel Silkiss as an Expert Witness

Cunningham called Emanuel Silkiss as an expert witness to establish that the clamp that broke should have been able to support the pipe. In his questioning of Silkiss plaintiff's attorney was greatly hindered by defense counsel's objections to the hypothetical questions he was posing. Although those questions sometimes covered over a page of printed transcript defense counsel always objected and claimed that plaintiff's attorney had misstated a minor point. These objections were sustained by the trial judge, and as a result Cunningham was unable to elicit helpful testimony from Silkiss. We feel the trial court's rulings were unduly restrictive. On retrial a better trial procedure would be for Cunningham's attorney to ask shorter, less detailed hypothetical questions. Then defense counsel should attack the expert's testimony by showing his conclusions would be different if certain facts were also assumed or if certain assumed facts were changed rather than by voicing picky objections to complicated hypothetical questions. Such a procedure has been advocated by many authorities. See, e.g., Proposed Federal Rule of Evidence 705 and advisory committee's note; C. McCormick, Evidence 16 (1972).

*   *   *

Because the trial judge's erroneous rulings on the admissibility of business records and the appropriateness of expert testimony were unduly restrictive, plaintiff was prevented from establishing his case. We think that the offered evidence should have been admitted, and that if it had been, plaintiff would have presented sufficient evidence to require submission of the case to a jury. Reversed and remanded for a new trial before a different judge.

There is, however, an exception to the exception to the hearsay rule provided by Rule 803(6), although it does not appear in the rule itself. Records that are prepared in anticipation of litigation or for trial are, quite reasonably, considered to lack the inherent trustworthiness of typical business records and thus are not covered by the rule, as the next case shows.

RUBRIGHT CO. V. INTERNATIONAL HARVESTER CO.
358 F.SUPP. 1388 (W.D.PA., 1973)

History

Plaintiff, W.D. Rubright Company, owned and operated a 1960 International six-wheel truck, Model No. COF192-AFA 6742 H.

On August 7, 1967, this International truck was being operated by an agent of Rubright when it was involved in an accident which inflicted considerable injuries upon one Jack Cowan.

Cowan brought suit against Rubright in the court of common pleas of Lawrence County, Pennsylvania, at No. 8 December term 1967.

Rubright joined International Harvester Company as an additional defendant in the Cowan suit.

On March 4, 1968, the claim of Cowan was settled for the sum of $180,000. Rubright paid the entire amount of the settlement which also released International from further liability.

When International refused to contribute to Rubright one half of the settlement, or the sum of $90,000, Rubright brought the present suit.

Immediately prior to trial, International stipulated that the $180,000 paid to Cowan was a reasonable fee in compensation for his injuries and other losses.

*   *   *

During the course of the trial, defense counsel attempted to offer investigative reports prepared by experts employed by the Pittsburgh Testing Laboratory. These reports were prepared at the request of plaintiff's counsel and recited conclusions based upon inspection of and testing of components from the rear axle braking system of the Rubright truck.

The theory behind defendant's offer was that these investigative reports were business records of Pittsburgh Testing Laboratory and as such were admissible as exceptions to the hearsay evidence rule. We rejected the offer as made and defendant now argues that the rejection constitutes reversible error. The hearsay rule has one basic purpose. When a statement is offered for the truth of that statement, the rule insists that the maker be brought before the jury so that it can evaluate his credibility and thereby gauge the truth of the statement itself. All the exceptions to the hearsay rule are based on the belief that something about the out-of-court statement insures or tends to insure its truthfulness, and therefore the jury need not evaluate the maker's demeanor for signs of credibility. The business records exception to the hearsay rule is in keeping with this theory of inherent believability. Giant businesses involve many departments which must interact as well as deal with outsiders over long periods of time. Precise communication and accurate records are extremely important if these interactions are to succeed. A company cannot lie to itself on a day-to-day basis and survive because business records serve as the corporation's memory.

So it follows that records made in the ordinary course of a company's business will be truthful. On the other hand, if records are made with the thought of using them at trial, they will not necessarily have the truthfulness inherent in the day-to-day records that are made in the ordinary course of business. Without this inherent believability, the jury should be permitted to view the demeanor of the maker in order to measure his credibility. The Pittsburgh Testing Laboratory reports do not qualify as business records because they were prepared specially for trial. As in this case, when expert reports are prepared at the behest of a party involved in litigation, it creates the possibility that an overzealous expert might abandon the impartial objectivity that is usually attributed to men of science or specialized learning, and move toward the role of an advocate. The right of cross-examination is the only effective means of dealing with this possibility. Moreover, when an expert performs a complex analytical procedure before arriving at some highly technical conclusions, the opposing party should always have the right to examine the validity of the methodology which brought the expert to his conclusions. Cross-examination of the expert is the best way to evaluate this methodology. We conclude that our refusal to admit the reports as offered was not error.

* * *

Defendant's motions for judgment N.O.V. and for a new trial must be denied.

The business records exception works in both directions. Just as Rule 803(6) makes the presence of an entry in the regularly kept business records admissible to prove that an event occurred, Rule 803(7) provides for the converse, that the absence of an entry is admissible to prove that the event did not occur.

FRE 803 (Cont'd.)

(7) Absence of entry in records kept in accordance with the provisions of paragraph (6).

Evidence that a matter is not included in the memoranda reports, records, or data compilations, in any form, kept in accordance with the provisions of paragraph (6), to prove the nonoccurrence or nonexistence of the matter, if the matter was of a kind of which a memorandum, report, record, or data compilation was regularly made and preserved, unless the sources of information or other circumstances indicate lack of trustworthiness.

The lesson here is that if you keep records you should keep accurate records. If your records are haphazard, you may lose out in various ways when you testify in court.

GOVERNMENT RECORDS

In the days before the business records rule included "nonprofit" records, some jurisdictions developed a separate rule for government records. In addition to Rule 803(6), the drafters of FRE included a separate rule for government records. Rule 803(8) is, however, somewhat restricted compared to the business records rule.

FRE Rule 803 (Cont'd.)

(8) Public records and reports.

Records, reports, statements, or data compilations, in any form, of public offices or agencies, setting forth (A) the activities of the office or agency, or (B) matters observed pursuant to duty imposed by law as to which matters there was a duty to report, excluding, however, in criminal cases matters observed by police officers and other law enforcement personnel, or (C) in civil actions and proceedings and against the Government in criminal cases, factual findings resulting from an investigation made pursuant to authority granted by law, unless the sources of information or other circumstances indicate lack of trustworthiness.

The limitation that must be noted is the "pursuant to duty imposed (or authority granted) by law" clause. The following case illustrates both this clause and the principle concerning unfair prejudice in Rule 403 (see Chapter 7).

BRADBURY V. FORD MOTOR CO., 333 N.W.2D 214 (MICH. APP. 1983)

John J. Bradbury, the plaintiff, appeals from a jury verdict of no cause of action in a case involving an allegedly defective transmission and linkage system on an automobile designed and manufactured by the Ford Motor Company, the defendant. On March 13, 1981, the Wayne County (Michigan) Circuit Court denied the plaintiff's motion for a new trial.

In March of 1977, the plaintiff's father purchased a new 1977 Ford Thunderbird from a Ford dealer. The car was equipped with a Ford FMX automatic transmission with the gear selector located on the steering column. The plaintiff testified that it was often extremely difficult to shift from reverse to drive, park to reverse, and reverse to park. Both the plaintiff and his father testified that they did not return the car to the dealership to discuss this problem.

On May 5, 1977, the plaintiff returned home after running errands with the car. He checked the mail and found that the post office had a registered letter for him. The plaintiff, using the Thunderbird, set out to get the letter. He saw the mail carrier's Jeep and, after asking the carrier if he had the letter, parked the car. The plaintiff testified that he put the gear selector in park and stepped out of the car. He testified that he had no problem shifting into park, and the car was stationary when he stepped out. He walked around the front of the car toward the carrier's Jeep. While the plaintiff was watching the carrier search for the letter, the carrier looked up and told the plaintiff to look at the car. The car was moving in reverse about 8 or 9 feet from the curb. Both the plaintiff and the carrier testified that about 30 seconds elapsed from the time the plaintiff left the car to the time it was seen moving. The plaintiff ran into the street and around the rear of the car attempting to get to the controls. When he was behind the car, the car pinned his leg against a light pole.

The plaintiff's theory at trial was that the transmission was negligently designed, manufactured, assembled, tested, and inspected and that Ford failed to adequately warn of the dangerous and defective condition. From an adverse jury verdict, the plaintiff appeals, raising six issues.

In his first issue, the plaintiff argues that the trial court erred in refusing to allow the admission into evidence of a National Highway Transportation Safety Administration (NHTSA) report examining the FMX and other transmissions. The plaintiff contends that the report was admissible under MRE 803(8)(B) as a public record, as rebuttal or impeachment evidence to counter an expert's testimony that Ford transmissions performed like transmissions by other U.S. manufacturers, and to show that Ford had notice of a defect, triggering a duty to warn.

Rule 803 provides:

"The following are not excluded by the hearsay rule, even though the declarant is available as a witness:

(8) Public records and reports. Records, reports, statements, or data compilations, in any form, of public offices or agencies, setting forth (A) the activities of the office or agency, or (B) matters observed pursuant to duty imposed by law as to which matters there was a duty to report, excluding, however, in criminal cases matters observed by police officers and other law enforcement personnel."

In Graham v. Ryerson, 96 Mich.App. 480, 490, 292 N.W.2d 704 (1980), lv. den. 410 Mich. 858 (1980), this Court concluded that an investigation report compiled by the NHTSA was prepared pursuant to a duty imposed by law and, therefore, would be admissible under MRE 803(8)(B). The duty is identical in our case, and we, therefore, reach the same conclusion. Rule 803(8)(B) is no bar to the admissibility of the report.

Those parts of the report comparing Ford FMX transmissions to transmissions manufactured by other automakers became relevant when a defense expert testified that Ford FMX transmissions were no worse than other transmissions. Thus, under MRE 402, this evidence was presumptively admissible unless prohibited by another rule. MRE 403 provides an exception:

"Although relevant, evidence may be excluded if its probative value is substantially outweighed by the danger of unfair prejudice, confusion of the issues, or misleading the jury, or by considerations of undue delay, waste of time, or needless presentation of cumulative evidence."

The defendant argues, and the trial court agreed, that the prejudicial effect of the report outweighs its probative value. We do not believe the probative value is substantially outweighed by the danger of unfair prejudice. We have no doubt that, if believed by the jury, evidence of a substantial performance difference would harm the defense, but we do not think this is unfair. "Damaging" is not equivalent to "prejudice." We have examined the relevant parts of the report and do not see how the wording, diagrams, or statistics could be unfairly prejudicial. Any inaccuracies are best considered by the jury when determining the weight to be given the report. In fact, many of the inaccuracies the defendant complains about (e.g., multiple reports of same incident) are cured by more refined statistics in the report (e.g., number of vehicles involved, including some compared by vehicle identification number). The court abused its discretion when it disallowed the admission of relevant parts of the report.

Those sections of the report showing that Ford knew of the possible defect also should have been admitted into evidence. First, they are relevant to the failure to warn issue. Second, they were not offered for a hearsay purpose. Third, for the reasons stated earlier, the probative value was not substantially outweighed by the danger of unfair prejudice.

*   *   *

Because we are reversing the trial court's judgment, it is unnecessary to address the question of cost levied against the plaintiff by the trial court.

Reversed and remanded.

Just as Rule 803(6) has its converse in Rule 803(7), Rule 803(8) has its converse in Rule 803(10).

FRE Rule 803 (Cont'd.)

(10) Absence of public record or entry.

To prove the absence of a record, report, statement, or data compilation, in any form, or the nonoccurrence or nonexistence of a matter of which a record, report, statement, or data compilation, in any form, was regularly made and preserved by a public office or agency, evidence in the form of a certification in accordance with rule 902, or testimony, that diligent search failed to disclose the record, report, statement, or data compilation, or entry.

The intervening Rule 803(9) deals with one particular type of government document with specific relevance for much medical testimony, especially in such fields as epidemiology and public health, and for showing the cause of death as determined by autopsy.

FRE Rule 803 (Cont'd.)

(9) Records of vital statistics.

Records or data compilations, in any form, of births, fetal deaths, deaths, or marriages, if the report thereof was made to a public office pursuant to requirements of law.

Despite these government records exceptions to the hearsay rule, however, the majority of government records introduced at trial are introduced under the business records exception when it is available in its expanded form that admits the records from an "institution, association, profession, occupation, and calling of every kind, whether or not conducted for profit."

CHAPTER 17

Hearsay Exceptions III — Printed Matter

The next major set of exceptions to the hearsay rule we must examine relates to printed materials from books, journals, and similar items. The first of these rules, which relates to commercial publications used by those in particular occupations, is closely related to the concepts regarding judicial notice, as discussed in Chapter 11.

FRE Rule 803 (Cont'd.)

(17) Market reports, commercial publications.

Market quotations, tabulations, lists, directories, or other published compilations, generally used and relied upon by the public or by persons in particular occupations.

Unlike judicial notice, Rule 803(17) relates merely to admissibility, not weight. Under judicial notice the matter is taken to be conclusively established as true, whereas here the matter is merely admitted into evidence for consideration by the fact finder, be it judge or jury. Examples of printed materials of this type include real estate sales in a given area compiled by a multiple listing agency, stock market reports in the newspaper, the Physician's Desk Reference, and engineering handbooks. The witness must only say, "This is a source that I regard as accurate and normally rely upon in my work," and the publication becomes admissible.

Since judicial notice is more powerful than this exception to the hearsay rule, one usually prefers to have judicial notice taken. You should inform your lawyer early in the course of your preparation for trial about whatever you wish to have admitted as evidence so the lawyer can attempt to convince the judge at the pretrial conference that judicial notice should be taken. If this fails, then you can fall back on Rule 803(17) to have the material admitted into evidence.

The other major hearsay exception for printed materials is the so-called learned treatise rule, which permits the use of materials from textbooks and journal articles.

FRE Rule 803 (Cont'd.)

(18) Learned treatises.

To the extent called to the attention of an expert witness upon cross-examination or relied upon by the expert witness in direct examination, statements contained in published treatises, periodicals, or pamphlets on a subject of history, medicine, or other science or art, established as a reliable authority by the testimony or admission of the witness or by other expert testimony or by judicial notice. If admitted, the statements may be read into evidence but may not be received as exhibits.

Rule 803(18) is not universal. Some jurisdictions permit the use of learned treatises only upon cross-examination, not in direct testimony. If there is something you wish to use in this manner, you should check with your lawyer regarding the version of the rule in use in your jurisdiction. The next case illustrates the full use of the rule in direct testimony.

BAIR V. AMERICAN MOTORS CORP., 473 F.2D 740 (3RD CIR. 1972)

This is an appeal from a judgment on a jury verdict in favor of the defendant American Motors Corporation. The plaintiff-appellant, Bair, was injured on October 26, 1966, when, in an automobile accident, she was ejected from an American Motors Rambler which she had purchased in August, 1966, from an American Motors' dealer. She sued American Motors on both negligence and strict liability theories, alleging that the defective design of the door latch on the Rambler failed to prevent the door from opening when the car was subjected to upward and longitudinal stresses in the accident, thus permitting her ejection and increasing her injuries. Pennsylvania law governs liability.

The case was submitted to the jury on three interrogatories:

1. Was plaintiff guilty of negligence which contributed to the happening of the collision between her Rambler and the Mustang?
2. Was defendant guilty of negligence in the design of the door latch on the 1966 Rambler?
3. Did defendant sell a product in a defective condition unreasonably dangerous to the user when it sold the 1966 Rambler equipped with the door latch described in this case?

To each interrogatory the jury answered no.

Bair contends on appeal that the negative answer[s] to the second and third interrogatories are the product of trial errors, and that a new trial should be granted. The errors alleged consist (1) of a ruling as to the admissibility of the results of statistical studies conducted by Cornell Aeronautical Laboratory, Inc., Automotive Crash Injury Research, offered during the testimony of the plaintiff's expert witness, Walter V.H. Pruyn; and (2) of allegedly disparaging treatment by the trial court of that witness.

Mr. Pruyn, an expert who gave opinion evidence, was the only liability witness for Bair, and American Motors did not put in any liability evidence. The district court held that plaintiff's liability case was sufficient to go to the jury. The jury, apparently, did not accept Pruyn's opinion. The excluded evidence was not cumulative of any other evidence in the case. Thus, if it was improperly excluded, and if it tended to support Pruyn's opinion, the error cannot be regarded as harmless.

The event was an intersection accident in which Bair's vehicle was struck on the left front fender by a vehicle traveling at 50 to 60 mph. Pruyn's theory of the accident was that after the initial impact there was a second impact, as the two cars swerved from a right angle to a parallel alignment, in which the right rear of the striking vehicle struck the Rambler, and that following this impact the left front (driver's) door of the Rambler opened. As the Rambler continued to rotate Bair was ejected. Pruyn claimed that had the Rambler been equipped with door latches then used by other automobile manufacturers to prevent opening when the vehicle was subjected to upward and longitudinal stress such as occurred in the accident, Bair would not have been ejected.

The door latch of the rambler was designed so that the bottom portion of the latch's rachet wheel teeth, mounted on the door, was, when the door was closed, enclosed by a steel retaining plate affixed to the left door striker pillar. The upper portion and sides of the ratchet wheel were not so enclosed. Thus, when the door was subjected to upward and longitudinal stress which lifted the teeth of the ratchet wheel above and out from behind the steel retaining plate the door was free to open. To prevent this occurrence some manufacturers had as early as the 1961–62 model year equipped their doors with a t-head type bolt assembly in which, when the door was closed, the bolt was totally enclosed at the top, bottom, and sides. Bair's claim, advanced through Pruyn's opinion testimony, was that American Motors' failure to adopt such a design by 1966 was negligent, and that the absence of such a latch mechanism made its product inherently defective.

The district court ruled that Pruyn was qualified to express such opinions; appellant claims unenthusiastically. During his direct testimony Bair sought to prove through him the findings of the three statistical surveys by automotive crash injury research of Cornell University as a basis for his opinion that the absence of the t-head type bolt assembly was a negligent design and produced an inherently unsafe vehicle. The surveys were objected to as hearsay, and the objection was sustained on the specific ground that since they were not made by Mr. Pruyn he could not testify to them.

Each of the surveys was made by automotive crash injury research [project] of Cornell Aeronautical Laboratory, Inc., Cornell University. That organization is engaged in the study of injury causes among occupants in automobile accidents. Its research has been supported by grants from the National Institutes of Health and the Division of Accident Prevention of the United States Public Health Service, the Automobile Manufacturers Association, Inc., and the United States Department of Transportation, National Highway Safety Bureau. The research method pursued by that organization, as described in the exhibits, is, with the cooperation of police and medical authorities around the country, the analysis after the event of large numbers of actual injury-producing accidents to determine the safety performance of various components having injury causative or preventive potential. The studies here in issue are:

1. "An evaluation of door lock effectiveness: pre-1956 vs. post-1955 automobiles," published in July, 1961.
2. "The safety performance of 1962–63 automobile door latches and comparison with earlier latch designs," published in November, 1964.
3. "Comparison of door opening frequency in 1967–1968 cars with earlier model U.S. cars," published as a final report in May, 1969.

These reports tend to support Pruyn's opinion that the t-head type bolt assembly was significantly more likely to prevent ejection. The first report referred to the pioneering 1954 automotive crash injury research report which established that, contrary to a widely held pre-1954 general belief, passenger car occupants ejected during an accident had a lower chance of avoiding serious injury or death than those not ejected. The 1961 report studied 14,135 automobiles from injury-producing accidents involving 31,855 occupants. It compared ejection rates for pre- and post-1956 automobiles, since in that model year American manufacturers for the first time introduced a modified safety door latch designed to reduce door opening on impact. It found a significant lowering of the incidence of ejectment. The 1964 report studied 24,342 cars from injury-producing accidents. It compared ejection rates for pre- and post-1963 automobiles, since in the 1962 and 1963 model years some manufacturers made further improvements in the door latch mechanism. It found a further significant lowering of the incidence of ejectment. Essentially, according to Pruyn, the 1966 Rambler had the type latch adopted by all manufacturers in 1956, while he contended it should have had the type latch adopted by other manufacturers in 1962–1963. Had Pruyn been permitted to support his opinion by reference to these studies, his contention that American Motors had neglected to incorporate in its 1966 door latch design the current state of the art in safe design would undoubtedly have been reinforced.

*   *   *

The information in the Cornell Aeronautical Laboratory reports, though not statistical tabulations of experiments conducted by that organization, and hence in one sense distinguishable from at least one of the three tests referred to in Western Assurance Co., is closely analogous. Timber can be subjected to crushing stresses in laboratory conditions, while people may not be. The compilation of data from the unfortunately all-too-frequent actual injury-producing accidents is the best substitute available. That courts must, on hearsay grounds, be deprived of the use of the collected data on which other departments of government, industry, and the engineering profession obviously rely, makes no more sense now than in 1897, when that notion was rejected by the second circuit.

* * *

Since it is possible that a retrial of this case might not be completed until after July 1, 1973, the effective date of the new rules of evidence for United States Courts and Magistrates, it is appropriate to comment that under those rules the new federal rule would be the same. Rule 803 governs hearsay exceptions. Rule 803(18) provides:

> Learned treatises. To the extent called to the attention of an expert witness upon cross-examination or relied upon by him in direct examination, statements contained in published treatises, periodicals, or pamphlets on a subject of history, medicine, or other science or art, established as a reliable authority by the testimony or admission of the witness or by other expert testimony or by judicial notice. If admitted, the statements may be read into evidence but may not be received as exhibits.

As originally proposed this rule would have permitted the treatises to go to the jury. The last sentence was added with the explanation:

> The rule avoids the danger of misunderstanding and misapplication by limiting the use of treatises as substantive evidence to situations in which an expert is on the stand and available to explain and assist in the application of the treatise if desired. The limitation upon receiving the publication itself physically in evidence, contained in the last sentence, is designed to further this policy....

* * *

Since the erroneous exclusion of evidence requires a new trial, there is no occasion to rule upon Bair's additional contention that the court unfairly disparaged her expert.

The judgment of the district court will be reversed and the case remanded for a new trial.

Cross-examination is one instance when you frequently encounter the use of learned treatises. The questioning would be somewhat as follows:

Q. Do you recognize Smith and Jones, *Principles of Junk,* as a recognized work in the field of junk?

or

Q. Do you recognize the journal *Junk: Concepts and Methods* as a major journal
    in the field?

or

Q. Do you recognize Prof. Trash as an authority in the field of junk?

This question is designed so you agree that the source cited is recognized as
standard in the field, thus satisfying the first part of the rule. If you agree that the
source is a standard or recognized authority, then you must answer, truthfully, "yes."
If you do not agree, however, you will not be able to avoid answering the question,
as the other side will offer its own expert witness to testify that this is a recognized
source (the "other expert testimony" clause).

You will not be asked this question unless the other side believes they have
something in the cited authority that contradicts your testimony. There are several
steps you should take to prepare for such questions.

1. Make sure that you keep up with the journals in your field. This does not mean
    you have to read every article in every issue, but you should at least scan the table
    of contents of every issue. More up-to-date research often renders the source cited
    outdated, and you can cite the more recent publication to support your position.
    Every field has at least two major journals that you should keep up with, one
    specific to your specialty and one more general to the overall field. Examples of
    major journals include *Analytic Chemistry* and *C&E News* for analytic chemists
    and *Circulation* and either *New England Journal of Medicine, Journal of the
    American Medical Association,* or *Lancet* for cardiologists.
2. Be careful about lawyers who quote out of context. If the quote read to you seems
    totally wrong (that is, you cannot believe anyone with knowledge in the field
    would say such a thing), it is your right as a witness to ask to see the original
    from which the lawyer is reading. You can then read the full paragraph into the
    record to show that the lawyer is quoting out of context.
3. Always remember that you are the "living, breathing" witness in front of the judge
    and jury and that the book or article is only paper. It is perfectly proper to say,
    "Well, Prof. Jones may say that, but I do not agree, and here's why," and then go
    on to explain why. Assuming, of course, that you do have valid reasons for
    disagreeing, the odds are better than even that you will be more convincing than
    the piece of paper from which the lawyer has just read.

CHAPTER 18

Hearsay Exceptions IV —
Miscellaneous

Rule 803 contains quite a few other exceptions to the hearsay rule, some of which we have not yet discussed. Since most of these exceptions are not of general interest to experts but may be applicable to certain specific types of experts, they are presented here in a body. After all the rules are presented, those which may be relevant are discussed briefly.

FRE Rule 803 (Cont'd.)

(11) Records of religious organizations.

Statements of births, marriages, divorces, deaths, legitimacy, ancestry, relationship by blood or marriage, or other similar facts of personal or family history, contained in a regularly kept record of a religious organization.

(12) Marriage, baptismal, and similar certificates.

Statements of fact contained in a certificate that the maker performed a marriage or other ceremony or administered a sacrament, made by a clergyman, public official, or other person authorized by the rules or practices of a religious organization or by law to perform the act certified, and purporting to have been issued at the time of the act or within a reasonable time thereafter.

(13) Family records.

Statements of fact concerning personal or family history contained in family Bibles, genealogies, charts, engravings on rings, inscriptions on family portraits, engravings on urns, crypts, or tombstones, or the like.

(14) Records of documents affecting an interest in property.

The record of a document purporting to establish or affect an interest in property, as proof of the content of the original recorded document and its execution and delivery by each person by whom it purports to have been executed, if the record is a record of a public office and an applicable statute authorizes the recording of documents of that kind in that office.

(15) Statements in documents affecting an interest in property.

A statement contained in a document purporting to establish or affect an interest in property if the matter stated was relevant to the purpose of the document, unless dealings with the property since the document was made have been inconsistent with the truth of the statement or the purport of the document.

(16) Statements in ancient documents.

Statements in a document in existence twenty years or more the authenticity of which is established.

*   *   *

(19) Reputation concerning personal or family history.

Reputation among members of a person's family by blood, adoption, or marriage, or a person's associates, or in the community, concerning a person's birth, adoption, marriage, divorce, death, legitimacy, relationship by blood, adoption, or marriage, ancestry, or other similar fact of personal or family history.

(20) Reputation concerning boundaries or general history.

Reputation in a community, arising before the controversy, as to boundaries of or customs affecting lands in the community, and reputation as to events of general history important to the community or State or nation in which located.

(21) Reputation as to character.

Reputation of a person's character among associates or in the community.

(22) Judgment of previous conviction.

Evidence of a final judgment, entered after a trial or upon a plea of guilty (but not upon a plea of nolo contendere), adjudging a person guilty of a crime punishable by death or imprisonment in excess of one year, to prove any fact essential to sustain the judgment, but not including, when offered by the Government in a criminal prosecution for purposes other than impeachment, judgments against persons other than the accused. The pendency of an appeal may be shown but does not affect admissibility.

(23) Judgment as to personal, family, or general history, or boundaries.

Judgments as proof of matters of personal, family or general history, or boundaries, essential to the judgment, if the same would be provable by evidence of reputation.

Exceptions 11 through 16 and 19 are important and relevant to genealogists and, very possibly, to medical genetics researchers. Exceptions 14, 15, 20, and 23 are useful to surveyors and others concerned with real property in cases of disputed boundaries, titles, etc. I suspect that experts may even find an occasional use for the other parts of Rule 803, but I am unable to think of any.

Keep in mind that all exceptions contained in Rule 803 apply regardless of whether the original declarant is available to testify or not. Rule 804, which is limited to cases in which the declarant is unavailable to testify, requires no commentary.

FRE Rule 804. Hearsay Exceptions; Declarant Unavailable

(a) Definition of unavailability.

"Unavailability as a witness" includes situations in which the declarant

(1) is exempted by ruling of the court on the ground of privilege from testifying concerning the subject matter of the declarant's statement; or

(2) persists in refusing to testify concerning the subject matter of the declarant's statement despite an order of the court to do so; or

(3) testifies to a lack of memory of the subject matter of the declarant's statement; or

(4) is unable to be present or to testify at the hearing because of death or then existing physical or mental illness or infirmity; or

(5) is absent from the hearing and the proponent of a statement has been unable to procure the declarant's attendance (or in the case of a hearsay exception under subdivision (b)(2), (3), or (4), the declarant's attendance or testimony) by process or other reasonable means.

A declarant is not unavailable as a witness if exemption, refusal, claim of lack of memory, inability, or absence is due to the procurement or wrongdoing of the proponent of a statement for the purpose of preventing the witness from attending or testifying.

(b) Hearsay exceptions.

The following are not excluded by the hearsay rule if the declarant is unavailable as a witness:

(1) Former testimony.

Testimony given as a witness at another hearing of the same or a different proceeding, or in a deposition taken in compliance with law in the course of the same or another proceeding, if the party against whom the testimony is now offered, or, in a civil action or proceeding, a predecessor in interest, had an opportunity and similar motive to develop the testimony by direct, cross, or redirect examination.

* * *

Another hearsay issue that needs to be discussed is multiple hearsay, or, as Rule 805 calls it, "hearsay within hearsay."

FRE Rule 805. Hearsay Within Hearsay

Hearsay included within hearsay is not excluded under the hearsay rule if each part of the combined statements conforms with an exception to the hearsay rule provided in these rules.

The result is admissible as long as there is an exception for each link in the chain of hearsay statements. For example, an excited utterance is recorded in a business record. The business record is then referred to by a physician taking a patient history and the physician then incorporates the business record with the excited utterance into his or her medical records. Since there is an exception at each step, the physician's medical records would be admissible to prove the truth of the contents of the original excited utterance.

In addition to all other exceptions to the hearsay rule, there is also a "catch-all" exception designed to deal with those rare instances when no other exception is available.

Rule 807. Residual Exception

A statement not specifically covered by Rule 803 or 804 but having equivalent circumstantial guarantees of trustworthiness, is not excluded by the hearsay rule, if the court determines that (A) the statement is offered as evidence of a material fact; (B) the statement is more probative on the point for which it is offered than any other evidence which the proponent can procure through reasonable efforts; and (C) the general purposes of these rules and the interests of justice will best be served by admission of the statement into evidence. However, a statement may not be admitted under this exception unless the proponent of it makes known to the adverse party sufficiently in advance of the trial or hearing to provide the adverse party with a fair opportunity to prepare to meet it, the proponent's intention to offer the statement and the particulars of it, including the name and address of the declarant.

A judge does not typically make this sort of decision during the course of a trial. If you think you might need to avail yourself of Rule 807, you should discuss the matter with your attorney well in advance of the trial, so your attorney can present the issue to the judge at the pretrial conference and the judge can consider the matter at leisure.

CHAPTER 19

Best Evidence Rule

Contrary to its name, the best evidence rule does not require that a party always introduce the best evidence available to prove a point. It is confined to proving the contents of documents. Rule 1002 states the best evidence rule.

FRE Rule 1002. Requirement of Original

To prove the content of a writing, recording, or photograph, the original writing, recording, or photograph is required, except as otherwise provided in these rules or by Act of Congress.

Rule 1001 contains the definitions for the terms used in Rule 1002.

FRE Rule 1001. Definitions

For purposes of this article the following definitions are applicable:

(1) Writings and recordings.
"Writings" and "recordings" consist of letters, words, or numbers, or their equivalent, set down by handwriting, typewriting, printing, photostating, photographing, magnetic impulse, mechanical or electronic recording, or other form of data compilation.
(2) Photographs.
"Photographs" include still photographs, X-ray films, video tapes, and motion pictures.

(3) Original.

An "original" of a writing or recording is the writing or recording itself or any counterpart intended to have the same effect by a person executing or issuing it. An "original" of a photograph includes the negative or any print therefrom. If data are stored in a computer or similar device, any printout or other output readable by sight, shown to reflect the data accurately, is an "original."

(4) Duplicate.

A "duplicate" is a counterpart produced by the same impression as the original, or from the same matrix, or by means of photography, including enlargements and miniatures, or by mechanical or electronic re-recording, or by chemical reproduction, or by other equivalent techniques which accurately reproduce the original.

As you can see, the definition of writing and recording is so broad as to include almost any conceivable type of document. If this definition were applied totally literally, it would severely limit the extent to which business could be conducted because half of the files would be in court at any one time. Fortunately, Rule 1003 provides the "exception which swallows the rule."

FRE Rule 1003. Admissibility of Duplicates

A duplicate is admissible to the same extent as an original unless (1) a genuine question is raised as to the authenticity of the original or (2) in the circumstances it would be unfair to admit the duplicate in lieu of the original.

Rule 1001(1) concerns the authenticity of the original, not the accuracy of the copy. It addresses such issues as forgery or the "accurate representation" of data stored on a computer as discussed in Rule 1001(3). If there is any question about the authenticity of the original, that is the perfect situation to use the request for admission, as discussed in Part I.

Rules 1004, 1005, 1006, and 1007 present other exceptions to the best evidence rule which apply to other situations.

FRE Rule 1004. Admissibility of Other Evidence of Contents

The original is not required, and other evidence of the contents of a writing, recording, or photograph is admissible if

(1) Originals lost or destroyed.

All originals are lost or have been destroyed, unless the proponent lost or destroyed them in bad faith; or

(2) Original not obtainable.

No original can be obtained by any available judicial process or procedure; or

(3) Original in possession of opponent.

At a time when an original was under the control of the party against whom offered, that party was put on notice, by the pleadings or otherwise, that the contents would be a subject of proof at the hearing, and that party does not produce the original at the hearing; or

(4) Collateral matters.

The writing, recording, or photograph is not closely related to a controlling issue.

FRE Rule 1005. Public Records

The contents of an official record, or of a document authorized to be recorded or filed and actually recorded or filed, including data compilations in any form, if otherwise admissible, may be proved by copy, certified as correct in accordance with Rule 902 or testified to be correct by a witness who has compared it with the original. If a copy which complies with the foregoing cannot be obtained by the exercise of reasonable diligence, then other evidence of the contents may be given.

FRE Rule 1006. Summaries

The contents of voluminous writings, recordings, or photographs which cannot conveniently be examined in court may be presented in the form of a chart, summary, or calculation. The originals, or duplicates, shall be made available for examination or copying, or both, by other parties at reasonable time and place. The court may order that they be produced in court.

FRE Rule 1007. Testimony or Written Admission of Party

Contents of writings, recordings, or photographs may be proved by the testimony or deposition of the party against whom offered or by that party's written admission, without accounting for the nonproduction of the original.

Rule 1004 deals in a simple and straightforward manner with the problem of missing, destroyed, or otherwise unobtainable originals. Rule 1005 confirms our common practice of accepting as accurate copies of public records which carry the official stamp or seal and which state they are, indeed, true copies. Alternatively, it also provides for bringing in a witness who has compared the copy with the original to testify the copy is accurate. Rule 1006 discusses summaries. If you need to rely on a summary of some sort, I suggest this is another good occasion to use the request for admission during the discovery process. Rule 1007 simply states that if the other side has admitted to the contents of a document, that is admissible to prove those contents.

A word is necessary here about the "shown to reflect the data accurately" requirement regarding computer-stored information. In the early 1970s some judges required complete "dumps" from computers to prove that the data being presented in court was not selected to give an advantage to the party introducing it. More recent cases appear to have abandoned this view and treat computer storage as just another way of handling data, thus accepting the metaphor of "the paperless office." Nevertheless, if you intend to use a computer printout in your testimony, it might be best to treat it as a summary under Rule 1006 and ensure that the lawyer raises the issue at the pretrial conference, in case the other side has any problems with the idea.

CHAPTER 20

A "Real" Case

Thus far, we have reviewed cases for the purpose of examining the interpretation of individual rules, or, at most, two or three issues. Here you are presented with the decision in an actual case which involved considerable expert testimony regarding a scientifically complex causation issue, problems of the weight of evidence, routine practice, and other concepts we examined previously.

IN RE SWINE FLU IMMUNIZATION; Bean v. United States, 533 F.Supp. 567 (D. Colo. 1980)

Memorandum Opinion and Order Background and Overview of the Case

On November 16, 1976, plaintiff Ellen Bean, age sixty-two and a resident of Jefferson County, Colorado, received a swine flu vaccination administered pursuant to the National Swine Flu Immunization Program of 1976. The program was designed to inoculate the country's adult population against the threat of a swine flu epidemic. Shortly after her vaccination, in December, 1976, plaintiff developed an illness known as drop foot. At the time of trial, plaintiff still suffered from this condition which requires her to wear a brace on her left foot in order to walk properly.

In this suit, brought under the Federal Tort Claims Act, 28 U.S.C. ss 1346(b), 2671 et seq., it is claimed that the defendant, United States, is liable to Mrs. Bean for her illness. Plaintiff seeks recovery based on theories of negligence, strict liability, breach of warranty, and failure to adequately warn her of possible adverse reactions to the vaccine. The government contends that there is no causal connection between the vaccination and her condition, and that even if a causal relation is proven, that plaintiff cannot establish any theory of recovery which would render defendant liable.

The questions presented are whether plaintiff's drop foot was caused by the vaccination, and if so, is defendant liable; also present is the issue of the adequacy of the warning given to plaintiff. On these pivotal issues, we find in favor of defendant, United States of America.

* * *

The program was prompted in part by the medical discovery in early February, 1976 at Fort Dix, New Jersey, of military servicemen having a new strain of influenza virus antigenically related to the virus prevalent during the 1918–19 swine flu pandemic. That pandemic was responsible for 20 million deaths worldwide, including 500,000 in the United States alone. Prior to 1930, this strain was the predominant cause of influenza in the United States. Since 1930, the virus had been limited to transmission among swine only with occasional transmission from swine to human, with no secondary person-to-person transmission.

In addition, the Swine Flu Act was prompted by the collapse of the commercial liability insurance market, both for vaccine manufacturers and other program participants. The cases of *Davis v. Wyeth Laboratories, Inc.*, 399 F.2d 121 (9th Cir. 1968), and *Reyes v. Wyeth Laboratories*, 498 F.2d 1264 (5th Cir. 1974), which held a manufacturer of polio vaccine strictly liable in tort, greatly contributed to the insurance problem. For this reason, the Swine Flu Act provided that the exclusive remedy for injury caused by the vaccine would be against the United States. However, since the manufacturers could still insure themselves against negligence liability, they may be liable in a suit by the United States (42 U.S.C. s 247b(k)(7) if the United States is found to be liable on a negligence theory.

History has demonstrated that no swine flu epidemic occurred during the winter of 1976–77. As can be expected, however, many people who were inoculated also incurred some type of illness, injury or adverse medical condition in a period relative to the vaccination. Lawsuits, such as the instant one, were filed throughout the country for illnesses allegedly resulting from the immunization. In addition, numerous administrative claims have been filed.

The critical question presented in these cases is the causal relationship between the immunization and claimed illness. However, mere temporal relation between the onset of a disease and the vaccination is insufficient to establish legal causation. Each plaintiff has the burden of proving that the swine flu inoculation was the proximate cause of a claimed injury or medical condition.

Adequacy of the Warning: Informed Consent

A.

On November 16, 1976, Mrs. Bean received a swine flu vaccination at a public health clinic in Jefferson County, Colorado. The testimony is in conflict as to whether she received adequate warning of the possible adverse effects of the vaccine prior to inoculation. Plaintiff testified that the only material distributed by the Jefferson County Health Department was a blue card (Plaintiff's Exhibit 3A) which advised her that she might suffer some minor discomfort such as redness and tenderness at the injection site, fever, chills, nausea, aches and other symptoms lasting less than 48 hours.

Testimony indicated that the Jefferson County Health Department has been unable to locate any executed consent forms for November 16. Ms. Virginia Wolf, Assistant Director of Nursing for the County Health Department, testified that she was a coordinator for the vaccination program in Jefferson County; that it was the routine practice at the health center to give each person a registration (consent) form and a national fact sheet containing information about swine flu and the immunization program; and that the signed consent form was exchanged for a blue card which informed the person administering the vaccine whether the vaccinee was to receive a bivalent or monovalent vaccination. The foregoing was prescribed as standard procedure by the State Health Department.

Mrs. Barbara Mertens, a communicable disease nurse, worked at several of the Jefferson County Health Centers during the immunization program. She testified that a person could not be inoculated without first presenting the blue card and that such a card was obtained only by exchanging an executed consent form. Both Wolf and Mertens testified that personnel were available to answer any questions a vaccinee might have, and that such questions were encouraged.

The question of whether evidence is admissible in a proceeding in federal courts is determined by reference to the Federal Rules of Evidence. With respect to evidence of habit and routine practice, Rule 406 of the Federal Rules of Evidence is instructive:

> Evidence of the habit of a person or of the routine of an organization, whether corroborated or not and regardless of the presence of eyewitnesses, is relevant to prove that the conduct of the person or organization on a particular occasion was in conformity with the habit or routine practice.

Several cases are informative on the effect of evidence of habit or routine practice. In *Meyer v. United States*, 464 F.Supp. 317, (D.Colo. 1979) aff'd 638 F.2d 155 (10th Cir. 1980) the trial court stated:

> In the context of Rule 406, habit is a person's or organization's practice of handling a particular kind of situation with a specific type of conduct. Habit is one's regular response to a repeated specific situation. In similar fashion, an organization's regularity of action is within the purview of Rule 406.

In *Meyer*, the trial court considered evidence of a dentist's regular and routine practice of warning patients of the risks involved in oral surgery as persuasive on the issue of whether he provided such warning to the plaintiff. At trial, plaintiff had unequivocally testified that she received no advice or warning concerning the dangers attending oral surgery. In affirming the district court, the Tenth Circuit held that evidence of habit "does not stand in a special light nor is it to be referred to a second-class category which automatically carries little weight.... [T]he weight to be given to it is dependent on the particular circumstances." 638 F.2d at 158.

*   *   *

We find that the Jefferson County Health Department's habit and routine practice of obtaining signed consent forms prior to administering the vaccine was present on November 16, 1976, and that the health center acted in conformity with the habit and custom in advising Mrs. Bean of the potential adverse effects of the swine flu vaccine.

*   *   *

In our view, the patient's right of self-determination shapes the boundaries of the duty to reveal. That right can be effectively exercised only if the patient possesses enough information to enable an intelligent choice. The scope of the physician's communications to the patient, then, must be measured by the patient's need, and that need is the information material to the decision. Thus the test for determining whether a particular peril must be divulged is its materiality to the particular decision: all risks potentially affecting the decision must be unmasked. And to safeguard the patient's interest in achieving his own determination of treatment, the law itself must set the standard for adequate disclosure...no less than any other aspect of negligence, the issue of non-disclosure must be approached from the viewpoint of the reasonableness of the physician's divulgence in terms of what he knows or should know to be the patient's informational needs. If, but only if, the fact-finder can say that the physician's communication was unreasonably inadequate is an imposition of liability legally or morally justified.

*   *   *

We find that the warning given to Mrs. Bean was sufficient to provide her with adequate information to make an informed decision as to whether she should be vaccinated. Resolving this issue adversely to plaintiff, we now consider the pivotal question of causation and the medical history of plaintiff prior to and after the swine flu immunization.

*   *   *

Expert Testimony

The testimony is in conflict as to whether the swine flu vaccine caused plaintiff's drop foot. In support of plaintiff's position, several doctors rendered their expert opinions and analyses.

Martin Lewis, M.D., Chairman of the Pathology Department at Georgetown University, Washington, D.C., has conducted several studies concerning the effect of vaccination on the immune system. His testimony at trial pertained to one such test which seeks to determine a nexus between the swine flu vaccine and Guillian-Barre Syndrome (GBS). The methodology utilized involves reacting a person's blood serum with both peripheral nerve antigen and the swine flu vaccine. Dr. Lewis analyzed over 100 sera in this manner.

*   *   *

At trial the government objected to the admissibility of Dr. Lewis' testimony on two grounds. First, it contends that plaintiff has not established an adequate chain of custody with respect to the blood samples of Mrs. Bean analyzed by Dr. Lewis; and second, the tests are not the type reasonably relied on by the medical profession in formulating opinions.

We have considered and overrule defendant's objection to the testimony of Dr. Lewis. The general purpose of requiring a chain of custody to be established is to insure that evidence being offered is what the proponent claims it to be. To establish a chain of custody, the proponent must trace the continuous whereabouts of the item in question. Here, plaintiff has submitted affidavits of: (a) the nurse who drew blood from Mrs. Bean and mailed it to plaintiff's attorney; (b) of plaintiff's attorney's secretary who received the blood and mailed it to Dr. Phillips at Georgetown University; and (c) of Dr. Phillips who received the blood and coded it in accordance with his laboratory's usual procedures. We are satisfied that these affidavits support a continuous chain of custody of Mrs. Bean's blood samples from the time it was drawn until it was analyzed.

Rule 703, Federal Rules of Evidence, upon which defendant's second objection is based, reads as follows:

> The facts or data in the particular case upon which an expert bases an opinion or inference may be those perceived by or made known to him at or before the hearing. If of a type reasonably relied upon by experts in the particular field in forming opinions or inferences upon the subject, the facts or data need not be admissible in evidence.

The government bases its objection to Dr. Lewis' testimony on what we believe to be an incorrect interpretation of the second sentence of Rule 703. The thrust of the government's objection is that the medical community has not yet accepted Dr. Lewis' conclusions. It has, however, accepted the methodology in which his tests were conducted. The second sentence of Rule 703 allows experts to render opinions based upon information that otherwise might be hearsay, if this information or data is routinely relied upon by experts in the field. Dr. Lewis, however, based his opinion upon tests conducted by laboratory personnel under his supervision. It is beyond question that physicians regularly base opinions on laboratory findings. Therefore, Dr. Lewis may base his opinion on the results of those tests.

The fact that Dr. Lewis could not state to a reasonable degree of medical certainty that the swine flu vaccine caused Mrs. Bean's illness goes to the weight we give his testimony, not to its admissibility. Similarly, the fact that the results are preliminary, and may not generally be accepted by the medical community goes to the weight we give Dr. Lewis' testimony, not to its admissibility.

We believe the test for the admissibility of this testimony is its usefulness to the fact finder. Reference to Rule 702, Federal Rules of Evidence is helpful:

If scientific, technical, or other specialized knowledge will assist the trier of fact to understand the evidence or to determine a fact in issue, a witness qualified as an expert by knowledge, skill, experience, training, or education, may testify thereto in the form of an opinion or otherwise.

The testimony of Dr. Lewis is admissible in evidence in the case. It is useful for a better understanding of the medical issues inherent in this litigation.

*   *   *

Under Colorado law, an event is the proximate cause of another's damage if in the natural and probable sequence of things, it produced the claimed injury. If more than one cause contributed to the alleged injury, then each cause may be considered a proximate cause. A proximate cause need not have been the only cause or the last or nearest cause. Such event is sufficient if it concurs with some other event, either in combination with it or separately, to cause the claimed injury....

In the instant case, if plaintiff establishes that the swine flu vaccination aggravated her previous back problems thereby causing her drop foot or that the vaccine singly caused the drop foot, then the vaccination is the proximate cause of her condition.

All that is necessary to establish a causal connection between the inoculation and plaintiff's illness is to show facts and circumstances as would indicate with a reasonable probability that the drop foot resulted from, or was precipitated by, the vaccine.

*   *   *

Burden of Proof

Plaintiff has the burden of proving by a preponderance of the evidence that the swine flu vaccine was the proximate cause of her drop foot. While plaintiff presented the testimony of widely respected doctors, we are not persuaded that she has met her burden of proof. We have found nothing persuasive in the evidence establishing a causal connection between drop foot and the swine flu vaccine. Additionally, two of the experts who testified in support of plaintiff's position (Dr. Lewis and Dr. Baisel) were unable to state with a reasonable degree of medical certainty that the inoculation caused plaintiff's condition. Dr. Lewis' serum analysis is not persuasive in the instant case. It purports to establish a relationship between the vaccine and Guillain-Barre Syndrome. In his own words, the study is preliminary and inconclusive....

Conclusion

We find and conclude that plaintiff has failed to establish by a preponderance of the evidence that the injuries she sustained were caused by the immunization.

Several possible causes of drop foot have been advanced; however, in our role as trier of fact, we are led to the inescapable conclusion that the evidence presents no more than equal probabilities as to the cause of Mrs. Bean's condition. All that has been shown here is a temporal relation; and that is insufficient to carry the burden of proof which rests upon plaintiff.

Order

We find the issues joined in favor of defendant, United States of America, and against plaintiff, Ellen Bean. The Clerk of the Court is directed to enter judgment in favor of defendant and against plaintiff and the complaint and action are dismissed. Each party to pay his or her own costs.

This Order constitutes the findings of fact and conclusions of law as required by the Federal Rules of Civil Procedure, Rule 52(a).

Suggestions and Hints for Expert Witnesses

CHAPTER 21

Presenting Direct Testimony

As the section heading states, Part III presents suggestions and hints for expert witnesses, based largely on my own experience as a trial lawyer.

If you are presenting your direct testimony as a response to a hypothetical question, then as discussed earlier in Chapter 9, you have to follow the rules regarding such questions. And, of course, you need to help the attorney draft the question.

ORGANIZING NARRATIVE TESTIMONY

The first step is to organize your narrative testimony. If the lawyer with whom you are working is willing to have you give narrative testimony, you should sit down and establish the sequence in which you want questions asked of you. The first thing you must decide is what point in your testimony is the strongest.

Points can be strong or weak in one of two ways, as Figure 21.1 illustrates. As you can see, on the vertical axis, a point may be strong or weak because it is either strongly supported by the facts already in evidence or it has weak factual support. On the horizontal axis, a point can strongly support the ultimate conclusion you intend to reach or it can weakly aid you in reaching that conclusion. The strongest possible point would be way off the scale at the upper right. The weakest possible point would be way off the scale at the lower left.

Assume that you have seven points you wish to make in support of your ultimate conclusion. The first thing you must do is rank them. Assuming these points are spread as are the points in Figure 21.1, you can see how I would number them from strongest (1) to weakest (7). You might disagree on the numbering of points 3 and 4, or points 5 and 6, and those numbers could be switched, but I hope we agree about the rest. Try to save your strongest point for last. People remember longest the point they hear most recently, so save Point 1 for your last point. On the other hand, we do not want to start with your weakest point, Point 7, because you would not sound

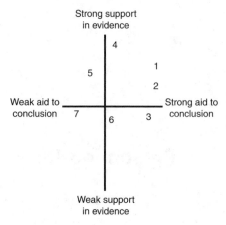

Figure 21.1 Strength of support for points.

very convincing when you start your testimony. The ideal scheme would be to proceed in the order of Point 3, Point 6, Point 7, Point 5, Point 4, Point 2, and Point 1. This way you will start fairly strongly, go quickly down to your weakest points, and then build up strongly to your conclusion.

Obviously, this arrangement is an abstraction. Do not let it detract from the technical merits of your arguments. If the technical requirements are such that you cannot discuss Point 3 until you have discussed Point 6, then you obviously must discuss Point 6 before you discuss Point 3. To the greatest extent possible, however, I recommend that you follow an organization of this type.

After you have ordered your points, write a question the lawyer can ask you that will raise each of the points. After the question, write some notes regarding your reply. Include in these notes the major sub-points you wish to discuss and any exhibits or illustrations you intend to use to explicate those points. I favor putting references to exhibits or illustrations in the answer at the point they are to be used inside {curly brackets}. For example:

Q. Is this groundwater contaminated and how do you know?
A. Five samples collected over 3 months. Samples tested on GC/MS. {Show reference profile of furan/profile of sample}.

I also favor a set of introductory questions of the: "What is your opinion about…" type. In the above example it would be:

Q. Do you have an opinion as to whether and how badly this groundwater is contaminated and what the source of that contamination is?
A. Yes, I have an opinion.
Q. What is your opinion?
A. My opinion is that the groundwater is contaminated by dibenzo furans, which makes it unsafe for people and that the source of the contamination is the XYZ Company's waste site.

The purpose of this introduction is to tell the judge and jury where you are going with your testimony. It will be much easier for them to follow if they know what conclusion you are leading them to. I admit, however, that this is a personal preference that is not shared by all attorneys.

Give a copy of this outline to your lawyer and go over it with her. You may find that she disagrees with something; especially how you ranked the strength of the points and the order in which you plan to cover them. This is something you can negotiate with her, but please remember that she has a lot more at stake in the case than you do, so she should have the final say.

After the final order is set, you and the attorney should both have a copy whenever you testify, either at the trial or a deposition. You can then both check points off from your respective copies as you go, ensuring that everything you have to say is covered in the correct sequence, and that all documents or other exhibits that you intend to rely upon are utilized. You may take your outline on the witness stand with you, since, as you may recall from FRE Rule 612 (Chapter 16), the only limitation is that the other side is entitled to see the document. There can be no problem with the other side seeing this outline of your testimony since the other side probably already has heard it in great detail at your deposition or, at least, has read all your written reports.

And almost all attorneys want you to have a final summary question in which you restate very briefly the bases of your conclusion; for example:

Q. Now, could you please briefly restate your reasons for reaching this conclusion?

A. Yes. I did several lab tests that showed that this water is contaminated by dibenzo furans, which are listed by the EPA as toxic and hazardous chemicals. The levels of these chemicals in the water far exceed the limits considered safe for human use. I consulted the geologic maps and hydrographic data that are available and determined that the water on this property arrives there after it leaves the XYZ Corporation property. Since the tests I performed on the water on the other side of the XYZ property show no contamination, and there is no dispute that XYZ disposed of chemicals on its property, I concluded that the XYZ property is the source of the contamination.

BE A TEACHER

In the event of a jury trial, in particular, always remember that part of your role is to be an educator. You need to educate the jury so that jury members learn enough about your technical field to understand what you are talking about and are convinced that you are right. This brings up the question, "What level of student am I addressing?" The general assumption one makes is that all jury members are high school graduates. If you have a judge-only trial you can, of course, safely assume that the judge is a college graduate, but you cannot assume the judge has any level of scientific or technical knowledge.

Some judges, however, are scientifically trained, and you may appear before such a judge in a nonjury case. Be sure to ask the lawyer if he or she has any idea of the extent of the judge's scientific training, and then adjust the level of your testimony accordingly. For example, some U.S. District Court judges have bachelor's degrees or even master's degrees in sciences ranging from chemistry to biology to electrical engineering. If you are discussing epidemiology before a judge with a background in physics, you will be able to assume some familiarity with the mathematics you will be using even if the judge is unfamiliar with the difference between case control and longitudinal studies.

Some judges are even experimenting with having a meeting with the experts, with or without the lawyers, long before trial in an informal setting. As one U.S. District Judge has written, it provides an opportunity

> "to tutor the judge on the complex issues present in the case. This is a good way for judges to learn the fundamentals of a particular discipline in a classroom-like setting, rather than in a courtroom. Often, this approach works better than having the judge piece together the basics from the often diametrically opposed party expert reports and testimony."[1]

One must be careful about the field of mathematics. There is a wonderful scene in a P. D. James mystery novel where a group of forensic scientists talk among themselves while waiting for the police:

"Juries hate scientific evidence."

"They think they won't be able to understand it so naturally they can't understand it. As soon as you step into the box you see a curtain of obstinate incomprehension clanging down over their minds. What they want is certainty. Did this paint article come from this car body? Answer yes or no. None of those nasty mathematical probabilities we're so fond of."

"If they hate scientific evidence they certainly hate arithmetic more. Give them a scientific opinion that depends on the ability to divide a factor by two thirds and what do you get from counsel? 'I'm afraid you'll have to explain yourself more simply, Mr. Middlemass. The jury and I haven't got a higher degree in mathematics, you know.' Inference: You're an arrogant bastard and the jury would be well advised not to believe a word you say."[2]

While the situation may not be as extreme as the novel suggests, it is difficult to present mathematical reasoning to juries. If it is mere arithmetic, I suggest showing it step by step on a flip-chart so the jury can follow every step. If you have to integrate numbers or calculate a Fourier transform or the like, however, I think it best just to tell the jury the result. Your lawyer may have some specific suggestions for your case.

PRESENTING THE TESTIMONY

The most important rule is to always make eye contact with the person you are trying to convince. In the jury situation you should make eye contact with individual members of the jury. Indeed, the attorney may be able to guess who will become the foreman of the jury, in which case you can concentrate the majority of your attention on that juror; but do not ignore the other jurors. We all listen more closely to people who look at us, so do not constantly look down and read your testimony. The paper you take on the stand is merely notes, not a verbatim script for you to follow. And definitely do not look only at the attorney who is questioning you.

Eye contact is also important in a judge-only trial. Remember the courtroom pictures from Chapter 13. Clearly, in the traditional courtroom you cannot directly address the judge while seated below and left of her. In that case you can carry on a conversation with the attorney who is asking the questions. But in the modern courtroom you are even with the judge and can turn in your seat and look at her when answering the question. It may well be that she is not looking at you but at some papers on her desk, but do not let that stop you from looking at her; at some point she will look up and you can make eye contact. In sum, do not enter into a conversation with your lawyer. You are not attempting to convince the lawyer. Look at the lawyer when the lawyer asks you a question, then turn and look at the jury or judge when answering.

If you are in a traditional courtroom and you have some mounted pictures, diagrams, or other items to help explain your testimony, make sure they are faced toward the decision maker (jury or judge). And when standing to explain them, make sure you are not blocking the decision maker's view. Why go to all the effort of preparing them if you get in the way of seeing them?

In the modern courtroom, however, you have no such problems. Everyone has a monitor they can easily see. In fact, some attorneys favor using a "slide show" of the PowerPoint© type that lists your points as you make them. The trick here is not to make the presentation too deep and complicated; keep it down to an outline of the major points and avoid getting bogged down with details. Otherwise the jury might be so busy reading that you will not be able to keep their attention.

Your testimony is very different from writing a report or a journal article. Always speak in the first person active voice. Never say, "The sample was tested and the following results were noted"; say instead, "I tested the sample and found the following results"; or "The sample was tested by Dr. X under my supervision"; or a similar statement. The passive voice not only sounds pedantic, it puts people to sleep.

Avoid technical terms as much as you can; and when you have to use one, explain it by analogy. Many years ago I heard an expert witness describe 1 ppm as a tablespoon of dye dumped into an Olympic swimming pool. I have never done the math, but I suspect it is the correct order of magnitude. And it certainly made clear how small a ppm was.

Then for five or six times you can use the technical term without redefining it. But then, the next time, remind everyone of the definition. Something like: "You remember, that's the tablespoon in the swimming pool."

You should also tell stories to illustrate your points; that is, stories unrelated to the exact case you are involved with (as I did two paragraphs ago). This serves several purposes. It helps illustrate the point, makes you appear friendlier and more "human," and gives everyone a break from the technical details of your testimony.

You also need to pay attention to your clothing when appearing in court. Many judges have the attitude that, if you are not dressed as they consider appropriate, then you are not showing respect for the formality of the courtroom setting. And a jury takes cues from the judge; if the judge is looking at you with disdain, the jury will tend to give your testimony less weight.

If you are in a uniformed service (police, military, USPHS, etc.), then you can wear your dress uniform if the attorney agrees. But do check with her; there are some courts where a uniform immediately raises negative attitudes, especially from a jury. If you do not wear a uniform then wear a conservative business suit.

Finally, remember that you are trying to appear both expert and personable. You want the decision maker to decide that you are an expert mechanic from whom he or she would buy a used car.

REFERENCES

1. Kaplan, L.A., Experts in the courtroom: Problems and opportunities, *Colum. Bus. L. Rev.,* 247 at 254, 2006.
2. James, P.D., *Death of an Expert Witness,* Warner, New York, 1977, 96.

CHAPTER 22

Withstanding Cross-Examination

Most expert witnesses who have not participated in many trials have a fear of cross-examination. This fear is unfounded, since it is virtually impossible to "destroy" on cross-examination an expert who knows what he or she is talking about. You should be aware of a few major legal rules that apply in this area.

First of all, you can take heart from the fact that an expert witness can always resort to saying, "That is my expert opinion." An opinion is something that exists only in your mind; it is not an objective fact capable of proof. Nobody can prove that you do not believe what you have testified to on direct examination. If "driven to the wall," you can always retreat to that position.

Remember our earlier discussion regarding the learned treatise exception to the hearsay rule, FRE Rule 803(18), and watch out for quotes out of context. Do not be upset that a written authority disagrees with you; you are in court in person and the jury can evaluate you and decide to believe you, whereas the author of the book or article is not present. The advantage in this situation is yours as long as you can reasonably explain why you disagree with the quoted "authority."

Be aware that it is perfectly proper for you to be cross-examined on the basis of what you previously said, or — more likely for experts — wrote, on the subject of your testimony. Rule 613 addresses this issue.

FRE Rule 613. Prior Statements of Witnesses

(a) Examining witness concerning prior statement.

In examining a witness concerning a prior statement made by the witness, whether written or not the statement need not be shown nor its contents disclosed to the witness at that time, but on request the same shall be shown or disclosed to opposing counsel.

In this situation you do not have the right to see the paper from which the lawyer is reading. Since it is your work being quoted, you should be familiar with it. This is not an infrequent occurrence for experts who pass through major changes in their fields during their professional lifetimes. The simple response in such situations is to explain why results since the time of your writing have convinced you that the approach to your subject has changed.

This cannot happen to you regarding your own testimony in court. If the lawyer starts to cross-examine you on something you said in your direct testimony and you believe that the reference is incorrect, you may ask to have the court reporter read back that section of your testimony. That is, after all, why we have court reporters instead of tape recorders. The reporter can find previous testimony without having to listen to a tape in "real time" to locate the referenced answer. You may not, however, request that your deposition testimony be read back to you. For this reason, you should always read over your deposition shortly before appearing in court so that you can be relatively certain as to what you said in it.

You should always remember that you are supposed to be an "objective" expert, not an advocate for one side in the case. The attorney is the advocate, not you. Nothing annoys a trial judge as much as expert witnesses who "overstate the certainty of their conclusions and ... gloss over important nuances in an effort to present the most uncompromising support for the lawyers' position."[1] This quote, from an active trial judge, should always be kept in mind when responding to cross-examination.

Witnesses frequently permit lawyers to cut them off in the middle of an answer. We all have seen television shows in which the lawyer holds up a hand and says, "Thank you, Witness, but I believe that is a sufficient answer." This has conditioned many experts to believe that this can really happen to them; and this can happen if you permit it to happen. Remember, as the expert, you know when you have finished your answer. All you have to do is say, "Excuse me, Attorney, but I have not finished answering that question," and then finish your answer. In the extreme case, the judge can say, "Witness, I believe you are done," and you will be unable to continue, but I have never heard of that happening to an expert witness in an actual case.

And remember, cross-examination can give you the chance to repeat your direct testimony by reemphasizing points you previously made. It is perfectly acceptable to preface an answer with, "Well, as I said earlier..." and then go on to reiterate that section of your direct testimony. A good cross-examiner, of course, will not give you that opportunity, but if you spot an opening, dive in.

Go back and reread the transcript of Kelly ex rel Michigan v. E.I. Dupont, et al. in Chapter 3. This is a reasonably good cross-examination. Notice that all of the questions are very short and provide almost no opportunity for the witness to expand beyond a few words. Also notice that the point the attorney is attempting to make is kept hidden until the attorney is ready to spring. There are no "Are you certain that these charges are all related to the project?" or "Have you audited these charges?" questions. That would have given the witness the opportunity to protect himself by saying something like, "Well, I haven't examined all the calls in detail, but they're probably all related," or some such "waffle."

If time permits, the lawyer with whom you are working will probably give you the opportunity to respond to a mock cross-examination before you reach court.

This is part of proper preparation by the lawyer and a definite aid to you, as it will give you the chance to see how you and your testimony stand up under pressure. The lawyer probably also will take you aside at some point and give you all sorts of little hints. The following are some hints I always gave my experts before they went to testify.

Keep your cool. No matter how intent the cross-examiner seems to be on getting you into an argument, do not lose your temper. If you are angry, you might speak without fully thinking out your answer. Keep in mind, you are trying to present yourself to the fact finder as the voice of "objective, technical truth," which requires some degree of calm detachment.

Make eye contact with the jury. Eye contact is even more important in cross-examination than in direct examination. Look at the lawyer when asked the question and then turn and answer to the jury or, if in a modern courtroom in a bench trial, the judge.

Do not answer a question unless you are sure what is being asked. If you are uncertain what is being asked, ask the lawyer to rephrase the question. If you are still not sure what is being asked, then you can attempt to rephrase the question yourself and ask the lawyer if that is what was meant. But never present the lawyer with two possible versions of the question; pick the version that is best for the points you are attempting to make.

"I don't know" is an acceptable answer. Nobody knows everything. Be sure to add "because I didn't consider it important in this case" or "but I can find out for you if you want me to."

"It's on the tip of my tongue" is also an acceptable answer. We all occasionally draw a blank when trying to recall something we know that we know. If this happens to you on the witness stand, say so, and ask the lawyer to go on to something else as you are sure you will soon remember whatever you cannot now recall.

Confine yourself to your specialty. We all know a great deal about closely related specialties, but we never know enough about them to satisfy a cross-examiner. The moment you wander outside your area, the lawyer will lead you further out until you eventually get lost. Stop this process before it starts by saying, "That's not my field; you want a whatsitologist for that."

Explain why you can't say if you "have stopped beating your spouse." This is what lawyers call an argumentative question. When asked a trick question, point out to all present that it is a trick question, and you cannot answer it in the format presented. You may even try to reword it in a different form and then answer it.

Watch out for breaks in rhythm. All conversations develop their own rhythm. Question, pause before answering, answer, pause before next question, next question; that is how the cross-examination will sound. At some point, however, the questioner will break the rhythm by not asking the next question. And, as the silence goes on, you will be tempted to fill it with whatever comes to mind. This can occasionally be dangerous as it violates the next recommendation.

"Be sure brain is engaged before putting mouth into gear." Take two seconds to think about your answer before you start verbalizing it.

Other lawyers will tell you about additional or different points, some important and some not so important. Listen to what the lawyer has to say, even if you believe you have heard all these suggestions previously, or read them in this book. It never hurts to have your memory refreshed on such topics. Always remember that your professional reputation is not really on the line in your courtroom appearances. Your professional peers probably will not even know you were there, and their opinion of you will not change because of what occurs when you appear as an expert witness.

In conclusion, approach the entire expert witness situation as an opportunity to participate in an exotic, unusual, and perhaps barbaric ritual. Use it to expand your own knowledge of some small area of your expertise while being paid for your time. Do not become "ego involved" in the situation. Have fun and make money while teaching the "heathen" about your specialty.

REFERENCE

1. Kaplan, L.A., Experts in the courtroom: Problems and opportunities. *Colum. Bus. L. Rev.*, 247 at 251, 2006.

Appendices and Case Listing

Appendix A

**EXTRACTS FROM THE FEDERAL RULES OF CIVIL PROCEDURE
(IN NUMERICAL ORDER)**

Rule 16. Pretrial Conferences; Scheduling; Management

(a) Pretrial Conferences; Objectives.

In any action, the court may in its discretion direct the attorneys for the parties and any unrepresented parties to appear before it for a conference or conferences before trial for such purposes as

(1) expediting the disposition of the action;

(2) establishing early and continuing control so that the case will not be protracted because of lack of management;

(3) discouraging wasteful pretrial activities;

(4) improving the quality of the trial through more thorough preparation, and;

(5) facilitating the settlement of the case.

(b) Scheduling and Planning.

Except in categories of actions exempted by district court rule as inappropriate, the district judge, or a magistrate judge when authorized by district court rule, shall, after receiving the report from the parties under Rule 26(f) or after consulting with the attorneys for the parties and any unrepresented parties by a scheduling conference, telephone, mail, or other suitable means, enter a scheduling order that limits the time

(1) to join other parties and to amend the pleadings;

(2) to file motions; and

(3) to complete discovery.

The scheduling order may also include

(4) modifications of the times for disclosures under Rules 26(a) and 26(e)(1) and of the extent of discovery to be permitted;

(5) the date or dates for conferences before trial, a final pretrial conference, and trial; and

(6) any other matters appropriate in the circumstances of the case.

The order shall issue as soon as practicable but in any event within 90 days after the appearance of a defendant and within 120 days after the complaint has been served on a defendant. A schedule shall not be modified except upon a showing of good cause by leave of the district judge or, when authorized by local rule, by a magistrate judge.

(c) Subjects for Consideration at Pretrial Conferences.

At any conference under this rule consideration may be given, and the court may take appropriate action, with respect to

(1) the formulation and simplification of the issues, including the elimination of frivolous claims or defenses;

(2) the necessity or desirability of amendments to the pleadings;

(3) the possibility of obtaining admissions of fact and of documents which will avoid unnecessary proof, stipulations regarding the authenticity of documents, and advance rulings from the court on the admissibility of evidence;

(4) the avoidance of unnecessary proof and of cumulative evidence, and limitations or restrictions on the use of testimony under Rule 702 of the Federal Rules of Evidence;

(5) the appropriateness and timing of summary adjudication under Rule 56;

(6) the control and scheduling of discovery, including orders affecting disclosures and discovery pursuant to Rule 26 and Rules 27 through 37;

(7) the identification of witnesses and documents, the need and schedule for filing and exchanging pretrial briefs, and the date or dates for further conferences and for trial;

(8) the advisability of referring matters to a magistrate judge or master;

(9) settlement and the use of special procedures to assist in resolving the dispute when authorized by statute or local rule;

(10) the form and substance of the pretrial order;

(11) the disposition of pending motions;

(12) the need for adopting special procedures for managing potentially difficult or protracted actions that may involve complex issues, multiple parties, difficult legal questions, or unusual proof problems;

(13) an order for a separate trial pursuant to Rule 42(b) with respect to a claim, counterclaim, cross-claim, or third-party claim, or with respect to any particular issue in the case;

(14) an order directing a party or parties to present evidence early in the trial with respect to a manageable issue that could, on the evidence, be the basis for a judgment as a matter of law under Rule 50(a) or a judgment on partial findings under Rule 52(c);

(15) an order establishing a reasonable limit on the time allowed for presenting evidence; and

(16) such other matters as may facilitate the just, speedy, and inexpensive disposition of the action.

At least one of the attorneys for each party participating in any conference before trial shall have authority to enter into stipulations and to make admissions regarding all matters that the participants may reasonably anticipate may be discussed. If appropriate, the court may require that a party or its representatives be present or reasonably available by telephone in order to consider possible settlement of the dispute.

(d) Final Pretrial Conference.

Any final pretrial conference shall be held as close to the time of trial as reasonable under the circumstances. The participants at such conference shall formulate a plan for trial, including a program for facilitating the admission of evidence. The conference shall be attended by at least one of the attorneys who will conduct the trial for each of the parties and by any unrepresented parties.

(e) Pretrial Orders.

After any conference held pursuant to this rule, an order shall be entered reciting the action taken. This order shall control the subsequent course of the action unless modified by a subsequent order. The order following a final pretrial conference shall be modified only to prevent manifest injustice.

(f) Sanctions.

If a party or party's attorney fails to obey a scheduling or pretrial order, or if no appearance is made on behalf of a party at a scheduling or pretrial conference, or if a party or party's attorney is substantially unprepared to participate in the conference, or if a party or party's attorney fails to participate in good faith, the judge, upon motion or the judge's own initiative, may make such orders with regard thereto as are just, and among others any of the orders provided in Rule 37(b)(2)(B), (C), (D). In lieu of or in addition to any other sanction, the judge shall require the party or the attorney representing the party or both to pay the reasonable expenses incurred because of any noncompliance with this rule, including attorney's fees, unless the judge finds that the noncompliance was substantially justified or that other circumstances make an award of expenses unjust.

Rule 26. General Provisions Governing Discovery; Duty of Disclosure

(a) Required Disclosures; Methods to Discover Additional Matter.

(1) Initial Disclosures. Except in categories of proceedings specified in Rule 26(a)(1)(E), or to the extent otherwise stipulated or directed by order, a party must, without awaiting a discovery request, provide to other parties:

(A) the name and, if known, the address and telephone number of each individual likely to have discoverable information that the disclosing party may use to support its claims or defenses, unless solely for impeachment, identifying the subjects of the information;

(B) a copy of, or a description by category and location of, all documents, electronically stored information, and tangible things that are in the possession, custody, or control of the party and that the disclosing party may use to support its claims or defenses, unless solely for impeachment;

(C) a computation of any category of damages claimed by the disclosing party, making available for inspection and copying as under Rule 34 the documents or other evidentiary material, not privileged or protected from disclosure, on which such computation is based, including materials bearing on the nature and extent of injuries suffered; and

(D) for inspection and copying as under Rule 34 any insurance agreement under which any person carrying on an insurance business may be liable to satisfy part or all of a judgment which may be entered in the action or to indemnify or reimburse for payments made to satisfy the judgment.

Unless otherwise stipulated or directed by the court, these disclosures shall be made at or within 10 days after the meeting of the parties under subdivision (f). A party shall make its initial disclosures based on the information then reasonably available to it and is not excused from making its disclosures because it has not fully completed its investigation of the case or because it challenges the sufficiency of another party's disclosures or because another party has not made its disclosures.

(2) Disclosure of Expert Testimony.

(A) In addition to the disclosures required by paragraph (1), a party shall disclose to other parties the identity of any person who may be used at trial to present evidence under Rules 702, 703, or 705 of the Federal Rules of Evidence.

(B) Except as otherwise stipulated or directed by the court, this disclosure shall, with respect to a witness who is retained or specially employed to provide expert testimony in the case or whose duties as an employee of the party regularly involve giving expert testimony, be accompanied by a written report prepared and signed by the witness. The report shall contain a complete statement of all opinions to be expressed and the basis and reasons therefor; the data or other information considered by the witness in forming the opinions; any exhibits to be used as a summary of or support for the opinions; the qualifications of the witness, including a list of all publications authored by the witness within the preceding ten years; the compensation to be paid for the study and testimony; and a listing of any other cases in which the witness has testified as an expert at trial or by deposition within the preceding four years.

(C) These disclosures shall be made at the times and in the sequence directed by the court. In the absence of other directions from the court or stipulation by the parties, the disclosures shall be made at least 90 days before the trial date or the date the case is to be ready for trial or, if the evidence is intended solely to contradict or rebut evidence on the same subject matter identified by another party under paragraph (2)(B), within 30 days after the disclosure made by the other party. The parties shall supplement these disclosures when required under subdivision (e)(1).

(3) Pretrial Disclosures.

In addition to the disclosures required in the preceding paragraphs, a party shall provide to other parties the following information regarding the evidence that it may present at trial other than solely for impeachment purposes:

(A) the name and, if not previously provided, the address and telephone number of each witness, separately identifying those whom the party expects to present and those whom the party may call if the need arises;

(B) the designation of those witnesses whose testimony is expected to be presented by means of a deposition and, if not taken stenographically, a transcript of the pertinent portions of the deposition testimony; and

(C) an appropriate identification of each document or other exhibit, including summaries of other evidence, separately identifying those which the party expects to offer and those which the party may offer if the need arises.

Unless otherwise directed by the court, these disclosures shall be made at least 30 days before trial. Within 14 days thereafter, unless a different time is specified by the court, a party may serve and file a list disclosing (i) any objections to the use under Rule 32(a) of a deposition designated by another party under subparagraph (B) and (ii) any objection, together with the grounds therefor, that may be made to the admissibility of materials identified under subparagraph (C). Objections not so disclosed, other than objections under Rules 402 and 403 of the Federal Rules of Evidence, shall be deemed waived unless excused by the court for good cause shown.

(4) Form of Disclosures; Filing.

Unless otherwise directed by order or local rule, all disclosures under paragraphs (1) through (3) shall be made in writing, signed, served, and promptly filed with the court.

(5) Methods to Discover Additional Matter.

Parties may obtain discovery by one or more of the following methods: depositions upon oral examination or written questions; written interrogatories; production of documents or things or permission to enter upon land or other property under Rule 34 or 45(a)(1)(C), for inspection and other purposes; physical and mental examinations; and requests for admission.

(b) Discovery Scope and Limits.

Unless otherwise limited by order of the court in accordance with these rules, the scope of discovery is as follows:

(1) In General.

Parties may obtain discovery regarding any matter, not privileged, which is relevant to the subject matter involved in the pending action, whether it relates to the claim or defense of the party seeking discovery or to the claim or defense of any other party, including the existence, description, nature, custody, condition, and location of any books, documents, or other tangible things and the identity and location of persons having knowledge of any discoverable matter. The information sought need not be admissible at the trial if the information sought appears reasonably calculated to lead to the discovery of admissible evidence.

(2) Limitations.

(A) By order, the court may alter the limits in these rules on the number of depositions and interrogatories or the length of depositions under Rule 30. By order or local rule, the court may also limit the number of requests under Rule 36.

(B) A party need not provide discovery of electronically stored information from sources that the party identifies as not reasonably accessible because of undue burden or cost. On motion to compel discovery or for a protective order, the party from whom discovery is sought must show that the information is not reasonably accessible because of undue burden or cost. If that showing is made, the court may nonetheless order discovery from such sources if the requesting party shows good cause, considering the limitations of Rule 26(b)(2)(C). The court may specify conditions for the discovery.

(C) The frequency or extent of use of the discovery methods otherwise permitted under these rules and by any local rule shall be limited by the court if it determines that: (i) the discovery sought is unreasonably cumulative or duplicative, or is obtainable from some other source that is more convenient, less burdensome, or less expensive; (ii) the party seeking discovery has had ample opportunity by discovery in the action to obtain the information sought; or (iii) the burden or expense of the proposed discovery outweighs its likely benefit, taking into account the needs of the case, the amount in controversy, the parties' resources, the importance of the issues at stake in the litigation, and the importance of the proposed discovery in resolving the issues. The court may act upon its own initiative after reasonable notice or pursuant to a motion under Rule 26(c).

(3) Trial Preparation: Materials.

Subject to the provisions of subdivision (b)(4) of this rule, a party may obtain discovery of documents and tangible things otherwise discoverable under subdivision (b)(1) of this rule and prepared in anticipation of litigation or for trial by or for another party or by or for that other party's representative (including the other party's attorney, consultant, surety, indemnity, insurer, or agent) only upon a showing that the party seeking discovery has substantial need of the materials in the preparation of the party's case and that the party is unable without undue hardship to obtain the substantial equivalent of the materials by other means. In ordering discovery of such materials when the required showing has been made the court shall protect against disclosure of the mental impressions, conclusions, opinions, or legal theories of an attorney or other representative of a party concerning the litigation.

A party may obtain without the required showing a statement concerning the action or its subject matter previously made by that party. Upon request, a person not a party may obtain without the required showing a statement concerning the action or its subject matter previously made by that person. If the request is refused, the person may move for a court order. The provisions of Rule 37(a)(4) apply to the award of expenses incurred in relation to the motion. For purposes of this paragraph, a statement previously made is (A) a written statement signed or otherwise adopted or approved by the person making it, or (B) a stenographic, mechanical, electrical, or other recording, or a transcription thereof, which is a substantially verbatim recital of an oral statement by the person making it and contemporaneously recorded.

(4) Trial Preparation: Experts.

(A) A party may depose any person who has been identified as an expert whose opinions may be presented at trial. If a report from the expert is required under subdivision (a)(2)(B), the deposition shall not be conducted until after the report is provided.

(B) A party may, through interrogatories or by deposition, discover factors known or opinions held by an expert who has been retained or specially employed by another party in anticipation of litigation or preparation for trial and who is not expected to be called as a witness at trial, only as provided in Rule 35(b) or upon a showing of exceptional circumstances under which it is impracticable for the party seeking discovery to obtain facts or opinions on the same subject by other means.

(C) Unless injustice would result, (i) the court shall require that the party seeking discovery pay the expert a reasonable fee for time spent in responding to discovery under this subdivision; and (ii) with respect to discovery obtained under subdivision (b)(4)(B) of this rule the court shall require the party seeking discovery to pay the other party a fair portion of the fees and expenses reasonably incurred by the latter party in obtaining facts and opinions from the expert.

(5) Claims of Privilege or Protection of Trial-Preparation Materials.

(A) Information Withheld. When a party withholds information otherwise discoverable under these rules by claiming that it is privileged or subject to protection as trial-preparation material, the party shall make the claim expressly and shall describe the nature of the documents, communications, or things not produced or disclosed in a manner that, without revealing information itself privileged or protected, will enable other parties to assess the applicability of the privilege or protection.

(B) Information Produced. If information is produced in discovery that is subject to a claim of privilege or of protection as trial-preparation material, the party making the claim may notify any party that received the information of the claim and the basis for it. After being notified, a party must promptly return, sequester, or destroy the specified information and any copies it has and may not use or disclose the information until the claim is resolved. A receiving party may promptly present the information to the court under seal for a determination of the claim. If the receiving party disclosed the information before being notified, it must take reasonable steps to retrieve it. The producing party must preserve the information until the claim is resolved.

(c) Protective Orders.

Upon motion by a party or by the person from whom discovery is sought, accompanied by a certification that the movant has in good faith conferred or attempted to confer with other affected parties in an effort to resolve the dispute without court action, and for good cause shown, the court in which the action is pending or alternatively, on matters relating to a deposition, the court in the district where the deposition is to be taken may take any order which justice requires to protect a party or person from annoyance, embarrassment, oppression, or undue burden or expense, including one or more of the following:

(1) that the disclosure or discovery not be had;

(2) that the disclosure or discovery may be had only on specified terms and conditions, including a designation of the time or place;

(3) that the discovery may be had only by a method of discovery other than that selected by the party seeking discovery;

(4) that certain matters not be inquired into, or that the scope of the disclosure or discovery be limited to certain matters;

(5) that discovery be conducted with no one present except persons designated by the court;

(6) that a deposition, after being sealed, be opened only by order of the court;

(7) that a trade secret or other confidential research, development, or commercial information not be revealed or be revealed in a designated way; and

(8) that the parties simultaneously file specified documents or information enclosed in sealed envelopes to be opened as directed by the court.

If the motion for a protective order is denied in whole or in part, the court may, on such terms and conditions as are just, order that any party or other person provide or permit discovery. The provisions of Rule 37(a)(4) apply to the award of expenses incurred in relation to the motion.

(d) Timing and Sequence of Discovery.

Except when authorized under these rules or by local rule, order, or agreement of the parties, a party may not seek discovery from any source before the parties have met and conferred as required by subdivision (f). Unless the court upon motion, for the convenience of parties and witnesses and in the interests of justice, orders otherwise, methods of discovery may be used in any sequence, and the fact that a party is conducting discovery, whether by deposition or otherwise, shall not operate to delay any other party's discovery.

(e) Supplementation of Disclosures and Responses.

A party who has made a disclosure under subdivision (a) or responded to a request for discovery with a disclosure or response is under a duty to supplement or correct the disclosure or response to include information thereafter acquired if ordered by the court or in the following circumstances:

(1) A party is under a duty to supplement at appropriate intervals its disclosures under subdivision (a) if the party learns that in some material respect the information disclosed is incomplete or incorrect and if the additional or corrective information has not otherwise been made known to the other parties during the discovery process or in writing. With respect to testimony of an expert from whom a report is required under subdivision (a)(2)(B) the duty extends both to information contained in the report and to information provided through a deposition of the expert, and any additions

or other changes to this information shall be disclosed by the time the party's disclosures under Rule 26(a)(3) are due.

(2) A party is under a duty seasonably to amend a prior response to an interrogatory, request for production, or request for admission if the party learns that the response is in some material respect incomplete or incorrect and if the additional or corrective information has not otherwise been made known to the other parties during the discovery process or in writing.

(f) Meeting of Parties; Planning for Discovery.

Except in actions exempted by local rule or when otherwise ordered, the parties shall, as soon as practicable and in any event at least 14 days before a scheduling conference is held or a scheduling order is due under Rule 16(b), meet to discuss the nature and basis of their claims and defenses and the possibilities for a prompt settlement or resolution of the case, to make or arrange for the disclosures required by subdivision (a)(1), and to develop a proposed discovery plan. The plan shall indicate the parties' views and proposals concerning:

(1) what changes should be made in the timing, form, or requirement for disclosures under subdivision (a) or local rule, including a statement as to when disclosures under subdivision (a)(1) were made or will be made;

(2) the subjects on which discovery may be needed, when discovery should be completed, and whether discovery should be conducted in phases or be limited to or focused upon particular issues;

(3) what changes should be made in the limitations on discovery imposed under these rules or by local rule, and what other limitations should be imposed; and

(4) any other orders that should be entered by the court under subdivision (c) or under Rule 16(b) and (c).

The attorneys of record and all unrepresented parties that have appeared in the case are jointly responsible for arranging and being present or represented at the meeting, for attempting in good faith to agree on the proposed discovery plan, and for submitting to the court within 10 days after the meeting a written report outlining the plan.

(g) Signing of Disclosures, Discovery Requests, Responses, and Objections.

(1) Every disclosure made pursuant to subdivision (a)(1) or subdivision (a)(3) shall be signed by at least one attorney of record in the attorney's individual name, whose address shall be stated. An unrepresented party shall sign the disclosure and state the party's address. The signature of the attorney or party constitutes a certification that to the best of the signer's knowledge, information, and belief, formed after a reasonable inquiry, the disclosure is complete and correct as of the time it is made.

(2) Every discovery request, response, or objection made by a party represented by an attorney shall be signed by at least one attorney of record in the attorney's individual name, whose address shall be stated. An unrepresented party shall sign the request, or objection and state the party's address. The signature of the attorney or party constitutes a certification that to the

best of the signer's knowledge, information, and belief, formed after a reasonable inquiry, the request, response, or objection is:

(A) consistent with these rules and warranted by existing law or a good faith argument for the extension, modification, or reversal of existing law;

(B) not interposed for any improper purpose, such as to harass or to cause unnecessary delay or needless increase in the cost of litigation; and

(C) not unreasonable or unduly burdensome or expensive, given the needs of the case, the discovery already had in the case, the amount in controversy, and the importance of the issues at stake in the litigation.

If a request, response, or objection is not signed, it shall be stricken unless it is signed promptly after the omission is called to the attention of the party making the request, response, or objection, and a party shall not be obligated to take any action with respect to it until it is signed.

(3) If without substantial justification a certification is made in violation of the rule, the court, upon motion or upon its own initiative, shall impose upon the person who made the certification, the party on whose behalf the disclosure, request, response, or objection is made, or both, an appropriate sanction, which may include an order to pay the amount of the reasonable expenses incurred because of the violation, including a reasonable attorney's fee.

Rule 30. Deposition Upon Oral Examination

(a) When Depositions May Be Taken; When Leave Required.

(1) A party may take the testimony of any person, including a party, by deposition upon oral examination without leave of court except as provided in paragraph (2). The attendance of witnesses may be compelled by subpoena as provided in Rule 45.

(2) A party must obtain leave of court, which shall be granted to the extent consistent with the principles stated in rule 26(b)(2), if the person to be examined is confined in prison or if, without the written stipulation of the parties.

(A) a proposed deposition would result in more than ten depositions being taken under this rule or Rule 31 by the plaintiffs, or by the defendants, or by third-party defendants;

(B) the person to be examined already has been deposed in the case; or

(C) a party seeks to take a deposition before the time specified in Rule 26(d) unless the notice contains a certification, with supporting facts, that the person to be examined is expected to leave the United States and be unavailable for examination in this country unless deposed before that time.

(b) Notice of Examination: General Requirements; Method of Recording; Production of Documents and Things; Deposition of Organization; Deposition by Telephone.

(1) A party desiring to take the deposition of any person upon oral examination shall give reasonable notice in writing to every other party to

the action. The notice shall state the time and place for taking the deposition and the name and address of each person to be examined, if known, and, if the name is not known, a general description sufficient to identify the person or the particular class or group to which the person belongs. If a subpoena duces tecum is to be served on the person to be examined, the designation of the materials to be produced as set forth in the subpoena shall be attached to, or included in, the notice.

(2) The party taking the deposition shall state in the notice the method by which the testimony shall be recorded. Unless the court orders otherwise, it may be recorded by sound, sound-and-visual, or stenographic means, and the party taking the deposition shall bear the cost of the recording. Any party may arrange for a transcription to be made from the recording of a deposition taken by nonstenographic means.

(3) With prior notice to the deponent and other parties, any party may designate another method to record the deponent's testimony in addition to the method specified by the person taking the deposition. The additional record or transcript shall be made at that party's expense unless the court otherwise orders.

(4) Unless otherwise agreed by the parties, a deposition shall be conducted before an officer appointed or designated under Rule 28 and shall begin with a statement on the record by the officer that includes (A) the officer's name and business address; (B) the date, time and place of the deposition; (C) the name of the deponent; (D) the administration of the oath or affirmation to the deponent; and (E) an identification of all persons present. If the deposition is recorded other than stenographically, the officer shall repeat items (A) through (C) at the beginning of each unit of recorded tape or other recording medium. The appearance or demeanor of deponents or attorneys shall not be distorted through camera or sound-recording techniques. At the end of the deposition, the officer shall state on the record that the deposition is complete and shall set forth any stipulations made by counsel concerning the custody of the transcript or recording and the exhibits, or concerning other pertinent matters.

(5) The notice to a party deponent may be accompanied by a request made in compliance with Rule 34 for the production of documents and tangible things at the taking of the deposition. The procedure of Rule 34 shall apply to the request.

(6) A party may in the party's notice and in a subpoena name as the deponent a public or private corporation or a partnership or association or governmental agency and describe with reasonable particularity the matters on which examination is requested. In that event, the organization so named shall designate one or more officers, directors, or managing agents, or other persons who consent to testify on its behalf, and may set forth, for each person designated, the matters on which the person will testify. A subpoena shall advise a non-party organization of its duty to make such a designation. The persons so designated shall testify as to matters known or reasonably available to the organization. This subdivision (b)(6) does not preclude taking a deposition by any other procedure authorized in these rules.

(7) The parties may stipulate in writing or the court may upon motion order that a deposition be taken by telephone or other remote electronic means. For the purposes of this rule and Rules 28(a), 37(a)(1), and 37(b)(1), a deposition taken by such means is taken in the district and at the place where the deponent is to answer questions.

(c) Examination and Cross-Examination; Record of Examination; Oath; Objections.

Examination and cross-examination of witnesses may proceed as permitted at the trial under the provisions of the Federal Rules of Evidence except Rules 103 and 615. The officer before whom the deposition is to be taken shall put the witness on oath or affirmation and shall personally, or by someone acting under the officer's direction and in the officer's presence, record the testimony of the witness. The testimony shall be taken stenographically or recorded by any other method authorized by subdivision (b)(2) of this rule. All objections made at the time of the examination to the qualifications of the officer taking the deposition, to the manner of taking it, to the evidence presented, to the conduct of any party, or to any other aspect of the proceedings shall be noted by the officer upon the record of the deposition; but the examination shall proceed, with the testimony being taken subject to the objections. In lieu of participating in the oral examination, parties may serve written questions in a sealed envelope on the party taking the deposition and the party taking the deposition shall transmit them to the officer, who shall propound them to the witness and record the answers verbatim.

(d) Schedule and Duration; Motion to Terminate or Limit Examination.

(1) Any objection to evidence during a deposition shall be stated concisely and in a non-argumentative and non-suggestive manner. A party may instruct a deponent not to answer only when necessary to preserve a privilege, to enforce a limitation on evidence directed by the court, or to present a motion under paragraph (3).

(2) By order or local rule, the court may limit the time permitted for the conduct of a deposition, but shall allow additional time consistently with Rule 26(b)(2) if needed for a fair examination of the deponent or if the deponent or another party impedes or delays the examination. If the court finds such an impediment, delay, or other conduct that has frustrated the fair examination of the deponent, it may impose upon the persons responsible an appropriate sanction, including the reasonable costs and attorney's fees incurred by any parties as a result thereof.

(3) At any time during a deposition, on motion of a party or of the deponent and upon a showing that the examination is being conducted in bad faith or in such manner as unreasonably to annoy, embarrass, or oppress the deponent or party, the court in which the action is pending or the court in the district where the deposition is being taken may order the officer conducting the examination to cease forthwith from taking the deposition, or may limit the scope and manner of the taking of the deposition as provided in Rule 26(c). If the order made terminates the examination, it shall be resumed thereafter only upon the order of the court in which the action is

pending. Upon demand of the objecting party or deponent, the taking of the deposition shall be suspended for the time necessary to make a motion for an order. The provisions of Rule 37(a)(4) apply to the award of expenses incurred in relation to the motion.

(e) Review by Witness; Changes; Signing.

If requested by the deponent or a party before completion of the deposition, the deponent shall have 30 days after being notified by the officer that the transcript or recording is available in which to review the transcript or recording and, if there are changes in form or substance, to sign a statement reciting such changes and the reasons given by the deponent for making them. The officer shall indicate in the certificate prescribed by subdivision (f)(1) whether any review was requested and, if so, shall append any changes made by the deponent during the period allowed.

(f) Certification and Filing by Officer; Exhibits; Copies; Notices of Filing.

(1) The officer shall certify that the witness was duly sworn by the officer and that the deposition is a true record of the testimony given by the witness. This certificate shall be in writing and accompany the record of the deposition. Unless otherwise ordered by the court, the officer shall securely seal the deposition in an envelope or package endorsed with the title of the action and marked "Deposition of [here insert name of witness]" and shall promptly file it with the court in which the action is pending or send it to the attorney who arranged for the transcript or recording, who shall store it under conditions that will protect it against loss, destruction, tampering, or deterioration. Documents and things produced for inspection during the examination of the witness, shall, upon the request of a party, be marked for identification and annexed to the deposition and may be inspected and copied by any party, except that if the person producing the materials desires to retain them the person may (A) offer copies to be marked for identification and annexed to the deposition and to serve thereafter as originals if the person affords to all parties fair opportunity to verify the copies by comparison with the originals, or (B) offer the originals to be marked for identification, after giving to each party an opportunity to inspect and copy them, in which event the materials may then be used in the same manner as if annexed to the deposition. Any party may move for an order that the original be annexed to and returned with the deposition to the court, pending final disposition of the case.

(2) Unless otherwise ordered by the court or agreed by the parties, the officer shall retain stenographic notes of any deposition taken stenographically or a copy of the recording of any deposition taken by another method. Upon payment of reasonable charges therefor, the officer shall furnish a copy of the transcript or other recording of the deposition to any party or to the deponent.

(3) The party taking the deposition shall give prompt notice of its filing to all parties.

(g) Failure to Attend or to Serve Subpoena; Expenses.

(1) If the party giving the notice of the taking of a deposition fails to attend and proceed therewith and another party attends in person or by attorney

pursuant to the notice, the court may order the party giving the notice to pay to such other party the reasonable expenses incurred by that party and that party's attorney in attending, including reasonable attorney's fees.

(2) If the party giving the notice of the taking of a deposition of a witness fails to serve a subpoena upon the witness and the witness because of such failure does not attend, and if another party attends in person or by attorney because that party expects the deposition of that witness to be taken, the court may order the party giving the notice to pay to such other party the reasonable expenses incurred by that party and that party's attorney in attending, including reasonable attorney's fees.

Rule 33. Interrogatories to Parties

(a) Availability.

Without leave of court or written stipulation, any party may serve upon any other party written interrogatories, not exceeding 25 in number including all discrete subparts, to be answered by the party served or, if the party served is a public or private corporation or a partnership or association or governmental agency, by any officer or agent, who shall furnish such information as is available to the party. Leave to serve additional interrogatories shall be granted to the extent consistent with the principles of Rule 26(b)(2). Without leave of court or written stipulation, interrogatories may not be served before the time specified in Rule 26(d).

(b) Answers and Objections.

(1) Each interrogatory shall be answered separately and fully in writing under oath, unless it is objected to, in which event the objecting party shall state the reasons for objection and shall answer to the extent the interrogatory is not objectionable.

(2) The answers are to be signed by the person making them, and the objections signed by the attorney making them.

(3) The party upon whom the interrogatories have been served shall serve a copy of the answers, and objections if any, within 30 days after the service of the interrogatories. A shorter or longer time may be directed by the court or, in the absence of such an order, agreed to in writing by the parties subject to Rule 29.

(4) All grounds for an objection to an interrogatory shall be stated with specificity. Any ground not stated in a timely objection is waived unless the party's failure to object is excused by the court for good cause shown.

(5) The party submitting the interrogatories may move for an order under Rule 37(a) with respect to any objection to or other failure to answer an interrogatory.

(c) Scope; Use at Trial.

Interrogatories may relate to any matters which can be inquired into under Rule 26(b)(1), and the answers may be used to the extent permitted by the rules of evidence.

An interrogatory otherwise proper is not necessarily objectionable merely because an answer to the interrogatory involves an opinion or contention that relates to fact or the application of law to fact, but the court may order that such an interrogatory need not be answered until after designated discovery has been completed or until a pretrial conference or other later time.

(d) Option to Produce Business Records.

Where the answer to an interrogatory may be derived or ascertained from the business records, including electronically stored information, of the party upon whom the interrogatory has been served or from an examination, audit or inspection of such business records, including a compilation, abstract or summary thereof, and the burden of deriving or ascertaining the answer is substantially the same for the party serving the interrogatory as for the party served, it is a sufficient answer to such interrogatory to specify the records from which the answer may be derived or ascertained and to afford to the party serving the interrogatory reasonable opportunity to examine, audit or inspect such records and to make copies, compilations, abstracts, or summaries.

Rule 34. Production of Documents, Electronically Stored Information, and Things and Entry Upon Land for Inspection and Other Purposes

(a) Scope.

Any party may serve on any other party a request (1) to produce and permit the party making the request, or someone acting on the requestor's behalf, to inspect, copy, test, or sample any designated documents or electronically stored information--including writings, drawings, graphs, charts, photographs, sound recordings, images, and other data or data compilations stored in any medium from which information can be obtained--translated, if necessary, by the respondent into reasonably usable form, or to inspect, copy, test, or sample any designated tangible things which constitute or contain matters within the scope of Rule 26(b) and which are in the possession, custody or control of the party upon whom the request is served; or (2) to permit entry upon designated land or other property in the possession or control of the party upon whom the request is served for the purpose of inspection and measuring, surveying, photographing, testing, or sampling the property or any designated object or operation thereon, within the scope of Rule 26(b).

(b) Procedure.

The request shall set forth, either by individual item or by category, the items to be inspected, and describe each with reasonable particularity. The request shall specify a reasonable time, place, and manner of making the inspection and performing the related acts. Without leave of court or written stipulation, a request may not be served before the time specified in Rule 26(d). The party upon whom the request is served shall serve a written response within 30 days after the service of the request. A shorter or longer time may be directed by the court or, in the absence of such an order, agreed to in writing by the parties, subject to Rule 29. The response shall state, with respect to each item or category, that inspection and related activities will be permitted as requested, unless the request is objected to, in which event the reasons for the objection shall be stated. If objection is made to part of an item or category, the part shall be specified and inspection permitted of the remaining parts. The party submitting the request may move for an order under Rule 37(a) with respect to any objection to or other failure to respond to the request or any part thereof, or any failure to permit inspection as requested.

A party who produces documents for inspection shall produce them as they are kept in the usual course of business or shall organize and label them to correspond with the categories in the request.

(c) Persons Not Parties.

A person not a party to the action may be compelled to produce documents and things or to submit to an inspection as provided in Rule 45.

Rule 35. Physical and Mental Examination of Persons

(a) Order for Examination.

When the mental or physical condition (including the blood group) of a party or of a person in the custody or under the legal control of a party, is in controversy, the court in which the action is pending may order the party to submit to a physical or mental examination by a suitably licensed or certified examiner or to produce for examination the person in the party's custody or legal control. The order may be made only on motion for good cause shown and upon notice to the person to be examined and to all parties and shall specify the time, place, manner, conditions, and scope of the examination and the person or persons by whom it is to be made.

(b) Report of Examiner.

(1) If requested by the party against whom an order is made under Rule 35(a) or the person examined, the party causing the examination to be made shall deliver to the requesting party a copy of the detailed written report of the examiner setting out the examiner's findings, including results of all tests made, diagnoses and conclusions, together with like reports of all earlier examinations of the same condition. After delivery the party causing the examination shall be entitled upon request to receive from the party against whom the order is made a like report of any examination, previously or thereafter made, of the same condition, unless, in the case of a report of examination of a person not a party, the party shows that the party is unable to obtain it. The court on motion may make an order against a party requiring delivery of a report on such terms as are just, and if an examiner fails or refuses to make a report the court may exclude the examiner's testimony if offered at trial.

(2) By requesting and obtaining a report of the examination so ordered or by taking the deposition of the examiner, the party examined waives any privilege the party may have in that action or any other involving the same controversy, regarding the testimony of every other person who has examined or may thereafter examine the party in respect of the same mental or physical condition.

(3) This subdivision applied to examinations made by agreement of the parties, unless the agreement expressly provides otherwise. The subdivision does not preclude discovery of a report of an examiner or the taking of a deposition of the examiner in accordance with the provisions of any other rule.

(c) Definitions.

For the purpose of this rule, a psychologist is a psychologist licensed or certified by a State or the District of Columbia.

Rule 36. Requests for Admission

(a) Request for Admission.

A party may serve upon any other party a written request for the admission, for purposes of the pending action only, of the truth of any matters within the scope of Rule 26(b)(l) set forth in the request that relate to statements or opinions of fact or of the application of law to fact, including the genuineness of any documents described in the request. Copies of documents shall be served with the request unless they have been or are otherwise furnished or made available for inspection and copying. Without leave of court or written stipulation, requests for admission may not be served before the time specified in Rule 26(d).

Each matter of which an admission is requested shall be separately set forth. The matter is admitted unless, within 30 days after service of the request, or within such shorter or longer time as the court may allow or as the parties may agree to in writing, subject to Rule 29, the party to whom the request is directed serves upon the party requesting the admission a written answer or objection addressed to the matter, signed by the party or by the party's attorney. If objection is made, the reasons therefor shall be stated. The answer shall specifically deny the matter or set forth in detail the reasons why the answering party cannot truthfully admit or deny the matter. A denial shall fairly meet the substance of the requested admission, and when good faith requires that a party qualify an answer or deny only a part of the matter of which an admission is requested, the party shall specify so much of it as is true and qualify or deny the remainder. An answering party may not give lack of information or knowledge as a reason for failure to admit or deny unless the party states that the party has made reasonable inquiry and that the information known or readily obtainable by the party is insufficient to enable the party to admit or deny. A party who considers that a matter of which an admission has been requested presents a genuine issue for trial may not, on that ground alone, object to the request; the party may, subject to the provisions of Rule 37(c), deny the matter or set forth reasons why the party cannot admit or deny it.

The party who has requested the admissions may move to determine the sufficiency of the answers or objections. Unless the court determines that an objection is justified, it shall order that an answer be served. If the court determines that an answer does not comply with the requirements of this rule, it may order either that the matter is admitted or that an amended answer be served. The court may, in lieu of these orders, determine that final disposition of the request be made at a pretrial conference or at a designated time prior to trial. The provisions of Rule 37(a)(4) apply to the award of expenses incurred in relation to the motion.

(b) Effect of Admission.

Any matter admitted under this rule is conclusively established unless the court on motion permits withdrawal or amendment of the admission. Subject to the provision of Rule 16 governing amendment of a pretrial order, the court may permit withdrawal or amendment when the presentation of the merits of the action will be subserved thereby and the party who obtained the admission fails to satisfy the court that withdrawal or amendment will prejudice that party in maintaining the action or defense on the merits. Any admission made by a party under this rule is for the purpose of the pending action only and is not an admission for any other purpose nor may it be used against the party in any other proceeding.

Rule 37. Failure to Make or Cooperate in Discovery; Sanctions

(a) Motion for Order Compelling Disclosure or Discovery.

A party, upon reasonable notice to other parties and all persons affected thereby, may apply for an order compelling disclosure or discovery as follows:

(1) Appropriate Court.

An application for an order to a party shall be made to the court in which the action is pending. An application for an order to a person who is not a party shall be made to the court in the district where the discovery is being, or is to be, taken.

(2) Motion.

(A) If a party fails to make a disclosure required by Rule 26(a), any other party may move to compel disclosure and for appropriate sanctions. The motion must include a certification that the movant has in good faith conferred or attempted to confer with the party not making the disclosure in an effort to secure the disclosure without court action.

(B) If a deponent fails to answer a question propounded or submitted under Rules 30 or 31, or a corporation or other entity fails to make a designation under Rule 30(b)(6) or 31(a), or a party fails to answer an interrogatory submitted under Rule 33, or if a party, in response to a request for inspection submitted under Rule 34, fails to respond that inspection will be permitted as requested or fails to permit inspection as requested, the discovering party may move for an order compelling answer, or a designation, or an order compelling inspection in accordance with the request. The motion must include a certification that the movant has in good faith conferred or attempted to confer with the person or party failing to make the discovery in an effort to secure the information or material without court action. When taking a deposition on oral examination, the proponent of the question may complete or adjourn the examination before applying for an order.

(3) Evasive or Incomplete Disclosure, Answer, or Response.

For purposes of this subdivision an evasive or incomplete disclosure, answer, or response is to be treated as a failure to disclose, answer, or respond.

(4) Expenses and Sanctions.

(A) If the motion is granted or if the disclosure or requested discovery is provided after the motion was filed, the court shall, after affording an opportunity to be heard, require the party or deponent whose conduct necessitated the motion or the party or attorney advising such conduct or both of them to pay to the moving party the reasonable expenses incurred in making the motion, including attorney's fees, unless the court finds that the motion was filed without the movant's first making a good faith effort to obtain the disclosure or discovery without court action, or that the opposing party's nondisclosure, response, or objection was substantially justified, or that other circumstances make an award of expenses unjust.

(B) If the motion is denied, the court may enter any protective order authorized under Rule 26(c) and shall, after affording an opportunity to be heard, require the moving party or the attorney filing the motion or both of them to pay to the party or deponent who opposed the motion the reasonable expenses incurred in opposing the motion, including attorney's fees, unless the court finds that the making of the motion was substantially justified or that other circumstances make an award of expenses unjust.

(C) If the motion is granted in part and denied in part, the court may enter any protective order authorized under Rule 26(c) and may, after affording an opportunity to be heard, apportion the reasonable expenses incurred in relation to the motion among the parties and persons in a just manner.

(b) Failure to Comply with Order.

(1) Sanctions by Court in District Where Deposition is Taken.

If a deponent fails to be sworn or to answer a question after being directed to do so by the court in the district in which the deposition is being taken, the failure may be considered a contempt of that court.

(2) Sanctions by Court in Which Action is Pending.

If a party or an officer, director, or managing agent of a party or a person designated under Rule 30(b)(6) or 31(a) to testify on behalf of a party fails to obey an order to provide or permit discovery, including an order made under subdivision (a) of this rule or Rule 35, or if a party fails to obey an order entered under Rule 26(f), the court in which the action is pending may make such orders in regard to the failure as are just, and among others the following:

(A) An order that the matters regarding which the order was made or any other designated facts shall be taken to be established for the purposes of the action in accordance with the claim of the party obtaining the order;

(B) An order refusing to allow the disobedient party to support or oppose designated claims or defenses, or prohibiting that party from introducing designated matters in evidence;

(C) An order striking out pleadings or parts thereof, or staying further proceedings until the order is obeyed, or dismissing the action or proceeding or any part thereof, or rendering a judgment by default against the disobedient party;

(D) In lieu of any of the foregoing orders or in addition thereto, an order treating as a contempt of court the failure to obey any orders except an order to submit to a physical or mental examination;

(E) Where a party has failed to comply with an order under Rule 35(a) requiring that party to produce another for examination, such orders as are listed in paragraphs (A), (B), and (C) of this subdivision, unless the party failing to comply shows that that party is unable to produce such person for examination.

In lieu of any of the foregoing orders or in addition thereto, the court shall require the party failing to obey the order or the attorney advising that party or both to pay the reasonable expenses, including attorney's fees, caused by the failure, unless the court finds that the failure was substantially justified or that other circumstances make an award of expenses unjust.

(c) Failure to Disclose, False or Misleading Disclosure; Refusal to Admit.

(1) A party that without substantial justification fails to disclose information required by Rule 26(a) or 26(e)(1) shall not, unless such failure is harmless, be permitted to use as evidence at a trial, at a hearing, or on a motion any witness or information not so disclosed. In addition to or in lieu of this sanction, the court, on motion and after affording an opportunity to be heard, may impose other appropriate sanctions. In addition to requiring payment of reasonable expenses, including attorney's fees, caused by the failure, these sanctions may include any of the sanctions authorized under subparagraphs (A), (B), and (C) of subdivision (b)(2) of this rule and may include informing the jury of the failure to make the disclosure.

(2) If a party fails to admit the genuineness of any document or the truth of any matter as requested under Rule 36, and if the party requesting the admissions thereafter proves the genuineness of the document or the truth of the matter, the requesting party may apply to the court for an order requiring the other party to pay the reasonable expenses incurred in making that proof, including reasonable attorney's fees. The court shall make the order unless it finds that (A) the request was held objectionable pursuant to Rule 36(a), or (B) the admission sought was of no substantial importance, or (C) the party failing to admit had reasonable ground to believe that the party might prevail on the matter, or (D) there was other good reason for the failure to admit.

(d) Failure of Party to Attend at Own Deposition or Serve Answers to Interrogatories or Respond to Request for Inspection.

If a party or an officer, director, or managing agent of a party or a person designated under Rule 30(b)(6) or 31(a) to testify on behalf of a party fails (1) to appear before the officer who is to take the deposition, after being served with a proper notice, or (2) to serve answers to objections to interrogatories submitted under Rule 33, after proper service of the interrogatories, or (3) to serve a written response to a request for inspection submitted under Rule 34, after proper service of the request, the court in which the action is pending on motion may make such orders in regard to the failure as are just, and among others it may take any action authorized under subparagraphs (A), (B), and (C) of subdivision (b)(2) of this rule. Any motion specifying a failure under clause (2) or (3) of this subdivision shall include a certification that the movant has in good faith conferred or attempted to confer with the party failing to answer or respond in an effort to obtain such answer without court action. In lieu of any order or in addition thereto, the court shall require the party failing to act or the attorney advising that party or both to pay the reasonable expenses, including attorney's fees, caused by the failure unless the court finds that the failure was substantially justified or that other circumstances make an award of expenses unjust.

The failure to act described in this subdivision may not be excused on the ground that the discovery sought is objectionable unless the party failing to act has a pending motion for a protective order as provided by Rule 26(c).

(f) Electronically Stored Information.

Absent exceptional circumstances, a court may not impose sanctions under these rules on a party for failing to provide electronically stored information lost as a result of the routine, good-faith operation of an electronic information system.

Appendix B

EXTRACTS FROM THE FEDERAL RULES OF EVIDENCE (IN NUMERICAL ORDER)

Rule 201. Judicial Notice of Adjudicative Facts

(a) Scope of rule.

This rule governs only judicial notice of adjudicative facts.

(b) Kinds of facts.

A judicially noticed fact must be one not subject to reasonable dispute in that it is either (1) generally known within the territorial jurisdiction of the trial court or (2) capable of accurate and ready determination by resort to sources whose accuracy cannot reasonably be questioned.

(c) When discretionary.

A court may take judicial notice, whether requested or not.

(d) When mandatory.

A court shall take judicial notice if requested by a party and supplied with the necessary information.

(e) Opportunity to be heard.

A party is entitled upon timely request to an opportunity to be heard as to the propriety of taking judicial notice and the tenor of the matter noticed. In the absence of prior notification, the request may be made after judicial notice has been taken.

(f) Time of taking notice.

Judicial notice may be taken at any stage of the proceeding.

(g) Instructing jury.

In a civil action or proceeding, the court shall instruct the jury to accept as conclusive any fact judicially noticed. In a criminal case, the court shall instruct the jury that it may, but is not required to, accept as conclusive any fact judicially noticed.

Rule 401. Definition of "Relevant Evidence"

"Relevant evidence" means evidence having any tendency to make the existence of any fact that is of consequence to the determination of the action more probable or less probable than it would be without the evidence.

Rule 402. Relevant Evidence Generally Admissible; Irrelevant Evidence Inadmissible

All relevant evidence is admissible, except as otherwise provided by the Constitution of the United States, by Act of Congress, by these rules, or by other rules prescribed by the Supreme Court pursuant to statutory authority. Evidence which is not relevant is not admissible.

Rule 403. Exclusion of Relevant Evidence on Grounds of Prejudice, Confusion, or Waste of Time

Although relevant, evidence may be excluded if its probative value is substantially outweighed by the danger of unfair prejudice, confusion of the issues, or misleading the jury, or by considerations of undue delay, waste of time, or needless presentation of cumulative evidence.

Rule 406. Habit; Routine Practice

Evidence of the habit of a person or of the routine practice of an organization, whether corroborated or not and regardless of the presence of eyewitnesses, is relevant to prove that the conduct of the person or organization on a particular occasion was in conformity with the habit or routine practice.

Rule 612. Writing Used to Refresh Memory

Except as otherwise provided in criminal proceedings by section 3500 of title 18, United States Code, if a witness uses a writing to refresh memory for the purpose of testifying, either
    (1) while testifying, or
    (2) before testifying, if the court in its discretion determines it is necessary in the interests of justice, an adverse party is entitled to having the writing produced at the hearing, to inspect it, to cross-examine the witness thereon, and to introduce in evidence those portions which relate to the testimony of the witness. If it is claimed that the writing contains matters not related to the subject matter of the testimony the court shall examine the writing in camera, excise any portions not so related and order delivery of

the remainder to the party entitled thereto. Any portion withheld over objections shall be preserved and made available to the appellate court in the event of an appeal. If a writing is not produced or delivered pursuant to order under this rule, the court shall make any order justice requires, except that in criminal cases when the prosecution elects not to comply, the order shall be one striking the testimony or, if the court in its discretion determines that the interests of justice so require, declaring a mistrial.

Rule 613. Prior Statements of Witnesses

(a) Examining witness concerning prior statement.

In examining a witness concerning a prior statement made by the witness whether written or not the statement need not be shown nor its contents disclosed to the witness at that time, but on request the same shall be shown or disclosed to opposing counsel.

* * *

Rule 701. Opinion Testimony by Lay Witnesses

If the witness is not testifying as an expert, the witness' testimony in the form of opinions or inferences is limited to those opinions or inferences which are (a) rationally based on the perception of the witness and (b) helpful to a clear understanding of the witness' testimony or the determination of a fact in issue.

Rule 702. Testimony by Experts

If scientific, technical, or other specialized knowledge will assist the trier of fact to understand the evidence or to determine a fact in issue, a witness qualified as an expert by knowledge, skill, experience, training, or education, may testify thereto in the form of an opinion or otherwise, if (1) the testimony is based upon sufficient facts or data, (2) the testimony is the product of reliable principles and methods, and (3) the witness has applied the principles and methods reliably to the facts of the case.

Rule 703. Bases of Opinion Testimony by Experts

The facts or data in the particular case upon which an expert bases an opinion or inference may be those perceived by or made known to the expert at or before the hearing. If of a type reasonably relied upon by experts in a particular field in forming opinions or inferences upon the subject, the facts or data need not be admissible in evidence.

Rule 704. Opinion on Ultimate Issues

Except as provided in subdivision (b), testimony in the form of an opinion or inference otherwise admissible is not objectionable because it embraces an ultimate issue to be decided by the trier of fact.

Rule 705. Disclosure of Facts or Data Underlying Expert Opinion

The expert may testify in terms of opinion or inference and give reasons therefor without first testifying to the underlying facts or data, unless the court requires otherwise. The expert may in any event be required to disclose the underlying facts or data on cross-examination.

Rule 706. Court Appointed Experts

(a) Appointment.

The court may on its own motion or on the motion of either party enter an order to show cause why expert witnesses should not be appointed, and may request the parties to submit nominations. The court may appoint any expert witnesses agreed upon by the parties, and may appoint expert witnesses of its own selection. An expert witness shall not be appointed by the court unless the witness consents to act. A witness so appointed shall be informed of the witness duties by the court in writing, a copy of which shall be filed with the clerk, or at a conference in which the parties shall have opportunity to participate. A witness so appointed shall advise the parties of the witness' findings, if any; the witness' deposition may be taken by any party; and the witness may be called to testify by the court or any party. The witness shall be subject to cross-examination by each party, including a party calling the witness.

(b) Compensation.

Expert witnesses so appointed are entitled to reasonable compensation in whatever sum the court may allow. The compensation thus fixed is payable from funds which may be provided by law in criminal cases and civil actions and proceedings involving just compensation under the fifth amendment. In other civil actions and proceedings the compensation shall be paid by the parties in such proportion and at such time as the court directs, and therefore charged in like manner as other costs.

(c) Disclosure of Appointment.

In the exercise of its discretion, the court may authorize disclosure to the jury of the fact that the court appointed the expert witness.

(d) Parties' Experts of Own Selection.

Nothing in this rule limits the parties in calling expert witnesses of their own selection.

Rule 801. Definitions

The following definitions apply under this article:

(a) Statement.

A "statement" is (1) an oral or written assertion or (2) nonverbal conduct of a person, if it is intended by the person as an assertion.

(b) Declarant.

A "declarant" is a person who makes a statement.

(c) Hearsay.

"Hearsay" is a statement, other than one made by the declarant while testifying at the trial or hearing, offered in evidence to prove the truth of the matter asserted.

(d) Statements which are not hearsay.

A statement is not hearsay if —

(1) Prior statement by witness.

The declarant testifies at the trial or hearing and is subject to cross-examination concerning the statement, and the statement is (A) inconsistent with the declarant's testimony, and was given under oath subject to the penalty of perjury at a trial, hearing, or other proceeding, or in a deposition, or (B) consistent with the declarant's testimony and is offered to rebut an express or implied charge against the declarant of recent fabrication or improper influence or motive, or (C) one of identification of a person made after perceiving the person; or

(2) Admission by party-opponent.

The statement is offered against a party and is (A) the party's own statement, in either an individual or a representative capacity or (B) a statement of which the party has manifested an adoption or belief in its truth, or (C) a statement by a person authorized by the party to make a statement concerning the subject, or (D) a statement by the party's agent or servant concerning a matter within the scope of the agency or employment, made during the existence of the relationship, or (E) a statement by a coconspirator of a party during the course and in furtherance of the conspiracy.

Rule 802. Hearsay Rule

Hearsay is not admissible except as provided by these rules or by other rules prescribed by the Supreme Court pursuant to statutory authority or by Act of Congress.

Rule 803. Hearsay Exceptions; Availability of Declarant Immaterial

The following are not excluded by the hearsay rule, even though the declarant is available as a witness:

(1) Present sense impression.

A statement describing or explaining an event or condition made while the declarant was perceiving the event or condition, or immediately thereafter.

(2) Excited utterance.

A statement relating to a startling event or condition made while the declarant was under the stress of excitement caused by the event or condition.

(3) Then existing mental, emotional, or physical condition.

A statement of the declarant's then existing state of mind, emotion, sensation, or physical condition (such as intent, plan, motive, design, mental feeling, pain, and bodily health), but not including a statement of memory or belief to prove the fact remembered or believed unless it relates to the execution, revocation, identification, or terms of declarant's will.

(4) Statements for purposes of medical diagnosis or treatment.

Statements made for purposes of medical diagnosis or treatment and describing medical history, or past or present symptoms, pain, or sensations, or the inception or general character of the cause or external source thereof insofar as reasonably pertinent to diagnosis or treatment.

(5) Recorded recollection.

A memorandum or record concerning a matter about which a witness once had knowledge but now has insufficient recollection to enable the witness to testify fully and accurately, shown to have been made or adopted by the witness when the matter was fresh in the witness' memory and to reflect that knowledge correctly. If admitted, the memorandum or record may be read into evidence but may not itself be received as an exhibit unless offered by an adverse party.

(6) Records of regularly conducted activity.

A memorandum, report, record, or data compilation, in any form, of acts, events, conditions, opinions, or diagnoses, made at or near the time by, or from information transmitted by, a person with knowledge, if kept in the course of a regularly conducted business activity, and if it was the regular practice of that business activity to make the memorandum, report, record, or data compilation, all as shown by the testimony of the custodian or other qualified witness, unless the source of information or the method or circumstances of preparation indicate lack of trustworthiness. The term "business" as used in this paragraph includes business, institution, association, profession, occupation, and calling of every kind, whether or not conducted for profit.

(7) Absence of entry in records kept in accordance with the provisions of paragraph (6).

Evidence that a matter is not included in the memoranda reports, records, or data compilations, in any form, kept in accordance with the provisions of paragraph (6), to prove the nonoccurrence or nonexistence of the matter, if the matter was of a kind of which a memorandum, report, record, or data compilation was regularly made and preserved, unless the sources of information or other circumstances indicate lack of trustworthiness.

(8) Public records and reports.

Records, reports, statements, or data compilations, in any form, of public offices or agencies, setting forth (A) the activities of the office or agency, or (B) matters observed pursuant to duty imposed by law as to which matters there was a duty to report, excluding, however, in criminal cases matters observed by police officers and other law enforcement personnel, or (C) in civil actions and proceedings and against the Government in criminal cases, factual findings resulting from an investigation made pursuant to authority granted by law, unless the sources of information or other circumstances indicate lack of trustworthiness.

(9) Records of vital statistics.

Records of data compilations, in any form, of births, fetal deaths, deaths, or marriages, if the report thereof was made to a public office pursuant to requirements of law.

(10) Absence of public record or entry.

To prove the absence of a record, report, statement, or data compilation, in any form, or the nonoccurrence or nonexistence of a matter of which a record, report, statement, or data compilation, in any form, was regularly made and preserved by a public office or agency, evidence in the form of a certification in accordance with Rule 902, or testimony, that diligent search failed to disclose the record, report, statement, or data compilation, or entry.

(11) Records of religious organizations.

Statements of births, marriages, divorces, deaths, legitimacy, ancestry, relationship by blood or marriage, or other similar facts of personal or family history, contained in a regularly kept record of a religious organization.

(12) Marriage, baptismal, and similar certificates.

Statements of fact contained in a certificate that the maker performed a marriage or other ceremony or administered a sacrament, made by a clergyman, public official, or other person authorized by the rules or practices of a religious organization or by law to perform the act certified, and purporting to have been issued at the time of the act or within a reasonable time thereafter.

(13) Family records.

Statements of fact concerning personal or family history contained in family Bibles, genealogies, charts, engravings on rings, inscriptions on family portraits, engravings on urns, crypts, or tombstones, or the like.

(14) Records of documents affecting an interest in property.

The record of a document purporting to establish or affect an interest in property, as proof of the content of the original recorded document and its execution and delivery by each person by whom it purports to have been executed, if the record is a record of a public office and an applicable statute authorizes the recording of documents of that kind in that office.

(15) Statements in documents affecting an interest in property.

A statement contained in a document purporting to establish or affect an interest in property if the matter stated was relevant to the purpose of the document, unless dealings with the property since the document was made have been inconsistent with the truth of the statement or the purport of the document.

(16) Statements in ancient documents.

Statements in a document in existence twenty years or more the authenticity of which is established.

(17) Market reports, commercial publications.

Market quotations, tabulations, lists, directories, or other published compilations, generally used and relied upon by the public or by persons in particular occupations.

(18) Learned treatises.

To the extent called to the attention of an expert witness upon cross-examination or relied upon by the expert witness in direct examination, statements contained in published treatises, periodicals, or pamphlets on a subject of history, medicine, or other science or art, established as a reliable authority by the testimony or admission of the witness or by other expert testimony or by judicial notice. If admitted, the statements may be read into evidence but may not be received as exhibits.

(19) Reputation concerning personal or family history.

Reputation among members of a person's family by blood, adoption, or marriage, or among a person's associates, or in the community, concerning a person's birth, adoption, or marriage, ancestry, or other similar fact of personal or family history.

(20) Reputation concerning boundaries or general history.

Reputation in a community, arising before the controversy, as to boundaries of or customs affecting lands in the community, and reputation as to events of general history important to the community or State or nation in which located.

(21) Reputation as to character.

Reputation of a person's character among associates or in the community.

(22) Judgment of previous conviction.

Evidence of a final judgment, entered after a trial or upon a plea of guilty (but not upon a plea of nolo contendere), adjudging a person guilty of a crime punishable by death or imprisonment in excess of one year, to prove any fact essential to sustain the judgment, but not including, when offered by the Government in a criminal prosecution for purposes other than impeachment, judgments against persons other than the accused. The pendency of an appeal may be shown but does not affect admissibility.

(23) Judgment as to personal, family, or general history, or boundaries.

Judgments as proof of matters of personal, family or general history, or boundaries, essential to the judgment, if the same would be provable by evidence of reputation.

Rule 804. Hearsay Exceptions: Declarant Unavailable

(a) Definition of unavailability.

"Unavailability as a witness" includes situations in which the declarant

(1) is exempted by ruling of the court on the ground of privilege from testifying concerning the subject matter of the declarant's statement; or

(2) persists in refusing to testify concerning the subject matter of the declarant's statement despite an order of the court to do so; or

(3) testifies to a lack of memory of the subject matter of the declarant's statement; or

(4) is unable to be present or to testify at the hearing because of death or then existing physical or mental illness or infirmity; or

(5) is absent from the hearing and the proponent of a statement has been unable to procure the declarant's attendance (or in the case of a hearsay exception under subdivision (b)(2), (3), or (4), the declarant's attendance or testimony) by process or other reasonable means.

A declarant is not unavailable as a witness if exemption, refusal, claim of lack of memory, inability, or absence is due to the procurement or wrongdoing of the proponent of a statement for the purpose of preventing the witness from attending or testifying.

(b) Hearsay exemptions.

The following are not excluded by the hearsay rule if the declarant is unavailable as a witness:

(1) Former testimony.

Testimony given as a witness at another hearing of the same or a different proceeding, or in a deposition taken in compliance with law in the course of the same or another proceeding, if the party against whom the testimony is now offered, or, in a civil action or proceeding, a predecessor in interest, had an opportunity and similar motive to develop the testimony by direct, cross, or redirect examination.

* * *

Rule 805. Hearsay Within Hearsay

Hearsay included within hearsay is not excluded under the hearsay rule if each part of the combined statements conforms with an exception to the hearsay rule provided in these rules.

Rule 807. Residual Exception

A statement not specifically covered by Rule 803 or 804 but having equivalent circumstantial guarantees of trustworthiness, is not excluded by the hearsay rule, if the court determines that (A) the statement is offered as evidence of a material fact; (B) the statement is more probative on the point for which it is offered than any other evidence which the proponent can procure through reasonable efforts; and (C) the general purposes of these rules and the inter-ests of justice will best be served by admission of the statement into evidence. However, a statement may not be admitted under this exception unless the proponent of it makes known to the adverse party sufficiently in advance of the trial or hearing to provide the adverse party with a fair opportunity to prepare to meet it, the proponent's intention to offer the statement and the particulars of it, including the name and address of the declarant.

Rule 1001. Definitions

For purposes of this article the following definitions are applicable:
(1) Writings and recordings.
"Writings" and "recordings" consist of letters, words, or numbers, or their equivalent, set down by handwriting, typewriting, printing, photostating, photographing, magnetic impulse, mechanical or electronic recording, or other form of data compilation.
(2) Photographs
"Photographs" include still photographs, x-ray films, video tapes, and motion pictures.
(3) Original.
An "original" of a writing or recording is the writing or recording itself or any counterpart intended to have the same effect by a person executing or issuing it. An "original" of a photograph includes the negative or any print therefrom. If data are stored in a computer or similar device, any printout or other output readable by sight, shown to reflect the data accurately, is an "original."
(4) Duplicate.
A "duplicate" is a counterpart produced by the same impression as the original, or from the same matrix, or by means of photography, including enlargements and miniatures, or by mechanical or electronic re-recording, or by chemical reproduction, or by other equivalent techniques which accurately reproduce the original.

Rule 1002. Requirement of Original

To prove the content of a writing, recording, or photograph, the original writing, recording, or photograph is required, except as otherwise provided in these rules or by Act of Congress.

Rule 1003. Admissibility of Duplicates

A duplicate is admissible to the same extent as an original unless (1) a genuine question is raised as to the authenticity of the original or (2) in the circum-stances it would be unfair to admit the duplicate in lieu of the original.

Rule 1004. Admissibility of Other Evidence of Contents

The original is not required, and other evidence of the contents of a writing, recording, or photograph is admissible if

(1) Originals lost or destroyed.

All originals are lost or have been destroyed, unless the proponent lost or destroyed them in bad faith; or

(2) Original not obtainable.

No original can be obtained by any available judicial process or procedure; or

(3) Original in possession of opponent.

At a time when an original was under the control of the party against whom offered, that party was put on notice, by the pleadings or otherwise, that the contents would be a subject of proof at the hearing, and that party does not produce the original at the hearing; or

(4) Collateral matters.

The writing, recording, or photograph is not closely related to a controlling issue.

Rule 1005. Public Records

The contents of an official record, or of a document authorized to be recorded or filed and actually recorded or filed, including data compilations in any form, if otherwise admissible, may be proved by copy, certified as correct in accordance with Rule 902 or testified to be correct by a witness who has compared it with the original. If a copy which complies with the foregoing cannot be obtained by the exercise of reasonable diligence, then other evidence of the contents may be given.

Rule 1006. Summaries

The contents of voluminous writings, recordings, or photographs which cannot conveniently be examined in court may be presented in the form of a chart, summary, or calculation. The originals, or duplicates, shall be made available for examination or copying, or both, by other parties at reasonable time and place. The court may order that they be produced in court.

Rule 1007. Testimony or Written Admission of Party

Contents of writings, recordings, or photographs may be proved by the testimony or deposition of the party against whom offered or by that party's written admission, without accounting for the nonproduction of the original.

Appendix C

TABLE OF ILLUSTRATIVE CASES

Index